❖   Women and American Politics

Gender and Politics represents the most recent scholarship in the areas of women, gender, and politics, and is explicitly cross-national in its organization and orientation. Recognizing the contribution of women's studies to gendered political analysis, the goal of *Gender and Politics* is to develop, and to publish, frontier analysis, the empirical research exemplary of the intersection between political studies and women's studies.

The series is edited by Professor Karen Beckwith at the Department of Political Science, College of Wooster and Professor Joni Lovenduski, Department of Politics and Sociology, Birkbeck College.

❖ Women and American Politics

New Questions, New Directions

edited by
Susan J. Carroll

OXFORD
UNIVERSITY PRESS

UNIVERSITY PRESS

Great Clarendon Street, Oxford OX2 6DP

Oxford University Press is a department of the University of Oxford.
It furthers the University's objective of excellence in research, scholarship,
and education by publishing worldwide in

Oxford New York

Auckland Cape Town Dar es Salaam Hong Kong Karachi
Kuala Lumpur Madrid Melbourne Mexico City Nairobi
New Delhi Taipei Toronto Shanghai

With offices in

Argentina Austria Brazil Chile Czech Republic France Greece
Gutemala Hungary Italy Japan South Korea Poland Portugal
Singapore Switzerland Thailand Turkey Ukraine Vietnam

Published in the United States
by Oxford University Press Inc., New York

British Library Cataloguing in Publication Data
data available

Library of Congress Cataloging in Publication Data
Women and American politics / edited by Susan J. Carroll.
  p. cm.
Includes bibliographical references.
1. Women in politics–United States. I. Carroll, Susan J., 1950–

HQ1236.5 U6 W64 2002 320′082–dc21 2002070189

ISBN 0–19–829347–X (hbk.)
ISBN 0–19–829348–8 (pbk.)

3 5 7 9 10 8 6 4

Typeset by SNP Best-set Typesetter Ltd., Hong Kong
Printed in Great Britain
on acid-free paper by Biddles Ltd
King's Lynn, Norfolk

❖ Preface

This volume had its origins in a conference entitled "Research on Women and American Politics: Agenda Setting for the Twenty-First Century." The three-day conference, held in April 1994, was organized by the Center for American Women and Politics at Rutgers University and funded by the Ford Foundation.

The purpose of the conference was to develop an agenda that could help guide research on women and American politics into the twenty-first century. The conference brought together 79 scholars, researchers, activists, and practitioners, all of whom were charged with identifying existing gaps in our knowledge, thinking about new directions for research, and imagining the kinds of research projects that would both enhance our understanding of the dynamics surrounding women's participation in American politics and facilitate the work of those trying to increase women's representation and influence in politics.

The original drafts of the essays that appear in much revised form in this volume were written for different working group sessions that occurred throughout the conference. Each author, a scholar with considerable expertise in the subject matter that was the focus of a particular workshop, was asked to look to the future and suggest an agenda for research that would move in new directions and address major unanswered research questions. Each paper was read in advance by conference participants who participated in the working group, and the workshop session itself was devoted to responding to the ideas of the author as well as providing additional ideas for research.

In the time that has passed since the conference, each author has revised her paper at least twice, incorporating the suggestions of conference participants and updating her essay to reflect developments since the conference took place. The end result is a volume of essays written by some of the foremost scholars in the field of women and politics, who have brought their considerable expertise and personal perspectives to their essays, but who have also benefitted from the collective insights and feedback of many researchers and activists at the forefront of academic and practical work on women and American politics.

This volume is deliberately forward looking. By reading any of the essays, the reader certainly develops a comprehensive understanding of, and appreciation for, what we have learned from previous research. However, the focus of this volume is less on what we do know than on what we do not know. The objective is to stimulate creative and original thinking and research about women's involvement in political life.

I am particularly grateful for the generous support that the Ford Foundation provided for the conference that laid the foundation for this volume. I especially want to thank Marcia Smith, formerly of the Ford Foundation, for her interest and assistance.

As with all CAWP projects, the conference was very much a collective endeavor and could not have happened without the assistance of my very willing and able colleagues at CAWP, and I very grateful to all of them. In particular, Debbie Walsh and Ruth Mandel played key roles. Debbie flawlessly handled the logistical planning for the conference and invited the practitioners and activists who participated. Ruth helped to conceive and conceptualize the project. Graduate assistants and other members of the CAWP staff who helped with the conference in various ways included: Kim Edens, Rose Harris, Michele Treadwell, Linda Phillips, Lucy Baruch, and Kathy Kleeman.

I am also thankful to the members of the advisory board for the conference— Sandy Aguilar, Jo Freeman, Marianne Githens, Elizabeth Hager, Jewel Prestage, and Linda Williams—who offered many valuable suggestions which helped to make the conference a success. In addition, I and the authors of the various chapters in this volume owe a great deal of gratitude to all the scholars, researchers, activists, and practitioners who attended the conference and provided valuable ideas and insights about research needs. Each of the essays in this volume is stronger because of the feedback provided by conference participants. We extend our thanks to: Deborah L. Alexander, Kristi J. Andersen, Polly B. Baca, Sylvia B. Bashevkin, Kathy L. Bonk, Linda B. Bowker, Nancy J. Brown, Nancy Burns, Barbara J. Callaway, Mary Ellen S. Capek, Cal Clark, Janet E. Clark, Betsy Crone, Barbara A. Crow, Cynthia R. Daniels, R. Darcy, Debra L. Dodson, Betty Dooley, Georgia Duerst-Lahti, Janet A. Flammang, Jo Freeman, Martha Gershun, Terry Gilmour, Lisa Goldberg, Gunnel Gustafsson, Carol Hardy-Fanta, Leonie Huddy, Jennifer Jackman, Kathleen Hall Jamieson, Jane Y. Junn, Kim Fridkin Kahn, Kate Karpilow, Lyn Kathlene, Rita Mae Kelly, Montague Kern, Bobbie Kilberg, Celinda Lake, Tanya M. Melich, Jody Newman, Karen M. Paget, Anita Perez-Ferguson, Beth Reingold, Virginia Sapiro, Ida Schmertz, Ronnee Schreiber, Christine M. Sierra, Roberta Sigel, Marian J. Simms, Eleanor Smeal, Adaljiza Sosa-Riddell, Jeanie R. Stanley, Candice Straight, Carol Swain, Paule Cruz Takash, Gayle T. Tate, Katherine Tate, Sue Tolleson-Rinehart, Toni-Michelle C. Travis, Marcia L. Whicker, Susan N. Wilson, Betsey Wright, and Linda Zerilli.

Susan J. Carroll

❖ Contents

❖ Part I
Running for Public Office

❖ Part II
Other Aspects of Women's Participation in Electoral Politics

❖ **Part III**

New Directions in Women and Politics Research

❖ List of Figures

❖ List of Tables

❖ List of Contributors

Martha A. Ackelsberg   is Professor of Government and Women's Studies at Smith College. She is the author of *Free Women of Spain: Anarchism and the Struggle for the Emancipation of Women* (1991) as well as of numerous articles on women's community activism and feminist theory. She is currently at work on *Making Democracy Work: Rethinking Politics Through the Lens of Women's Activism* (forthcoming).

Denise L. Baer   is President of Strategic Research Concepts, a Washington, DC, area consulting firm, and a Professorial Lecturer with the Graduate School of Political Management, George Washington University. Her current research focuses on party institutionalization, women candidates, and voter mobilization and campaign strategy based on gender gap issues.

Barbara C. Burrell   is Associate Professor of Political Science and Associate Director of the Public Opinion Laboratory, Northern Illinois University. She is the author of *A Women's Place Is in the House: Campaigning for Congress in the Feminist Era* (1994) and *Public Opinion, the First Ladyship and Hillary Rodham Clinton*, rev. ed. (2001).

Susan J. Carroll   is Professor of Political Science and Women's and Gender Studies at Rutgers University as well as Senior Scholar at the Center for American Women and Politics (CAWP). She is the author of *Women as Candidates in American Politics* (2nd ed., 1994) and the editor of *The Impact of Women in Public Office* (2001). Carroll has also co-authored several CAWP publications focusing on the recruitment and impact of women state legislators and members of Congress, including *Reshaping the Agenda: Women in State Legislatures*; *Women's Routes to Elective Office: A Comparison With Men's*; and *Voices, Views, Votes: The Impact of Women in the 103rd Congress*.

Cathy J. Cohen   is Professor of Political Science at the University of Chicago. She is the author of *The Boundaries of Blackness: AIDS and the Breakdown of Black Politics* (1999) and the co-editor (with Kathleen Jones and Joan Tronto) of *Women Transforming Politics: An Alternative Reader* (1997). Cohen has been published in numerous journals and edited volumes, including the *American Political Science Review* and *GL/Q*.

MARIANNE GITHENS is Professor of Comparative Politics at Goucher College. Among her publications are *A Portrait of Marginality* (1977), co-edited with Jewel Prestage; *Different Roles, Different Voices* (1994), co-edited with Pippa Norris and Joni Lovenduski; and *Abortion Politics: Public Policy in Cross-Cultural Perspective* (1996), co-edited with Dorothy McBride Stetson. She has written extensively in the area of women and politics and has served as a major research consultant to the European Women Project, sponsored by the European Union, and to the television series *Shoulder to Shoulder*, which dealt with the British suffrage movement.

KIM FRIDKIN KAHN is Professor of Political Science at Arizona State University. She has contributed articles to the *American Political Science Review*, *American Journal of Politics*, and the *Journal of Politics*. She is the co-author of *The Spectacle of U.S. Senate Campaigns* (1999) and the author of *The Political Consequences of Being a Woman* (1996). Professor Kahn's current research interests focus on negativity in campaigns and women and politics.

DEBRA J. LIEBOWITZ is Assistant Professor of Women's Studies and Political Science at Drew University. Her research focuses on gender and transnational political organizing with an emphasis on debates in international political economy and U.S.–Latin American relations. Most recently, she served as guest editor of a special issue of the *International Feminist Journal of Politics* on gender politics in the wake of the North American Free Trade Agreement (NAFTA).

JOAN E. MCLEAN is Associate Professor at Ohio Wesleyan University where she has taught politics and government since 1990. Before entering academia, she was active in national politics as political director for the National Women's Political Caucus, a founder of EMILY's List, and a political adviser to Geraldine Ferraro during her 1984 Vice Presidential race. Professor McLean is currently conducting research on the effect of term limits on the career decisions of state legislators.

PIPPA NORRIS is McGuire Lecturer in Comparative Politics at the John F. Kennedy School of Government, Harvard University. She has published more than two dozen books comparing gender politics, elections and voting behavior, and political communications. Recent books include *Democratic Phoenix: Political Activism Worldwide* (2002) and *Rising Tide: Gender Equality and Cultural Change* (with Ronald Inglehart, 2003).

SUE THOMAS formerly Associate Professor and Director of Women's Studies at Georgetown University, works as senior policy researcher for Pacific Institute for Research and Evaluation. Her research interests center on women and politics and women's issues generally. She has published widely in professional journals, and her books include *How Women Legislate* (1994) and *Women and Elective Office: Past, Present, and Future* (with Clyde Wilcox, 1998), both by Oxford University Press. Most recently, she has concentrated on women's health issues.

❖ Introduction: New Challenges, New Questions, New Directions[1]

Susan J. Carroll and Debra J. Liebowitz

More than two decades have passed since a few pioneering political scientists began to raise questions about why women were so underrepresented in the political life of the United States (Kirkpatrick 1974; Tolchin and Tolchin 1976; Diamond 1977; Githens and Prestage 1977). In particular, these early women and politics scholars noticed that relatively few women served in positions of political leadership and asked: Who are these women? What are their backgrounds and their characteristics? And why are there so few of them? Their questions and their studies gave rise to more questions and more research, and over the years women and politics developed into a major area of scholarly inquiry within, and to a lesser extent outside, the discipline of political science.

We have learned a great deal during the past two decades about the participation of women in American politics, especially electoral politics which has been the focus of most research. As a result of studies conducted both by the Center for American Women and Politics (CAWP)[2] and by individual researchers, we now have considerable knowledge about the backgrounds of women who serve in public office in the United States, the obstacles they face in winning election, and their interests, attitudes, and priorities as officeholders (e.g., Johnson and Carroll 1978; Carroll and Strimling 1983; Dodson and Carroll 1991; Darcy, Welch, and Clark 1994; Carroll 1994; Burrell 1994; Thomas 1994; Gertzog 1995; Fox 1997; Rosenthal 1998; Swers 2001; Carroll 2001). Similarly, research has greatly enhanced our understanding of the factors that facilitate and impede women's participation in other aspects of electoral politics—e.g., as voters and party activists (Freeman 2000; Sapiro 1983; Klein 1984; Burns, Schlozman, and Verba 2001; Schlozman, Burns, and Verba 1994; Schlozman, Burns, Verba, and Donahue 1995; Jennings and Farah 1981).

However, while much has been learned over the past 25 years about women's participation in American politics, especially electoral politics, many questions remain. Developments in politics have presented new questions for scholars of women and politics. The number of women has increased substantially at some levels of office since the mid-1970s although women still remain vastly under-represented at the highest levels. The increased numbers of women public officials have raised new questions about their potential impact: What difference, if any, does their presence make? To what extent have the increased numbers of women officeholders influenced public policy outcomes? Have women public officials helped to bring about noticeable changes in the political process or the way the business of politics is conducted? Under what circumstances do we see women in office making a difference? What effects do different institutional contexts and varying proportions of women among officeholders have on the extent to which women public officials have a distinctive, gender-related impact?

Similarly, the emergence (or at least public recognition) of gender differences in voting preferences, party identification, and other political attitudes and predispositions in the 1980s has posed a host of new questions for researchers. To what extent do the gender differences evident since the 1980s represent new developments and to what extent are they simply old differences that previously had been overlooked? What political and social developments caused these differences? How can gender differences in voting behavior and political orientations be explained? And what is their political significance?

Major shifts in the political climate and changes in the political context also have raised new questions for women and politics researchers. For example, the euphoria among feminists following the election of record numbers of women to Congress in the 1992 elections, all of whom were pro-choice, quickly vanished in 1994 with the election of several right-wing, pro-life congresswomen. What motivates strongly conservative women to run for office? How do conservative women see their gender influencing their political priorities and behavior? What impact has the presence of more conservative women had on the ability of women public officials to advance a collective agenda? What are the implications of the increasing presence of right-wing women for theories of representation and how we conceptualize the relationship between the numbers of women in office and the representation of "women's interests?"

Talk radio and televised talk shows have played an increasingly important role in influencing political attitudes and perceptions in recent years, thereby raising new questions for women and politics scholars. Similarly, the Internet is fast becoming a key tool for communicating political messages, raising money in campaigns, and garnering information; yet, we know little about the ways this rapidly changing technology has influenced the political participation of women as voters and candidates. What effect have these media had on public

❖ Susan J. Carroll and Debra J. Liebowitz

attitudes toward politically active women? In what ways have they made the political climate more or less hospitable to women's involvement? Do gendered expectations about technology have an impact on its use by women candidates?

Just as political developments have raised new questions, so too have recent intellectual developments within the academy posed important challenges to women and politics researchers. The most important of these challenges have come from interdisciplinary feminist scholarship in the field of women's studies. Most research on women and American politics has employed frameworks from political science and utilized scientific methodology, frequently relying on survey research. Because most of the existing work on women and politics has been conducted by scholars whose home discipline has viewed their research interests as marginal, the disciplinary and scientific orientation of much of the existing work on women and politics is understandable. In an attempt to achieve greater legitimacy for the study of women and politics and gain a foothold within their discipline, political scientists who study women and politics have generally adopted frameworks and methods favored by other political scientists. Yet, in striving for acceptance within political science, women and politics scholars have narrowed the range of questions they address, the frameworks they utilize, and the methods they employ. Interdisciplinary feminist scholarship provides alternative frameworks to those that are prevalent in political science and can suggest different ways of thinking about the possible effects of gender on political behavior. For example, work by feminist historians on women's activism suggests that women have been politically active in ways and locations overlooked by political scientists and that political science operates with too narrow a definition of politics, centering on the electoral arena (Baker 1990; Lebsock 1990). Feminist scholarship has also provided powerful critiques of scientific epistemology and methodology, pointing to the biases and limitations of scientific approaches and suggesting the need for alternative methodologies, especially methodologies that are historically and culturally specific (e.g., Potter 2001; Harding 1986, 1998; Bleier 1986).

The fact that scholars of women and politics have had to strive for legitimacy within academia also means that it has been difficult to concentrate on designing research useful to practitioners and activists who are working to advance women's status in American politics or improve their plight in society more generally. Most women and politics research, like academic research more generally, has been written for an academic audience. For the most part, the questions of greatest interest to academics have not been those of greatest concern to practitioners. And any results generated by academic research that might interest political practitioners have seldom reached this audience because mechanisms for communication and information dissemination have been extremely limited.

The study of women and politics stands at an important transition point. Women and politics scholarship, while still more on the margins than at the center of political science and other disciplines, has achieved a fairly secure foothold in academia. As evidence of this, the Organized Section for Women and Politics Research within the American Political Science Association currently has more than 500 members, and many scholars of women and politics have received tenure. Nevertheless, while the study of women and politics has achieved greater legitimacy, it currently faces new challenges posed by recent developments in both politics and interdisciplinary feminist scholarship.

The purpose of this volume is to help move the study of women and American politics through this transition into its next era. This volume presents a research agenda, developed by leading scholars of women and American politics, suggesting directions that could fruitfully shape the study of women and American politics in the early twenty-first century. While each chapter reviews current knowledge about a particular aspect of women's involvement in American politics, the emphasis of each chapter is on what we do *not* yet know, rather than on what we do know. The focus is forward, on research needs for the future, rather than backward, on what we have learned in the past.

We hope that this volume will stimulate more innovative and creative research projects employing a diversity of research methods. Certainly there is a need for research that will fill the gaps in our existing knowledge, and the various chapters of this book identify many questions that remain unanswered in existing research as well as the types of studies that are needed to address them. However, there also is a need for new research that examines the implications of recent political developments and that responds to the challenges posed by interdisciplinary feminist scholarship. We need not only to fill in the parts that are missing in existing pictures, but also to break out of the old frames and create new pictures.

Subsequent chapters will examine specific research needs on nine subjects of special interest to scholars of women and American politics: political recruitment, campaign strategy, money, political leadership, parties and women's organizations, the gender gap in voting, media, women of color, and participation outside of electoral politics. In this introductory chapter we set the stage for subsequent chapters by highlighting more general research needs and directions for research on women and American politics—needs and directions that cut across and transcend the nine subject areas. Our discussion of general research needs and directions illustrates some of the major ways in which recent developments in politics and interdisciplinary feminist scholarship have posed new challenges for scholars of women and politics.

❖ Susan J. Carroll and Debra J. Liebowitz

❖ COMPLICATING OUR CONCEPTION OF THE CATEGORY "WOMEN"

Recent work in feminist scholarship has called into question the very category, "women," which has constituted the epistemological foundation for the empirical work on women and American politics (e.g., Zerilli 1998; Butler 1990; Flax 1990; Alcoff 1988; Scott 1986; Young 1994). Many interdisciplinary feminist scholars, influenced by postmodern thinking, reject as essentialist the idea that all or most women share a common identity or a common set of interests, characteristics, or experiences. These scholars, who tend to be anti-foundationalist, resist totalizing generalizations and call into question the assumptions that there are underlying, discoverable truths or that people have stable, fixed identities. Rather, they see identities as fluid and provisional and believe that categories, such as the category "woman," serve to reify one difference while erasing and obscuring other differences.

More empirically oriented scholars, trained in scientific methodology, often dismiss the writings of those influenced by postmodernism as irrelevant for their work because the anti-foundationalist assumptions that underlie postmodern thought are so fundamentally different from the Enlightenment assumptions upon which scientific work is based. Indeed, critical differences in assumptions certainly do exist. Nevertheless, we believe that postmodern feminist critiques raise important theoretical issues for empirically oriented scholars of women and American politics, especially regarding the category "women" and the way we think about gender difference. In particular, these critiques would seem to suggest that women and politics scholars should, at a minimum, be more self-conscious about the assumptions that we make in using the category and the ways in which those assumptions are structured into our research. The use of the category "women," except when employed merely as a political strategy, is premised on the idea that certain commonalities exist among members of the category, and as scholars of women and politics we could be more self-reflective and explicit about what we assume those commonalities to be. Too often the category "women" is employed in empirical analysis without explanation as though the presumed commonalities are self-evident. Also, empirical scholars might more carefully consider whose experiences we may be downplaying or erasing in employing the category. Postmodern feminist writings have suggested that emphasizing one type of difference, such as gender difference, necessitates the suppression or erasure of other types of differences. As empirical scholars we should be ever mindful that members of the category "women" vary in the way in which, and the extent to which, they possess whatever characteristics or experiences are assumed to constitute commonality. Much variation and diversity exist within the category; it is hardly fixed. In short, postmodern feminist critiques suggest that the category "women" may be less stable and more complicated than we have generally assumed in empirical research. Therefore, we should perhaps be more careful and reflective in our use of the category and more explicit about the assumptions which underlie its use.

Both in the academy and in the political world outside the academy, many women of color, lesbians, and others whose work focuses on issues of diversity among women—some but not all of whom have been influenced by postmodernism—have also called the category "women" into question. They have suggested that the category "women" has generally meant "white, heterosexual, middle-class women" and that the experiences of other women have been overlooked and/or erased. Scholars have put forward various alternative models for conceptualizing the relationships among gender, race, ethnicity, sexual orientation, and class (e.g., Spelman 1988; King 1988; Collins 1990; Wing 1997), but increasingly theorists have opted for more complex conceptualizations that treat race, gender, and sometimes class and sexual orientation as mutually constitutive (e.g., Higginbotham 1992; Glenn 1992; Kempadoo 1999). In this view the experiences of African American women, for example, are not simply a function of experiences they have because of their gender and experiences they have because of their race. African American women cannot separate their identities into a race component and a gender component. Rather, their experiences as African American women are uniquely shaped by a complex interplay of race and gender. Because race and gender are mutually constitutive and the effects of gender and race are analytically intertwined, African American women's experiences of gender are shaped by, and cannot be analytically separated from, their race, and their experiences as African Americans are shaped by, and cannot be separated from, their gender. The same is true for Anglo women, Anglo men, and African American men, whose race and gender are similarly analytically intertwined.

Most empirical research on women and American politics focuses on gender differences in political attitudes and behavior, examining differences between the category "women" and the category "men." Women and politics scholars have long recognized that women (and men) are not monolithic groupings and that important differences exist in the life experiences of different subgroups of women (and men). In order to account for these differences, they have usually imposed statistical controls for variables such as race, occupation, income, and age in their analyses. This procedure assumes that gender and race, for example, are discrete categories, that their effects are analytically distinct, and that their effects can be measured separately. However, all of these assumptions are inconsistent with a theoretical perspective that views race and gender as mutually constitutive. In assuming that the effects of race are separable from the effects of gender and can be isolated and controlled for statistically, our statistical

❖ SUSAN J. CARROLL AND DEBRA J. LIEBOWITZ

analyses are based on an understanding of the effects of race and gender that resemble what Deborah King (1988) has termed an "additive" model, in which the effects of gender are distinct from the effects of race and the effects of one are merely added to the effects of the other. This clearly is a very different understanding of the relationship between gender and race than the more complex understanding, prevalent in current feminist theorizing, of race and gender as mutually constitutive.

The critiques of the category "women" by those whose work focuses on issues of diversity among women, like the critiques by those who have been influenced by postmodern thinking, suggest that women and politics scholars need to think in more complex and critical ways about the category "women" and to consider employing alternative methods, such as intensive interviews and historical case studies, which can better reflect the complexity of the category, instead of, or in addition to, standard statistical analyses. The critiques by women of color, lesbians, and others who emphasize diversity among women also point to several other, very concrete, suggestions about future research on women and American politics. Most studies of American women and politics are based on predominantly white samples or populations of women. Conclusions drawn about "women" based on these studies thus reflect the experiences of Anglo women to a far greater degree than they reflect the experiences of women of color. Relatively little research has explicitly and intensively examined the political orientations or behavior of women of color. (See Chapter Eight in this volume for an overview of the literature that does exist.) As a result, much more research focusing specifically on women of color is needed that takes the information we have about "women's" political involvement, based on studies of predominantly white women, and determines the ways in which the experiences of African American women, Latinas, Asian American women, and other women of color are similar to and different from those of white women and each other. Similarly, research is needed that focuses on the political involvement and experiences of lesbian and bisexual women, working-class women, women of the Christian right, and other politically significant subgroups of women whose experiences have seldom been the subject of intensive analysis.

In order to understand fully the involvement of women of color in American politics, future research projects should be devised in such a way that Anglo women's experiences are not used as the sole basis for formulating research questions. Researchers need to be sensitive to the distinctive experiences of various subgroups of women of color and to the ways in which the forms and location of their participation, the factors that motivate their involvement, and their priorities in the political arena may be very different from those of white women and from each other. In many cases new and different questions (for example, about the role of churches, participation in indigenous community groups, and immigration experiences) must be asked to understand fully the participation of women of color and their contributions to politics.

Of course, because of their life experiences and their understanding of their communities, women of color themselves may be most aware of the limitations of existing research for explaining the political participation and contributions of women of color and more likely to design studies that accurately assess the involvement and impact of women of color. The fact that there is so little research on the involvement of women of color in American politics is undoubtedly related to the fact that the vast majority of scholars conducting research on women and American politics are white. Consequently, there is an obvious need for political science, other academic disciplines, foundations, and individual scholars and activists to encourage and facilitate the education and the research of women of color who have an interest in studying women and American politics. However, enhancing the understanding of the participation and contributions of women of color to American politics is a collective responsibility that belongs to all researchers in this field, not just to those who themselves are women of color. One of the major challenges for scholars of women and politics is to develop a base of knowledge that far better reflects the full range and multiplicity of political experiences of those encompassed by the category "women."

Feminist critiques of the category "women" have also revealed the fundamentally "gendered" nature of politics itself. Feminists have argued that political life is produced through a socially and culturally constructed system where characteristics such as rationality, strength, and political or public activity are associated with masculinity, and, by virtue of that, men. Their opposites—irrationality, weakness, and the home or private sphere activity—are quintessentially feminized and consequently associated with the "weaker sex," women. For scholars of women and American politics this theoretical insight points to a host of unanswered research questions: In what ways are gendered assumptions and understandings written into the institutions that populate and the rules that guide the American political landscape? How does the gendered construction of the American political system affect individual candidates, both women and men, as they run for office? How do gendered expectations about family, a woman's ability to raise money, and the like affect her decision about whether to run for office? How does the gendered construction of policy issues affect who gets assigned to particular committees and who does not?

❖ DIVERSIFYING OUR CHOICE OF RESEARCH METHODS

To date most research on women and American politics has been done by political scientists employing disciplinary frameworks and relying primarily on quantitative analyses, often using survey data. This research has made, and will continue to make, invaluable contributions to our understanding of the opportunities and constraints faced by women in politics. Even so, it is clear that the almost exclusive reliance on quantitative approaches has narrowed the range of research questions that have been investigated as well as the types of knowledge that have been acquired. In order to address gaps in our knowledge and expand the focus of research on women and American politics, scholars in the future will need to employ a greater diversity of methodological approaches.

The heavy reliance of women and politics researchers on quantitative analysis, particularly of survey data, is due in large part to data availability and disciplinary reward structures. Researchers often make choices to use data that are available because there are substantial costs, in time and money, associated with original data collection. Academic funding sources and foundations that support the collection of new data, such as the National Science Foundation, have for a variety of reasons rarely given money to projects focusing on women and politics. First, many of the established scholars who have the greatest influence on the decisions of foundations (i.e., the academic gatekeepers) have viewed the study of women and politics as marginal—as outside the mainstream and peripheral to the most important work being done. Second, scholars who do research on women and politics often are perceived by these gatekeepers as advocates for a particular political agenda and thus are considered insufficiently "objective" in their work. Third, academic funding sources and foundations in the social sciences often have a strong bias toward supporting work that is highly scientific in nature and seeks to explain variations in human behavior with parsimonious models consisting of a small number of variables. Although much of the work on women and politics has been based on quantitative analysis, most of it has not employed the types of models and quantitative techniques that are commonly viewed as the most "sophisticated" and "rigorous."

In addition, most women and politics scholars work within a discipline which rewards certain types of work and not others. The choice to use methods that are viewed as unconventional can be a difficult one for women and politics researchers whose scholarship is already viewed as marginal to the discipline of political science. In broadening our methodological approaches, we may rely on methods that the majority of political scientists consider to be less scientific and thus less legitimate. In addition, most political science journals show a preference for publishing quantitative work that makes using alternative methods even more challenging. Nevertheless, as several of the chapters in this edited volume make clear, many women and politics researchers believe that more diverse and alternative approaches to research are necessary if we are to answer some of the most compelling questions about women's participation in American politics.

Interdisciplinary feminist scholars have raised many questions about the use of scientific methodology. The specifics of the critiques made by feminist critics of science vary, but all share the view that the current practice of science embodies strong androcentric biases. Feminist critics of science, many of whom are scientists themselves (e.g., feminist biologists or physicists like Bleier 1986; Hubbard 1990; Fausto-Sterling 2000; Rosser 1987), argue that sexist and androcentric biases are socially produced and individually located. These biases enter the research project at a number of different points: in the identification and definition of scientific problems, in the design of research projects and questions, and in the collection and interpretation of data. (See Keller, 1992, for a thorough review of these arguments.) Some feminist critics of science argue that values and biases can be expunged from the scientific process altogether by more strictly adhering to the scientific method; "bad" science, affected by cultural biases and the researcher's values, can be replaced by "good" science. Others, however, contend that adherence to even flawless scientific method will not eliminate gender, race, and class biases since bias stems from the inquiry process itself, via the identification and definition of research problems. Despite these differences, all feminist critics of science agree that uncritical and unreflective use of scientific methods, in failing to recognize the extent to which the research process is affected by cultural values and the perspective of the researcher, will produce inadequate, biased, and incomplete results.

Some feminist critics of science focus on the situatedness and complexity of knowledge. They argue that there exists no impartial, value-neutral, Archimedean perspective from which to view the world in hierarchically organized societies. Consequently, all knowledge is situated knowledge. Feminist standpoint theorists,[3] for example, assert that claims to knowledge are unable to transcend the hierarchical organization of society by race, gender, and class. Rather, each person can achieve only a partial perspective of the world from her or his "standpoint" in the social order. In other words, it is impossible to separate social structure and the content of knowledge claims from the social, cultural, historical, and material conditions influencing the lives of knowledge producers. Thus, knowledge and reality itself are theorized as "situated" in a specific temporal, spatial, historical, and experiential moment. Indeed, feminist standpoint theorists seek to locate and situate all knowledge claims. These feminist theorists share a commitment to elucidating the politics of knowledge production by questioning the adequacy of any epistemological framework that ignores the role of politics in knowledge production or the role that one's "standpoint" plays in helping to shape the types of issues and the particular questions that garner investigative attention. This means rejecting the hierarchical valuing of objectivity over subjectivity as well as the traditional definitions associated with these concepts. The writings of standpoint theorists suggest that we must ask ourselves whether a notion of objectivity that expects and requires a certain distance between the "knower" and the "known" is possible or desirable and whether the data that are generated from "scientific" research projects can be unbiased or value-free.

Feminist critiques of science and discussions of knowledge as contextually bound are important, for example, in thinking about the limitations of survey data. In using questions from large surveys like the National Election Studies, researchers make two critical and problematic assumptions that have long troubled some scholars of women and American politics. First, the researcher assumes that the questions asked are good measures of the underlying phenomena with which the researcher is concerned. The operationalization of key concepts is always difficult and nuances and subtleties are necessarily lost in the process. Second, the researcher assumes that complex cultural phenomena, like gender and race, which exist in dynamic relationships with each other, can be reduced to discrete variables that can be employed in statistical analyses.

Yet, despite such problems, researchers interested in questions concerning the political participation of women in the United States have often turned to readily available, large-scale data sources like the National Elections Studies and the General Social Survey. While analyses of these data sets have yielded important research findings, we hope that future research on women's participation in American political life will employ a greater diversity of methods of analysis and data collection. Finding answers to many of the most pressing substantive questions in the field of women and politics requires the use of less frequently employed methods such as in-depth interviews, participant observation, focus groups, case studies, content analysis, or some combination of these approaches.

In fact, whenever possible, multiple methods (for example, a combination of surveys, quantitative data analysis, in-depth interviewing, and participant observation) should be used. Relying on any one particular method, no matter what the approach, constrains both the questions that can be asked and the findings that are generated. Utilizing quantitative and qualitative methods as complementary research tools will further strengthen women and politics scholarship.

In examining the dominant methodological approaches to the study of women and politics, it is also important to consider the way that the scope of the research affects the questions that can be asked and the results that can be derived. With few exceptions such as the nationwide studies conducted by the Center for American Women and Politics, most studies of women in American politics are small in scale, geographically limited, and focused on a single level of government. This pattern reflects the fact that funding for more ambitious, large-scale research projects on women and politics has seldom been available.

Indeed, many unanswered questions require analyzing and comparing women's participation at different levels—local, state, and federal. It is not clear whether research findings concerning the state level, for example, are generalizable to the federal or local levels. Moreover, answers to research questions may vary across jurisdictions within the same level of government—for example, from state to state or from one locality to another. For these reasons more multisite, large-scale, and comparative (within the U.S.) research is desirable. For example, we could learn more about the dynamics and underlying causes of the "gender gap" if we had studies examining voting behavior and perceptions of candidates and issues in congressional, state legislative, and local races in addition to presidential and major statewide races, where the existence of data from publicly released exit polls has made research easier.

Access to resources poses the most significant obstacle to doing research that is large-scale, comparative (both within the U.S. and with other countries), and uses multiple methods. Often researchers with ambitious and imaginative ideas have scaled back projects in order to undertake them with minimal resources. Yet, large-scale research projects combining qualitative and quantitative methods would aid in developing more complex and nuanced models for understanding the nature of women's political activities and the ways in which those activities are affected by different political environments and contexts.

❖ EXPANDING OUR CONCEPTION OF "THE POLITICAL"

Political scientists have traditionally defined the study of politics in such a way that much of women's political activity has been overlooked. A full appreciation of women's contributions to American political life requires that we expand existing conceptions of what constitutes "political" activity.

Three interrelated problems have led political scientists who study American politics to dismiss much of what women do as nonpolitical. The first is the discipline's preoccupation with electoral politics and governmental institutions. The second is the focus on national-level politics, and the third is the legacy of the public/private split. Most research on political participation in the United States, including that conducted by researchers who study women and politics, has focused on electoral politics and formal governmental structures and institutions. Yet work by feminist historians would suggest that women have been politically active in ways that fall outside the parameters of electoral politics and formal government institutions. Suzanne Lebsock, for example, has observed that women historically have engaged in many activities that could have been viewed as political but instead have been considered "philanthropy" or "service" or "disorderly conduct" (1990, 35). In an attempt to develop a more comprehensive understanding of women's political involvement in the United States, feminist historians have studied women's participation in voluntary associations, the temperance movement, the women's club movement, the social settlement movement, and the trade union movement, among other activities (see Norton 1986; Lebsock 1990). In doing so, they have helped to broaden the conception of the "political" within the discipline of history (Norton 1986).

However, many of the types of involvement viewed as political by feminist historians still lie outside the normal parameters of political science research. Although there is, for example, considerable evidence from disciplines such as history and sociology suggesting that women have frequently been active participants in social movements, political scientists have generally left the study of social movements to those in other disciplines, examining social movement organizations only when they become "interest groups" attempting to influence the formal public policy-making process through lobbying efforts. Consequently, most of women's activism in social movements has not been viewed as political activity. Although political scientists have paid some attention to women's social movement activity (e.g., Freeman 1975; Costain 1998; Katzenstein and Mueller 1987; Katzenstein 1998), tremendous gaps in our knowledge still remain.

In large part because of the availability of data collected as part of the National Election Studies and other major national survey efforts, most studies of political behavior and public opinion in the United States have focused on national-level politics. Mirroring the research on participation more generally, much of the research on women's participation in American politics also has relied on national surveys and focused on voting and public opinion during presidential and congressional elections. The most consistent exception to this generalization is the research on women public officials, which until recently has tended to focus on state legislatures in large part because of the small number of women serving in Congress. However, even the study of women officeholders has shown an anti-grassroots bias; few studies focus on women holding municipal or local offices even though the numbers of women serving in local office are far greater than the numbers who serve at state and national levels.[4] Non-electoral forms of community and grassroots participation by women have been studied even less frequently. One of the few examples of such studies is *Women and the Politics of Empowerment* (1988), edited by Ann Bookman and Sandra Morgen, which includes several case studies of activism among working-class women. Included in this volume are studies of women who organized to obtain higher quality education for their children, fought to re-open a prenatal and gynecology clinic, organized a clerical union, and led a campaign to obtain better neighborhood services.[5] More recently, *Women Transforming Politics* (1997), edited by Cathy Cohen, Kathleen Jones, and Joan Tronto, examines a broad range of cases of women's political engagement that moves well beyond the national and electoral foci of most research. Their definition of politics is not limited by traditional disciplinary strictures and instead shows the multiplicity and breadth of women's political activities.

Finally, the legacy of the public/private split also has led political scientists to overlook much of women's activism and to dismiss much of what they do as nonpolitical activity. Feminist political theorists have clearly demonstrated the extent to which classic political theorists from Plato to Hegel naturalized the family and women's place in it. In the conceptions of the classic political theorists, men's participation in public life was premised on women's exclusion from public life and their relegation to the private sphere. Women were assumed because of their natures to be primarily oriented toward responsibilities and activities in the home (Okin 1979; Elshtain 1974, 1979; Pateman 1988). Jean Bethke Elshtain has described the implications of the public/private split for the way that women and their activities traditionally have been viewed:

> Man . . . has two statuses: as a public person and as a private person; therefore men are subject to two disparate judgments in their capacities as public and private persons. Woman, however, is totally immersed in the private, non-public realm and is judged by the single standard appropriate to that realm alone. . . . According to this system, if a woman should "go public" (or attempt to) she is still judged as a *private* person. All that women were in private (kind, virtuous, loving, responsible) men could attempt to become with the aid and succor of women; but women could not "become" what men were (responsible public persons) without forsaking their womanhood by definition. (1974, 459–60)

Historically, when women did venture into the realm of public life, they often justified their public involvement as motivated by their family responsibilities and as an extension of their "private" roles. Women's activities outside the parameters of home and family were always tainted with the view of women as inherently "private" creatures. Consequently, their activities could never be viewed as "political" in the same way as men's because only deviant, unfeminine women forsaking their "natural" interests and roles would engage in politics.

Both contemporary feminist theorists and more empirically oriented scholars have challenged the conceptualization of life as divided into public and private spheres and have suggested that the public/private dichotomy is an artificial construct. Nevertheless, the public/private split has had and continues to have a strong impact on the way women's activities outside the context of home and family are judged. Because of the legacy of the public/private split and the strong association of women with the private, much activity on the part of women has either been dismissed as nonpolitical or overlooked altogether. Although women's political involvement is generally viewed as primarily a post-suffrage phenomenon, Glenna Matthews (1992) has traced how American women since colonial times have engaged in activities aimed at influencing public opinion or bringing about social change. Among other

❖ Susan J. Carroll and Debra J. Liebowitz

activities, women boycotted British consumer goods prior to the Revolution, raised money for George Washington's troops, wrote novels such as Harriet Beecher Stowe's *Uncle Tom's Cabin*, spoke out publicly, formed voluntary associations, and in a variety of ways supported the efforts of soldiers in the Civil War. In a contemporary context, whenever women organize to have better street lighting or a stop sign installed in their neighborhood, protest the location of an incinerator or a toxic waste site in their community, or set up a domestic violence hotline, they are engaging in political activity that merits our research attention.

Scholars of American women and politics should adopt a broader, more expansive view of what constitutes "political" activity. Paula Baker has suggested that we might want to adopt John Dewey's definition of the "public" as our definition of the "political" (Baker 1990, 77). Dewey's definition focused on "all modes of associated behavior . . . [tha t] have exclusive and enduring consequences which involve others beyond those directly engaged in them" (1927, 27). As an alternative to Dewey's or some other more expansive definition, we would suggest that scholars of women and politics might adopt a more inductive approach to studying women's political behavior and arriving at a definition of the political. Scholars could begin by examining the activities in which women are engaged and by asking, "In what ways, if any, can these activities be considered to be political?" Certainly, we need to look outside as well as inside formal governmental institutions, at non-electoral as well as electoral forms of involvement, and at the grassroots as well as the national level. While looking in these alternative locations is important for women generally, it is particularly important for developing a more comprehensive understanding of the political involvement of women of color and working-class and poor women who have traditionally had more limited access to governmental institutions and more conventional forms of political participation.

Finally, we need to consider the connections between non-electoral and electoral forms of activism. Under what circumstances does involvement in the former lead to involvement in the latter? Similarly, the relationships between women active in social movements and grassroots politics (commonly viewed as "outsiders") and women who occupy formal positions of power within institutions ("insiders") would seem a fruitful topic for future research.

❖ BRIDGING THE ACADEMIC/ACTIVIST DIVIDE

Despite a shared interest in increasing the participation of women in American politics, scholars and activists concentrating on issues of women and politics have had limited channels for communication and few strategic conversations. One of the primary reasons for the limited communication is that scholars and practitioners confront different career-related demands and time constraints.

The information needs of political practitioners change as rapidly as does the political environment in which they operate, and practitioners need rapidly generated and timely information. Academic researchers operate on a much slower and more deliberative schedule, often taking years to go from a research idea to published research findings. Similarly, activists need information that is written in accessible language and can be easily communicated to the public. However, academics tend to utilize theoretical frameworks and statistical techniques that are understood only by those who have advanced training in an academic discipline. The type of research that is needed by practitioners is not the type of research that is valued by academic institutions or likely to lead to tenure and promotions for the researcher.

Although both activists/practitioners and scholars/researchers are concerned with promoting women's increased participation in politics, academic research is generally conceptualized and executed without consultation or communication between researchers and relevant political practitioners. However, it is important not to mistake the lack of communication between scholars and practitioners as indicative of a lack of interest on the part of either group. Rather, the lack of communication seems more often the result of insufficient opportunities to transcend and span different worlds.[6]

One of the primary goals of the contemporary U.S. women's movement has been to focus public attention on women's near absence from political life. As feminists began to make their way into the academy, they started teaching courses focusing on women and creating women's studies programs. This infiltration was seen by many as the development of an academic or scholarly branch of the movement for women's liberation. Thus, women's studies as an academic enterprise was stimulated by, and has evolved along with, the contemporary women's movement. In essence, the philosophy behind the development of women's studies was, in part, to demonstrate the artificiality of the division between the world of academic inquiry and the reality of women's lives and to promote academic work that explains and critiques women's political subordination.[7]

The birth of women and politics research within the discipline of political science is one example of the movement for women's liberation's journey into the academy. In the 1970s women in political science began to argue that women and politics scholarship was needed to fill a glaring "research gap" (Amundsen 1971; Bourque and Grossholtz 1974; Carroll 1979; Githens and Prestage 1977). Political science research, many argued, paid little attention to the participation, or lack thereof, of women in American political life. Given its roots in the movement for women's liberation, early women and politics research was concerned with challenging the frameworks provided by the discipline of political science. It revealed the androcentric biases of existing paradigms and demonstrated why and how it was that these frameworks failed to conceptualize

✦ SUSAN J. CARROLL AND DEBRA J. LIEBOWITZ

adequately the implications of, and reasons for, women's minimal role in the American political system.

Over the years feminist scholarship has become more integrated into the traditional academic disciplines, including political science, and women studies has become more institutionally secure in universities throughout the U.S. However, while feminist scholars have gained a strong foothold in American universities and have become centrally engaged in academic debates, little progress has been made in reducing the distance between scholars and political practitioners. In fact, one could argue that the success of women's studies within academia to some extent has come at the cost of buying into prevailing academic norms and increasing the distance between academic feminism and the activist feminist movement. Nevertheless, many feminist scholars, having been strongly influenced by the contemporary women's movement, are discontent with the rigid boundaries that academia constructs between itself and the outside world and are disturbed by the gap they see between feminist research within the academy and feminist practice outside the academy. Bridging the gap—developing spaces and methods for ongoing communication between those engaged in academic and activist work—is currently one of the most important challenges facing women's studies scholars generally, and women and politics scholars specifically.

Despite the obvious conflict between practitioners' needs for timely and accessible information and the very different conditions under which academics conduct research, we believe that women and politics researchers, both individually and collectively, can do more than they have done in the past to generate knowledge and information that activists can use to enhance women's political representation and influence. Women and politics scholars can begin by challenging the idea that researchers must necessarily distance themselves from the objects of their research in order to maintain their objectivity. When research is developed in consultation with practitioners, the research not only is potentially more useful, but also is more likely to reflect political reality. Interactions with practitioners can help a researcher to ask more realistic questions and to have a better understanding of her or his research topic; such interactions can actually improve, rather than jeopardize, the quality of research. Engaging in research that is sensitive to the information needs of political practitioners does not necessarily mean abandoning questions of theoretical import; rather, in many cases research can have both theoretical and practical implications. Indeed, perhaps the most desirable research is that which has both theoretical and practical relevance.

In addition to the efforts of individual researchers, more collective and institutionalized mechanisms are needed to help bridge the gap which currently exists between activists and scholars. Ways must be found to translate and disseminate scholarly research to a broader audience. Avenues are needed for academics to disseminate their research findings in a timely manner and in a form that is accessible to political practitioners. Recent advances in computer technology and communications, such as e-mail and the Internet, offer interesting possibilities for establishing ongoing forums for communications between scholars and activists.

Although the development of mechanisms to facilitate greater communication and collaboration between scholars and practitioners is likely to be a significant undertaking, the potential benefits are equally substantial. The end result may be research that proves to be more useful to practitioners who are concerned with increasing women's participation, impact, and effectiveness in political life at the same time that it provides a richer, more comprehensive understanding of political reality.

❖ CONDUCTING MORE COMPARATIVE RESEARCH

Future research on women and American politics would benefit from comparing the political situation of women in the U.S. to that of women in other countries. A comparative perspective helps us see that the problems we are concerned with are not unique to us and that the questions we ask are similar to questions that others are asking, albeit under different social, political, economic, and cultural circumstances. By comparing the United States to other countries, we gain the potential to find solutions to political problems and answers to research questions in places we may not have thought to look.

The development of research on women and politics has emulated the organization of the major subfields in the discipline of political science in that research on women in American politics has been largely separate from research on the political participation of women in other countries. Moreover, although the literature in the area of gender and comparative politics has grown considerably, it consists primarily of studies of countries other than the United States. Works on gender and comparative politics shed light on the situation of women in varying national contexts, but very few of them include the United States as a case. In fact, the largest portion of the work on gender and comparative politics has focused on comparing countries within a single region—e.g., Latin America, Western Europe, or Eastern Europe.[8] As women and politics scholarship confronts the realities of an increasingly globalizing world, works comparing the situation of women in the U.S. with those of women in other countries can shed new light on persistent problems and questions.

One of the reasons that comparative analyses have been underutilized in women and American politics scholarship is that it is difficult to conduct case studies with methodologies that are sufficiently similar to result in comparable data. However, *Women and Politics Worldwide* (1994), edited by Barbara

Nelson and Najma Chowdhury, demonstrates that this impediment is not insurmountable. This volume, which examines women's political engagement in 43 different countries, provides a useful methodological model for conducting comparative studies by constructing case studies which are genuinely comparable. As another example, *Negotiating Reproductive Rights: Women's Perspectives Across Countries and Cultures* (1998), edited by Rosalind Petchesky and Karen Judd, is a product of four years of collaborative research by the International Reproductive Rights Research Action Group, a consortium of women's health movement activists, researchers, and physicians in seven countries. Working together, the research teams developed comparative methodologies for conducting in-depth primary research on the meaning and practices of reproductive and sexual rights in a range of national contexts. The volume presents an interesting model for constructing comparative case studies that successfully transcends the activist/researcher divide.[9]

Comparative research, using the U.S. as one case, will contribute to the development of women and American politics scholarship in a number of ways. First, comparative research can facilitate our understanding of the effects of structural and institutional factors on women's opportunities in American politics. Second, comparative scholarship accents the variety of ways that women make political demands, organize themselves, and engage in informal and formal political processes, therefore demonstrating how diverse groups of women articulate demands around particular issues. Cross-national comparisons highlight the assumptions which undergird research in women and American politics, allowing us to see the extent to which culturally bound assumptions condition research development and design.

An examination of the strategies of women's movements in different countries is one area where comparative research might strengthen analysis of women and politics in the U.S. Relative to many other countries, women's organizations in the United States have concentrated more attention on legal and electoral remedies to address discrimination and gender inequities. In contrast, in other countries like Brazil and Australia, women have sought to create specific institutions within the state as a means for minimizing the impact of inequality and constructing affirmative strategies or alternatives. Indeed, some feminist scholars have begun to grapple with the limitations of a political strategy that relies heavily on legal contestation. While access to the legal and electoral systems for women in the United States is of the utmost importance, it is equally important, for example, to understand the limitations and possibilities posed by political strategies that focus primarily on these venues. Comparative research in this area could highlight the limitations, as well as benefits, of a particular strategic and research focus.

The study of political participation in the U.S. could also benefit from comparative analyses with other countries. As discussed in an earlier section of this chapter, one of the main challenges facing scholars of women and American politics is that of broadening the scope of research beyond the arena of electoral politics by redefining what constitutes politics and political participation. Research on grassroots activism by women and American politics scholars remains relatively underdeveloped; much of women's activism has not been recognized, theorized, and researched as a legitimate area of inquiry. By contrast, feminist scholars of and from developing countries have long examined grassroots activists and their political strategies (Ortiz 2001; Kaplan 1997; Stephen 1997; Kumar 1993). Indeed, many third-world countries have well-developed women's movements as well as established traditions of feminist scholarship that can provide useful models for deepening the research agenda on women and American politics.

Comparative political analysis can also help to inform the analysis and development of institutional, legal, and party rule changes that might further "level the playing field" of American politics. Comparative research may even provide alternative testing grounds for research hypotheses and ideas about American political strategies. Research on gender and political parties, for instance, could benefit a great deal from comparative inquiry. Political parties play an important role in structuring the opportunities that are available to women in American electoral politics. A broad array of policies and rule changes have been implemented by political parties in other countries (e.g., France, Norway, Mexico, Sweden, and Taiwan) that are designed to promote women's political participation. In anticipating the potential benefits and problems that would accompany a move to get U.S. political parties to pledge to appoint approximately equal numbers of men and women to office, a comparative analysis of countries (or states within the U.S.) which have gone through similar debates could elucidate some of the pitfalls and strengths of different approaches. In this manner comparative research could inform the development of methods and strategies for political change in the U.S. political context.

Work on women and politics that is focused outside the United States could also be particularly useful in challenging researchers to think more about the way gender is central to the construction of the U.S. political system. Scholars of gender and international politics have long recognized that a research agenda focused primarily on the formal political participation of women at the level of international politics and policy-making would result in rather sparse findings. While such studies are important to building our knowledge base, the paucity of women operating at the international level has forced scholars of gender and international politics to look elsewhere. Instead, such scholars have both examined the grassroots political participation of women and identified the ways that "gender makes the world go round."[10] In her trendsetting work *Bananas, Beaches and Bases: Making Feminist Sense of International Politics* (1990), Cynthia Enloe demonstrates the ways that wives of diplomats and household laborers, among others, are important cogs in an international political system that relies on gendered hierarchies to function. In examining the myriad ways that gender functions to create hierarchies of inclusion and exclusion in the realm of international politics, the work of Enloe (and others like Molyneux 2001; Tickner 2001; Chin 1998; Hooper 2001) could be useful to scholars looking to take women and American politics research in new directions.

There are many other areas of women and American politics scholarship that would be enhanced by comparative political investigation. This is especially true when it comes to dealing with political issues with which feminists in countries other than the United States have more experience. For example, what might women dealing with the policies put forth, and enacted by, right-wing religious fundamentalists in the United States learn from a comparative analysis of women's political challenges to religious fundamentalism in the Middle East, Northern Africa, South Asia, or Europe? What political lessons could be derived by doing a comparative analysis of efforts by U.S. women's organizations and the international network *Women Living Under Muslim Laws* to address fundamentalism? At first glance it may appear that women's resistance to religious fundamentalism in Algeria, for example, has no relationship to the politics of the right-wing militia movement or the increased prevalence of anti-lesbian and gay or choice ballot initiatives in the U.S. However, in-depth cross-national comparisons may demonstrate that insights gleaned from one situation can facilitate political understanding and strategizing in another national context. By expanding our range of vision and moving us beyond our ordinary frame of reference, comparative approaches to the study of women and politics can shed fresh light on persistent problems and place new questions in a different perspective.

❖ Overview of Other Chapters in this Volume

In this chapter we have highlighted general themes and concerns that we believe should inform future research on women and American politics. The remaining chapters in this volume are more specific; each one explores major research questions and future directions for research in one substantive area of inquiry. Much of the research on women's participation in American politics has focused on the electoral arena, and this volume reflects a continuing concern with understanding and enhancing women's involvement in the electoral process. The first section of the book examines women's participation as candidates running for office, and the second section looks at other aspects of women's participation in electoral politics (e.g., as officeholders and as voters). However, this volume also draws attention to the importance of expanding our research agenda into new areas. Consequently, the third section of the book focuses on new directions in research on women and politics, highlighting emerging, but as yet underdeveloped, areas for research.

The three chapters in Part I of this volume focus on various aspects of women's candidacies for public office. In Chapter One Marianne Githens examines the "perennial problem of recruitment." Githens calls for increased attention to the relationship between involvement in electoral politics and involvement in social movements and civic organizations. She suggests that researchers should re-conceptualize recruitment more as an ongoing process rather than a one-time occurrence, examine the role that groups based on identity politics (e.g., gender, race, ethnicity, social class) play in the recruitment of women to politics, investigate the effects that normative standards of behavior set by male politicians have on the recruitment of women candidates, and pay more attention to women's *perceptions* of the extent to which the political system is open to their participation.

In Chapter Two Joan McLean examines an aspect of women's candidacies that has not received much research attention—their campaign strategies. As more women run for office, the need for research examining how gender may affect the dynamics of campaigns grows ever more critical. McLean calls for more research on five components of women's campaigns: decision-making, staffing, media strategy, fund raising, and voter targeting.

Barbara C. Burrell focuses intensively on one important aspect of women's candidacies for public office—campaign finance. In Chapter Three Burrell observes that research, at least at the national level, has proven wrong the conventional wisdom that suggests women candidates are disadvantaged in fund raising. Nevertheless, more research is needed, especially at the state level and for races for executive offices. Burrell suggests that future research might examine whether approaches to raising and spending money in campaigns differ both between women and men and between white women and women of color. In addition, giving by women, especially to women candidates, and the relationship between women's PACs and women candidates need more research attention.

Part II examines aspects of women's involvement in electoral politics other than running for office. Sue Thomas in Chapter Four calls both for an expansion of the range and diversity of political leaders studied in future research and for more large-scale, collaborative, and multi-method research designs. She suggests that future research needs to examine the impact of women leaders not just on issues traditionally associated with women, but also on policy issues that are not explicitly gender-related. Future research also should more fully explore how women's impact on public policy is affected by the numbers and proportions of women and by whether they have reached or surpassed a "critical mass." Also important are questions about how women exercise leadership and influence the political process.

In Chapter Five Denise L. Baer argues that we still have much to learn about collective efforts by women in both nonpartisan and partisan contexts. She

❖ SUSAN J. CARROLL AND DEBRA J. LIEBOWITZ

suggests that we need more "theory-relevant" research on women's organizations with greater attention to historical context, and she calls for more research on a variety of topics including interactions between traditional and feminist women's organizations, issue networks, organizations of women of color, the implications of declining organizational membership, and lobbying by women's groups. As for women's relationships with the parties, Baer urges researchers to move beyond a concern with the numbers of women involved to develop more sophisticated ways of measuring women's influence and clout as an organized force within the parties.

Pippa Norris in Chapter Six examines the gender realignment that has taken place in American elections since 1980 with women more likely than men to vote Democratic. After examining explanations for the gender gap in voting based on issue voting, structural change, political mobilization, and generational value change, Norris calls for more multi-method approaches to studying the gender gap. Norris also suggests that future research needs to be more sensitive to contextual factors, including variations in the size of the gender gap over time, the diversity among women, and cross-cultural differences.

Part III focuses on new directions in research on women and politics, examining emerging areas for research. In Chapter Seven Kim Fridkin Kahn examines an area of research that has received little systematic attention —the relationship between the media and women and politics. She suggests several topics for future research, including news treatment of women public officials, the effectiveness of media strategies employed by women who run for office, possible gender differences in politicians' relationships with the press, the possible influence of a journalist's gender on the public's understanding of politics, and the effects of the media in socializing children about the role of women in the political arena.

In Chapter Eight Cathy J. Cohen examines the near-invisibility of women of color in research on American politics. Cohen points to the need for more research on the historical political activity of women of color as well as their current policy preferences, political views, and involvement. In order to gain a better understanding of the participation of women of color and their contributions to American politics, Cohen suggests that we need both to disaggregate the category "women of color" and to broaden our definition of political activity to include the actions that women of color are taking locally to affect change in the conditions most immediate to their lives. She calls on scholars to be "politically conscious," conducting research that can help to empower and improve the lives of women of color.

In Chapter Nine, the final chapter in this volume, Martha A. Ackelsberg examines the need to broaden the study of women's participation in American politics beyond the study of their involvement in the electoral process. The almost exclusive focus on electoral politics has caused researchers to overlook much of women's activism, both historically and in a contemporary context. Ackelsberg calls for the employment of a broader array of more qualitative methods. She also suggests the need for more research that explores why women get involved in activism, how activism changes women's political consciousness, what the relationship is between politically active women inside and outside formal governmental institutions, and what the relationships are among identity, activism, and coalition-building.

Considered as a whole, the chapters in this volume demonstrate both the wealth of information that has been generated by women and American politics scholarship and the vast array of questions that remain unanswered. Through highlighting critical gaps in our knowledge, this book will, we hope, help to shape and encourage further research on women and politics. In drawing attention to what we do not know as well as what we do know, the contributors to this volume suggest approaches, methods, and research questions which can lead to a more comprehensive understanding of women's involvement in, and contributions to, American politics.

❖ NOTES

1 Many of the ideas reviewed in this chapter emerged in discussions that took place at the conference, "Research on Women and American Politics: Agenda Setting for the 21st Century," organized by the Center for American Women and Politics in April 1994. We are grateful to conference participants for their insights and the contributions they made to our thinking about these issues.

2 In 1999 CAWP changed its name from the Center for the American Woman and Politics to the Center for American Women and Politics. The former name is used throughout this volume for references to pre-1999 publications and materials while the latter name is used for post-1999 references.

3 For examples of feminist standpoint epistemology, see Nancy Hartsock's now classic article, 1983; Collins 1989 and 1990; Rose 1983; hooks 1984; and Harding 1986 and 1991.

4 For notable exceptions see Stewart 1980; Flammang 1985; Hardy-Fanta 1993; Beck 2001; Boles 2001; Tolleson-Rinehart 2001.

5 Another excellent, but less recent, example is Kathleen McCourt 1977.

6 A caveat must be offered. In highlighting a communication and research gap between scholars and activists, we do not mean to make these categories of identity seem more stable and dichotomous than they really are. We recognize that absolute distinctions cannot be drawn between these two categories since many scholars are activists and many activists engage in scholarly research.

7 As one manifestation of this philosophy, the Center for American Women and Politics (CAWP) has been in the forefront of applied academic research since the early 1970s when it commissioned the first major book examining women serving in public office, Jeane J. Kirkpatrick's *Political Woman* (1974). CAWP, with its close ties to both the

academic and political worlds, has from its inception been concerned with conducting applied research and designing programs to bridge the gap between scholars and practitioners interested in women and politics.

8 Although this is, in general, an accurate statement, some important exceptions exist (e.g., Bystydzienski and Sekhon 1999; Jaquette and Wolchik 1998; Gelb 1989; Randall 1987; Katzenstein and Mueller 1987).

9 In addition, the June 2001 issue of *PS: Political Science & Politics* highlights articles that put women and politics scholarship in the United States in comparative perspective. The issue has a section entitled "Women in Comparative Perspective: Japan and the United States."

10 "Gender Makes the World Go Round" is the title of the first chapter of Cynthia Enloe's book.

❖ REFERENCES

Alcoff, Linda. 1988. "Cultural Feminism Versus Post-Structuralism." *Signs* 13: 405–36.

Amundsen, Kirsten. 1971. *The Silenced Majority: Women and American Democracy.* Englewood Cliffs: Prentice-Hall.

Baker, Paula. 1990. "The Domestication of Politics: Women and American Political Society, 1780–1920." In *Women, the State, and Welfare,* ed. Linda Gordon. Madison, Wis.: University of Wisconsin Press.

Beck, Susan Abrams. 2001. "Acting as Women: The Effects and Limitations of Gender in Local Governance." In *The Impact of Women in Public Office,* ed. Susan J. Carroll. Bloomington: Indiana University Press.

Bleier, Ruth, ed. 1986. *Feminist Approaches to Science.* New York: Pergamon.

Boles, Janet K. 2001. "Local Elected Women and Policy-Making: Movement Delegates or Feminist Trustees?" In *The Impact of Women in Public Office,* ed. Susan J. Carroll. Bloomington: Indiana University Press.

Bookman, Ann, and Sandra Morgen, eds. 1988. *Women and the Politics of Empowerment.* Philadelphia: Temple University Press.

Bourque, Susan C., and Jean Grossholtz. 1974. "Politics an Unnatural Practice: Political Science Looks at Female Participation." *Politics and Society* 4: 225–66.

Burns, Nancy, Kay Lehman Schlozman, and Sidney Verba. 2001. *The Private Roots of Public Action: Gender, Equality, and Political Participation.* Cambridge, Mass.: Harvard University Press.

Burrell, Barbara. 1994. *A Woman's Place Is in the House.* Ann Arbor: University of Michigan Press.

Butler, Judith. 1990. "Gender Trouble, Feminist Theory, and Psychoanalytic Discourse." In *Feminism/Postmodernism,* ed. Linda J. Nicholson. New York: Routledge.

Bystdzienski, Jill M., and Joti Sekhon. 1999. *Democratization and Women's Grassroots Movements.* Bloomington: Indiana University Press.

Carroll, Berenice A. 1979. "Political Science, Part I: American Politics and Political Behavior." *Signs* 5: 289–306.

Carroll, Susan J. 1994. *Women as Candidates in American Politics.* 2nd ed. Bloomington: Indiana University Press.

Carroll, Susan J., ed. 2001. *The Impact of Women in Public Office.* Bloomington: Indiana University Press.

—— and Wendy S. Strimling. 1983. *Women's Routes to Elective Office: A Comparison with Men's.* New Brunswick: Center for the American Woman and Politics.

Chin, Christine B. N. 1998. In *Service and Servitude: Foreign Domestic Workers and the Malaysian "Modernity" Project.* New York: Columbia University Press.

Cohen, Cathy J., Kathleen B. Jones, and Joan C. Tronto, eds. 1997. *Women Transforming Politics: An Alternative Reader.* New York: New York University Press.

Collins, Patricia Hill. 1989. "The Social Construction of Black Feminist Thought." *Signs* 14: 745–73.

—— 1990. *Black Feminist Thought: Knowledge, Consciousness, and the Politics of Empowerment.* New York: Routledge.

Costain, Anne N. 1998. "Women Lobby Congress." In *Social Movements and American Political Institutions,* ed. Anne N. Costain and Andrew S. McFarland. Lanham, Md.: Rowman and Littlefield Publishers, Inc.

Darcy, R., Susan Welch, and Janet Clark. 1994. *Women, Elections, and Representation.* 2nd ed. Lincoln, Neb.: University of Nebraska Press.

Dewey, John. 1927. *The Public and Its Problems.* New York: Henry Holt.

Diamond, Irene. 1977. *Sex Roles in the State House.* New Haven: Yale University Press.

Dodson, Debra L., and Susan J. Carroll. 1991. *Reshaping the Agenda: Women in State Legislatures.* New Brunswick, NJ: Center for the American Woman and Politics.

Elshtain, Jean Bethke. 1974. "Moral Woman and Immoral Man: A Consideration of the Public-Private Split and Its Political Ramifications." *Politics and Society* 4: 453–73.

—— 1979. *Public Man, Private Women.* Princeton: Princeton University Press.

Enloe, Cynthia. 1990. *Bananas, Beaches & Bases: Making Feminist Sense of International Politics.* Berkeley: University of California Press.

Fausto-Sterling, Anne. 2000. *Sexing the Body: Gender Politics and the Construction of Sexuality.* New York: Basic Books.

Flammang, Janet A. 1985. "Female Officials in the Feminist Capital: The Case of Santa Clara County." *Western Political Quarterly* 38: 94–118.

Flax, Jane. 1990. "Postmodernism and Gender Relations in Feminist Theory." In *Feminism/Postmodernism,* ed. Linda J. Nicholson. New York: Routledge.

Fox, Richard Logan. 1997. *Gender Dynamics in Congressional Elections.* Thousand Oaks, Calif.: Sage.

Freeman, Jo. 1975. *The Politics of Women's Liberation.* New York: Longman.

—— 2000. *A Room at a Time: How Women Entered Party Politics.* Lanham, Md.: Rowman and Littlefield Publishers, Inc.

Gelb, Joyce. 1989. *Feminism and Politics: A Comparative Perspective.* Berkeley: University of California Press.

Gertzog, Irwin N. 1995. *Congressional Women.* 2nd ed. Westport, Conn.: Praeger.

Githens, Marianne, and Jewel L. Prestage, eds. 1977. *A Portrait of Marginality: The Political Behavior of the American Woman.* New York: McKay.

Glenn, Evelyn Nakano. 1992. "From Servitude to Service Work: Historical Continuities in the Racial Division of Paid Reproductive Labor." *Signs* 18: 1–43.

❖ SUSAN J. CARROLL AND DEBRA J. LIEBOWITZ

Harding, Sandra. 1986. *The Science Question in Feminism*. Ithaca, N.Y.: Cornell University Press.

——1991. *Whose Science? Whose Knowledge?* Ithaca, N.Y.: Cornell University Press.

——1998. *Is Science Multicultural? Postcolonialisms, Feminisms, and Epistemologies*. Bloomington: Indiana University Press.

Hartsock, Nancy. 1983. "The Feminist Standpoint: Developing Grounds for a Specifically Feminist Historical Materialism." In *Discovering Reality: Feminist Perspectives on Epistemology, Metaphysics, Methodology and Philosophy of Science*, ed. Sandra Harding and Merrill Hintikka. Boston: D. Reidel.

Hardy-Fanta, Carol. 1993. *Latina Politics, Latino Politics*. Philadelphia: Temple University Press.

Hekman, Susan. 1987. "The Feminization of Epistemology: Gender and the Social Sciences." *Women & Politics* 7(3): 65–83.

Higginbotham, Evelyn Brooks. 1992. "African-American Women's History and the Metalanguage of Race." *Signs* 17: 251–74.

Hooper, Charlotte. 2001. *Manly States: Masculinities, International Relations, and Gender Politics*. New York: Columbia University Press.

Hubbard, Ruth. 1990. *The Politics of Women's Biology*. New York: Routledge.

hooks, bell. 1984. *Feminist Theory: From Margin to Center*. Boston: South End.

Jaquette, Jane S., and Sharon L. Wolchik, eds. 1998. *Women and Democracy: Latin America and Central and Eastern Europe*. Baltimore: Johns Hopkins University Press.

Jennings, M. Kent, and Barbara G. Farah. 1981. "Social Roles and Political Resources: An Over-Time Study of Men and Women in Party Elites." *American Journal of Political Science* 25: 462–82.

Johnson, Marilyn, and Susan Carroll. 1978. *Profile of Women Holding Office II*. New Brunswick: Center for the American Woman and Politics.

Kaplan, Temma. 1997. *Crazy for Democracy: Women in Grassroots Movements*. New York: Routledge.

Katzenstein, Mary Fainsod. 1998. *Faithful and Fearless: Moving Feminist Protest Inside the Church and Military*. Princeton: Princeton University Press.

—— and Carol McClurg Mueller, eds. 1987. *The Women's Movements of the United States and Western Europe*. Philadelphia: Temple University Press.

Keller, Evelyn Fox. 1992. "Feminism and Science." In *Women, Knowledge, and Reality: Explorations In Feminist Philosophy*, ed. Ann Garry and Marilyn Pearsall. New York: Routledge.

Kempadoo, Kamala. 1999. "Continuities and Change: Five Centuries of Prostitution in the Caribbean." In *Sun, Sex, and Gold: Tourism and Sex Work in the Caribbean*, ed. Kamala Kempadoo. New York: Rowman & Littlefield Publishers, Inc.

King, Deborah K. 1988. "Multiple Jeopardy, Multiple Consciousness: The Context of a Black Feminist Ideology." *Signs* 14: 42–72.

Kirkpatrick, Jeane J. 1974. *Political Woman*. New York: Basic Books.

Klein, Ethel. 1984. *Gender Politics*. Cambridge, Mass.: Harvard University Press.

Kumar, Radha. 1993. *The History of Doing: An Illustrated Account of Movements for Women's Rights and Feminism in India*. New York: Routledge, Chapman and Hall, Inc.

Lebsock, Suzanne. 1990. "Women and American Politics, 1880–1920." In *Women, Politics, and Change*, ed. Louise A. Tilly and Patricia Gurin. New York: Russell Sage Foundation.

Matthews, Glenna. 1992. *The Rise of Public Woman*. New York: Oxford.

McCourt, Kathleen. 1977. *Working-Class Women and Grass-roots Politics*. Bloomington: Indiana.

Molyneux, Maxine. 2001. *Women's Movements in International Perspective: Latin America and Beyond*. New York: Palgrave.

Nelson, Barbara J., and Najma Chowdhury, eds. 1994. *Women and Politics Worldwide*. New Haven: Yale University Press.

Norton, Mary Beth. 1986. "Is Clio A Feminist? The New History." *New York Times Book Review*, April 13.

Okin, Susan Moller. 1979. *Women in Western Political Thought*. Princeton: Princeton University Press.

Ortiz, Teresa. 2001. *Never Again a World Without Us: Voices of Mayan Women in Chiapas, Mexico*. Washington, DC: EPICA.

Pateman, Carole. 1988. *The Sexual Contract*. Stanford: Stanford University Press.

Petchesky, Rosalind P., and Karen Judd, eds. 1998. *Negotiating Reproductive Rights: Women's Perspectives Across Countries and Cultures*. New York: Zed Books Ltd.

Potter, Elizabeth. 2001. *Gender and Boyle's Law of Gases*. Bloomington: Indiana University Press.

Randall, Vicky. 1987. *Women and Politics: An International Perspective*. 2nd ed. Chicago: University of Chicago Press.

Tolleson-Rinehart, Sue. 2001. "Do Women Leaders Make a Difference? Substance, Style, and Perceptions." In *The Impact of Women in Public Office*, ed. Susan J. Carroll. Bloomington: Indiana University Press.

Rose, Hillary. 1983. "Hand, Brain and Heart: A Feminist Epistemology for the Natural Sciences." *Signs* 9: 73–90.

Rosenthal, Cindy Simon. 1998. *When Women Lead: Integrative Leadership in State Legislatures*. New York: Oxford University Press.

Rosser, Sue. 1987. "Feminist Scholarship in the Sciences: Where Are We Now and When Can We Expect a Theoretical Breakthrough?" *Hypatia* 2(3): 5–17.

Sapiro, Virginia. 1983. *The Political Integration of Women: Roles, Socialization, and Politics*. Urbana, Ill.: University of Illinois Press.

Schlozman, Kay Lehman, Nancy Burns, and Sidney Verba. 1994. "Gender and the Pathways to Participation: The Role of Resources." *Journal of Politics* 56: 963–90.

Schlozman, Kay Lehman, Nancy Burns, Sidney Verba, and Jesse Donahue. 1995. "Gender and Citizen Participation: Is There a Different Voice?" *American Journal of Political Science* 39: 267–93.

Scott, Joan. 1986. "Gender: A Useful Category of Historical Analysis." *American Historical Review* 91: 1053–75.

Spelman, Elizabeth V. 1988. *Inessential Woman: Problems of Exclusion in Feminist Thought*. Boston: Beacon.

Stephen, Lynn. 1997. *Woman and Social Movements in Latin America: Power from Below*. Austin: University of Texas Press.

❖ Susan J. Carroll and Debra J. Liebowitz

Stewart, Debra W. 1980. *Women in Local Politics*. Metuchen, NJ: Scarecrow.

Thomas, Sue. 1994. *How Women Legislate*. New York: Oxford University Press.

Tickner, J. Ann. 2001. *Gendering World Politics: Issues and Approaches in the Post-Cold War Era*. New York: Columbia University Press.

Tolchin, Susan, and Martin Tolchin. 1976. *Clout: Womanpower and Politics*. New York: G. P. Putnam's Sons, Capricorn Books.

Wing, Adrien Katherine. 1997. "Brief Reflections toward a Multiplicative Theory and Praxis of Being." In *Critical Race Feminism*, ed. Adrien Katherine Wing. New York: New York University Press.

Young, Iris Marion. 1994. "Gender as Seriality: Thinking about Women as a Social Collective." *Signs* 19: 713–38.

Zerilli, Linda M. G. 1998. "Doing Without Knowing: Feminism's Politics of the Ordinary." *Political Theory* 26(4): 435–59.

❖ **Part I**

Running for Public Office

1 ❖ Accounting for Women's Political Involvement: The Perennial Problem of Recruitment

Marianne Githens

The term recruitment may mean the act of enlisting new members, the consequences of that action (i.e., the new members of an organization), or the process
for enlisting new members. Since political science uses all three meanings inter-
changeably, recruitment may refer to the individuals recruited to politics, or to
the activity of gatekeepers who do the recruiting, or to the impact of opportunity structures on the recruitment process. Even the *Encyclopedia of the Social
Sciences* provides no criteria for distinguishing among these meanings, instead
simply listing a variety of approaches to the study of elite selection. The resulting confusion is further compounded by geographic and political party variations in political recruitment (Katz and Mair 1994; Lovenduski and Norris 1993)
and by the different traditions for recruiting men and women into the political
arena.

Any discussion of political recruitment must certainly take gender into
account for whereas there is a well-established tradition of male participation
in electoral politics in nineteenth-century America, the same cannot be said of
women. Opportunities and career aspirations in electoral politics were legally
or culturally closed to them. Prior to 1920 women could not vote in federal
elections. With very few exceptions they were also barred from exercising
the franchise at the state and local levels. Regardless of their social class or
achievements, they were not recruited to run for public office and for the
most part did not view themselves as eligible. Even when women like Victoria
Woodhull and Belva Lockwood sought the office of president of the United
States in the later part of the nineteenth century, they saw their candidacy
as a vehicle for garnering public support for particular reforms rather than as
a chance to win public office. The situation did not substantially change
after women obtained the vote. There continued to be little support for their

involvement in electoral politics with negative attitudes about their suitability to hold public office persisting for a number of years. Even as late as 1959 a noted political scientist counseled against women's active political participation on the grounds that it would contribute to juvenile delinquency and homosexuality (Lane 1959, 356).

Although the tradition of women's involvement in electoral politics is relatively recent, their presence in the political arena is not. Women have a long history of political activism in social movements and civic organizations where they often have held leadership positions and wielded considerable clout. It was through their efforts in various movements and organizations that important changes were adopted in public policy on issues as wide ranging as occupational safety, social welfare, social security, prohibition, family planning, and suffrage. For example, women were the backbone of the anti-slavery movement. In the nineteenth century they succeeded in getting penal reforms enacted and were responsible for ensuring a more humane treatment of the mentally ill. They were in the forefront of the peace movements of both the nineteenth and twentieth centuries and worked to make family planning available to all women. Yet all the while they were absent from or minimally represented in elected office, and rarely were they recruited to run as candidates for public office. Any discussion of women and political recruitment must, therefore, take into account their participation in social movements, civic organizations, and grassroots activism as well as in electoral politics.

❖ RECRUITMENT TO ELECTORAL POLITICS

Although women's recruitment to electoral politics is a more recent phenomenon, it is appropriate to start with it since the early research on women and politics focused on their participation in and recruitment to "conventional" political activity, such as voting and getting elected to public office. Drawing on the approaches used to study men's recruitment, scholars employed elite selection models, similar to those listed in the *Encyclopedia of the Social Sciences*. They looked at factors affecting women's recruitment, including social class and professional and occupational backgrounds; the role of political parties; and the perceptions of women officeholders about their constituencies. The circumstances leading to women's increased visibility in politics, particularly the impact of rapid social change and constraints on their recruitment and participation, were also explored. Subsequently research was expanded to an examination of the "gender gap."

A considerable volume of work dealing with women's participation in and recruitment to electoral politics now exists. The first wave scrutinized the kind of woman who was recruited into the political arena. Women's educational and professional backgrounds, their social class, and their economic situation were investigated.[1] Some research looking at the development of political under-standing in girls (Iglitzin 1974; Orum et al. 1977; Kelly and Boutilier 1978) and the relationship between socialization and political ambition (Perkins and Fowlkes 1980; Farah 1976) emphasized the effects of socialization to gender roles on their political aspirations. The implications of the widely accepted notion that women's primary, and perhaps even exclusive, role was that of wife and mother were also explored as were the effects of dividing the world into public and private spheres (Stoper 1977; Githens and Prestage 1977; Elshtain 1981).

Spurred on by the question "why were there so few women holding public office?" scholarly attention quickly turned from the "enlisted" to two other aspects of recruitment: the role of gatekeepers and opportunity structures. By the middle of the 1970s, explanations focusing on the barriers imposed by gatekeepers and the institutional arrangements that discouraged women from entering the political arena were advanced. For example, Jeane Kirkpatrick (1974) argued that there were four hypothetical constraints: physiological, cul-tural, role, and male conspiracy.[2] Others attributed women's limited participa-tion to either institutional constraints or constraints arising from prevailing societal perceptions of appropriate gender roles. Githens and Prestage (1977) argued that women holding public office were caught between the male world of politics and the female roles society assigned them and that this condition of "marginality" had important consequences for both their recruitment and their behavior. Diamond (1977) claimed that the size and degree to which a legisla-ture was "professionalized" affected women's recruitment. Githens (1977) saw a connection between recruitment and the situation of being a numerical minority in an elective body. Welch (1978) pointed to the small number of women lawyers in state legislatures and other factors that discouraged the elec-tion of women. Later, Rule (1981, 1987; Rule and Zimmerman 1992) examined the consequences of single-member versus multi-member electoral districts on women's success in gaining elective office. Cook (1980, 1984) and Githens (1995) pointed to the role of gatekeepers in women's appointment to the judiciary. In her path-breaking work Prestage (1977, 1992) expanded the notion of barriers by examining the significance of race for the recruitment process.

The research continues to concentrate on the multiple meanings of political recruitment. Some deals with the effects of opportunity structures on women's recruitment to politics (Diamond 1983; Githens and Prestage 1979; Fowlkes 1984; Beckwith 1989; Darcy, Welch, and Clark 1987; Clark 1991). The ramifica-tions of open seats versus incumbency, the type of electoral districts, the prac-tices of political parties, and the selection process for candidates have been carefully scrutinized (Rule 1987; Studlar and Welch 1991; Bullock and Mac-Manus 1991; Studlar and McAllister 1991; Norris 1994). Duerst-Lahti and Kelly

(1995) have examined gender power within the context of leadership and governance. Some scholarly work has extended the definition of opportunity structures to include the role of the print media and television. It has explored the media's treatment of women in terms of reinforcing stereotypes and its effects on women's efforts to run for public office (Carter, Branston, and Allan 1998; Kahn 1994; Kahn and Goldenberg 1991; Norris 1997).

In a number of instances there have been attempts to synthesize the various aspects of recruitment by simultaneously looking at the recruits themselves, their interactions with the gatekeepers, and their efforts to deal with the institutions in which they found themselves. *A Portrait of Marginality* (1977) was perhaps the earliest example of this approach. Since then a number of excellent studies have looked in depth at women as candidates (Carroll 1994; Clark 1991; Clark, Hadley, and Darcy 1989; Darcy, Welch, and Clark 1987). Prestage's and subsequently Cohen's work (see Chapter Eight, this volume) has been crucial in pointing to the complex situation confronting women of color. Others have examined closely the behavior and characteristics of women holding public office (Thomas 1994; Foerstel and Foerstel 1996; Tolleson-Rinehart and Stanley 1994; Carroll and Strimling 1993; Burrell 1996).

Discussions of women in electoral politics prompted some to scrutinize their impact on public policy affecting women. Most frequently the thrust of this research was on women as objects of public policy. For example, Boneparth (1982) looked at a broad range of policies affecting women's lives. In an effort to broaden the scope of discussion, Gelb and Palley explored an array of policies affecting women in America and elsewhere in their 1982 study and in a subsequent edition. In contrast Piven (1985), Pascall (1986), Gordon (1990), and Sainsbury (1994) focused on a specific area: gender and welfare policy. Explorations of the impact of public policy on women's lives also awakened interest in women's use of social movements to bring about changes in public policy, particularly in the areas of reproductive rights and sex discrimination (Dahlerup 1986; Lovenduski and Outshoorn 1986; Ackelsberg and Diamond 1987).

The work on women's recruitment to electoral politics has been invaluable. It has provided a snapshot of the women recruited to electoral politics, the positions that they held, the values that they brought with them into the public arena, and the routes they followed in achieving public office. It has permitted us to look at women's leadership styles and to contrast the situations of white women and women of color. It has given us a chance to evaluate the significance of women officeholders for public policy affecting women. It has also allowed for comparisons among women recruited to politics, less politicized women, and men. Moreover, in blending the three different notions of recruitment, it has produced a nuanced picture of those women participating in the electoral arena.

❖ MARIANNE GITHENS

❖ WOMEN'S OTHER ROUTE INTO THE POLITICAL ARENA

While some scholars were analyzing women's participation and recruitment to electoral politics, others started to explore women's participation in social movements and civic organizations. Findings in the newly emerging field of women's history indicated that contrary to widely held perceptions, women had long been active politically. Few women held public office as Duverger (1955) and others observed, but that did not mean that women were absent from the political arena. Quite the contrary. For example, between October 1914 and January 1915 some 40,000 women were mobilized to form the Woman's Peace Party (Degan 1939), and thousands of women were recruited into the suffrage, the settlement house, and the temperance movements. Sometimes women's political activity was directed toward the improvement of their own status. For example, in the nineteenth century they fought to gain the right to vote and to inherit and manage their own property. In the twentieth century they waged battles in the public arena to secure reproductive freedom and equal rights. In other instances they took up issues of community concern, including temperance, peace, and the establishment or expansion of social welfare programs. They were also involved in organizing workers and trade unions, especially the International Workers of the World (IWW). And American women were not the only ones to be active in social movements and civic organizations. Elsewhere in the world, women took part in a host of revolutionary and reform movements. They participated in the overthrow of the monarchy in France and the bread riots that sparked the 1917 revolution in Czarist Russia. They were actively involved in the Algerian war for independence. More recently their protests against human rights violations in Argentina contributed to the collapse of the government there.

Upon closer scrutiny it became clear that the contradictory images of women as politically passive and as movers and shakers in social movements and civic organizations resulted from a gendered understanding of what constituted political participation. As long as definitions of political participation were predicated exclusively on male patterns of voting, campaigning, elections, and officeholding, women's contributions in the public sphere would be overlooked. A more gender sensitive understanding was clearly needed.

At the same time that the definition of political participation was being broadened to include social movements, civic associations, and grassroots activism, research also noted some women's lack of interest in electoral politics. In an effort to account for this reluctance, the idea of difference was advanced. Ackelsberg and Diamond (1987) and Elshtain (1982), among others, argued that women, as an oppressed group, had been defined too long in terms of their oppression. As a result their difference and culture were ignored or denigrated. However, the truth was that women had interests, needs, and psyches that were unlike those of men. It was these gender differences in attitudes, values, and perhaps moral reasoning that made some women indifferent to electoral politics and agendas that addressed only the needs of men.

Difference soon became the defining paradigm for a number of feminist scholars. But although many embraced the idea of difference, they could not agree about its cause. For some, difference stemmed from the dominance of home and family in the lives of women or perhaps from something even more basic to their nature than that. The disparate expectations, ethical and emotional commitments, and work both at home and in the marketplace for men and women produced a distinctive set of assumptions, patterns of interactions, and policy agendas (Chodorow 1978; Gilligan 1982; Elshtain 1982).

For others difference was the legacy of patriarchy that created and perpetuated a condition of inferiority for women (Eisenstein 1979, 1989; MacKinnon 1989; Pateman 1988). Difference was seen as tied to structured relationships of domination and subordination that shaped identity (Lovenduski and Randall 1993, Moghadam 1994; Bock and James 1992). Emphasizing the concept of "otherness," some feminist scholars argued that as long as the idea of male-defined values and institutions was accepted as universal, women would be labeled deviant and discussed in an ahistorical framework that neglected their integrity, values, and contributions. Only when women were recognized as "other," rather than subordinate, would they experience genuine equality. As an Italian feminist scholar put it:

> female sexual difference (il pensiero della differenza sensuale) experiences the principle of equality as an effect of exclusion and homologization, camouflages itself in social stratification as an inferiorizing condition of human existence, and is caught by centuries of tradition in the domestic sphere where it appears in a role of obligatory unpaid service. (Cavarero 1992, 44)

One solution to a subordinate status was for women to find their own authentic voice. This would allow them to be seen as different and not deviant. Expanding on this idea some maintained that women had to explore the nature, origins, and implications of their own consciousness. This required a "feminist standpoint" reflecting women's needs and world-view. One of the primary vehicles for the articulation of this "feminist standpoint" was a women's movement or interest group where women could "find their own voice" and express a feminist consciousness. Participating in the affairs of established political parties, running for public office, seeking political appointment in the executive branch of government, and filling positions in the governmental bureaucracy simply interfered with the development of this consciousness and the articulation of issues of genuine concern to women.

If women had a different perception of politics and their role in it, electoral politics would be less relevant to them than to men. Gilligan (1982) provided some support for this contention in her claim that girls and boys reacted differently to determining the rules by which they played. She reported that boys enjoyed arguing about the rules, whereas girls stopped playing rather than argue. This suggested that women might be uncomfortable with, or even repulsed by, the dynamics of electoral politics and its emphasis on bargaining over rules. Cockburn, a British feminist scholar, expanded on this point, writing that "women are drawn by the thousands to movements, like peace and animal rights, whose purpose is closer to their hearts, but are repelled by the shenanigans of the House of Commons" (1991).

Just as the research exploring women's participation in electoral politics provided valuable insights into the political behavior of women, so too has the work on social movements and on difference and equality. The importance of gender for defining interests, however, sparked criticism. Difference, some contended, encouraged a view of women as peripheral to the community and diverted attention from their contributions to the broader community.[3] Some thought that difference and identity politics also encouraged fragmentation since it implied that one group of woman could not speak for another.[4] For example, was it appropriate for white women to speak for women of color, or Asian women to speak for Hispanic women? Could middle-class, professional African American women speak for impoverished African American women? For others objections to the notion of difference were based on their concern that it might signal support for the position of sociobiologists that equated difference with subordination. As Pateman (1992) and Italian and French feminists argued, gender difference was always recognized in both the public and private spheres. The problem was not acknowledging difference but associating it with subordination. What was needed, in Pateman's opinion, was the transformation of patriarchal social and sexual relations into free relations and the establishment of a genuine democratic citizenship that did not espouse subordination.

Nevertheless, research on women's roles in social movements and organizations expanded our appreciation of the diverse patterns of women's political participation and gave us a better understanding of women's contributions to the community. It forced us to rethink some of the assumptions in political science about what was political and to realize the extent to which gender specific frameworks influenced work in the field. At the same time though, the research told us little about what kind of woman joined social movements and civic organizations, how women were recruited into them, and what the recruitment process was for social movements. Yet, such information is critically important if we are to understand how and why women participate in this form of politics.

❖ Reformulating a Research Agenda for Political Recruitment

Research focusing on electoral politics minimized women's role in the political arena. Work emphasizing women's role in social movements corrected this distortion but told us little about what kind of woman was recruited to and participated in this form of political activity. Scholarship on difference suggested that some women avoided electoral politics because it did not address their interests and argued that women required a "special space," to be apart until they knew and understood their own voice. Although each of these research approaches contributed to our understanding of women's participation in specific types of politics, none explored the interplay among these forms of political activity. For example, little attention was given to the connection between women's recruitment to electoral politics and their participation in social movements or grassroots activism. It is true that some researchers looked at women officials' memberships in women's and other community organizations (Johnson and Carroll 1977; Carroll 1994), and Carroll and Strimling (1983, 83–109) explored in some detail the connections between women's organizations and the recruitment of women for public office. However, the relationship of American women's activism in broad-based social movements and grassroots organizations such as the environmental movement or Mothers Against Drunk Driving to their recruitment to elective office has received little scrutiny. In contrast there has been an effort in Britain to examine the significance of women's involvement in grassroots organizing such as the Greenham peace camp for their involvement in electoral politics. The role difference played in women's recruitment to social movements and grassroots organizations rather than electoral politics has also been ignored. Furthermore, emphasis on difference has obscured women's contributions in the area of public policy.

It is now time to turn our attention to the interplay among these different patterns of participation and recruitment. After all, women do participate in both electoral and social movement politics. Bella Abzug, who played a prominent leadership role in the women's movement and also served as an elected member of the House of Representatives, is perhaps the most obvious example.

When the various forms of participation and the possibility of a relationship among them are recognized, a number of interesting questions emerge. Is women's involvement in social movement politics simply a function of the opportunity structures in electoral politics? Did the women's movements of the nineteenth and twentieth centuries come into being because there were no other means available to women to place their issues on the public agenda? Are women's movements a way for women to organize themselves to achieve specific goals when the traditional methods for affecting political outcomes are not available to them? Are social movements temporary in nature, organized to achieve a limited, specific goal when women's access to electoral politics is only partial?[5] If so, will these movements become increasingly less important as women's access to political office improves? Or do women participate in politics differently and through grassroots organizations and social movements because they anticipate some form of societal punishment from their participation in electoral politics? Is the self-aggrandizement that is so intrinsic to professional politics contrary to the widely accepted norms of behavior for women? As a result, do they turn to "movement" politics instead? If the norms for appropriate behavior are modified, will women's recruitment to electoral as opposed to "movement" politics change? Or does women's involvement simply reflect different interests? Are social movements, particularly women's movements, a means for women to find their own voice? If so, what is the link between the articulation of that voice and political action, or is its articulation sufficient?

These kinds of questions suggest the need to expand the current research agenda on women and politics. Approaches that look at patterns of recruitment to and participation in either electoral or "movement" politics need to be blended into a coherent whole if there is to be a fuller recognition of the multidimensional political role of women. Building on existing research, this new agenda might focus on the following.

❖ 1. Identity Politics and Its Implications for the Recruitment of Women to Politics

Future research might begin by examining the implications of identity politics for women's recruitment to both electoral and "movement" politics more closely. Several questions need to be addressed. What role does identity politics play in the recruitment process? Do identity groups encourage the recruitment of women to "movement" politics? To seeking public office? To both? Does recruitment in all of its meanings—that is, the gatekeepers, those who are enlisted, and the process of enlisting—differ when the identity group consists only of women? When it is ethnically mixed? When it is racially mixed? Do some identity groups, but not others, reinforce prevailing norms concerning gender roles? Do women members perceive their identity groups as supportive of their political aspirations? Are there differences among ethnic and racial identity groups? Is double identity—that is, gender as well as ethnicity or race—more likely to contribute to women's recruitment to electoral politics? To "movement" politics? Does double identity fragment the base of support for women's recruitment to electoral politics? Identity may sometimes be closely tied to a profession or occupation. Do groups such as nursing associations, public health associations, and women's law centers affect the political recruitment process differently than groups whose membership is more closely linked to race, religion, or ethnicity?

Women grassroots community activists have been the subjects of study, but the relationship of their community involvement to their recruitment to electoral politics has not been fully explored.[6] Women and politics now needs to direct specific attention to the role of identity groups in encouraging the recruitment of women to politics. For example, African American sororities and professional women's groups, such as LINKS, have been studied, but their impact on the recruitment of women to both electoral and "movement" politics has not been carefully investigated. Similarly, studies have suggested that more traditional conceptions about gender equality in politics are found among those who regularly attend church or a synagogue (Bennett and Bennett, 1992), but little specific attention has been directed toward the role of religious groups in recruiting women to politics. For example, does identity group membership resulting from regular Roman Catholic church attendance encourage the recruitment of women to pro-life movement politics, but discourage those same women from running for and holding public office? Do fundamentalist Christian religions play a comparable role with regard to women's political recruitment?

Of course, identity is not always a matter of choice. Others may impose an identity on us. Eisenberg (1994) argued that identity may involve voluntary, nonvoluntary, and involuntary association. All women have a nonvoluntary association based on their physical characteristics, but they may have a voluntary or involuntary association with the identity group, women, as well. It is involuntary when negative qualities are associated with the identity of women. In such a case, a woman's preference for another identity may be irrelevant. In contrast, it is voluntary when women accept the identity of a woman and define it as a positive characteristic. If identity with the group, women, is equated with negative stereotypes of feminism in the mind of the general community, there may be important consequences for both voluntary and involuntary association that affect their political recruitment.

❖ 2. The Impact of Reference Groups

Reference group theory perhaps holds the key to a number of puzzling aspects of political recruitment and may shed some light on the concept of "critical mass"[7] discussed by Dahlerup (1986), Haavio-Mannila (1985), and others. Reference group, a term originally coined by Herbert Hyman, is a social group used by individuals as a standard for evaluating their behavior. Reference groups may be normative, that is they set the standards for those behaviors and attitudes that are "appropriate," or they may be evaluative, that is they enable individuals to compare themselves with others in order to assess their behavior and abilities. Individuals do not have to be members of a reference group; what is important is that they identify with the group and use it as a standard for behavior and evaluation. In fact, reference groups may have boundaries that brand as "outsiders" even those individuals who have adopted the group's norms. In some instances, individuals who find themselves excluded from membership in a reference group and who no longer feel fully at home in their original membership group create their own hybrid, sheltering, alternative culture. In this "marginal culture" individuals can interact with each other, share their concerns, and act as supports to one another.

Women involved in electoral politics are seeking entrance into a group where both the dominant culture and the numerical majority are male. This group, "politician," sets both the normative standards describing how women should behave and the evaluative standards for judging women's effectiveness. Even when the group, politician, is amenable to women's entrance, it sets normative standards for behavior which stress an equality based on the assumption of male values as universally valid.[8] As a consequence, women in the public arena may find themselves in a difficult position; the gendered nature of the evaluative standards of their reference group "politician" may make it difficult for them to judge themselves as highly effective. Similarly, the same evaluative standards may make it difficult for constituents to perceive them as highly effective. Moreover in accepting male values and behavior as universal, women are faced with "Hobson's Choice." Male behavior is considered inappropriate for a woman and female behavior typified as caring, compassionate, sensitive, and non-aggressive is inappropriate for a politician. As a consequence women find themselves in a classic double bind.

Research on the political recruitment of women needs to examine what function, if any, normative standards for behavior set by the male culture of politicians plays in the recruitment of women to "electoral" politics and to "movement" politics. What roles do evaluative standards, that is judgments of effectiveness, play in the recruitment of women to electoral and "movement" politics? Are women more likely to participate in politics at the elective and appointive level if an alternative or marginal culture such as a women's legislative caucus exists? Is the recruitment to movements that are predominantly or exclusively female an expression of the need for both normative and evaluative standards to be less skewed to male values? Do women's movements and groups and women politicians themselves play a role in modifying or changing the normative and evaluative standards of the reference group, politician? If so, what is the nature of that role? What are the implications for women's recruitment?

The concept of a critical mass contends that a certain percentage of women legislators is required to advance an agenda reflective of women's needs and concerns. Is the concept of critical mass important because it affects the normative or evaluative standards of the reference group, politician? Have, in fact, normative and evaluative standards been changed in countries such as Norway where there is a critical mass of women legislators? Does the existence of a critical mass affect recruitment by making women more likely to seek public office? Does it encourage women to participate in electoral politics? In the absence of a critical mass in a legislature, do women's movements and groups contribute to a similar sense of critical mass by linking women politicians to women in the wider community? Does this linkage provide support for women public officials who do not possess the critical mass capable of redefining normative and evaluative standards?

Last but certainly not least, there needs to be a much fuller exploration of the impact of state feminism on women's recruitment to electoral politics. Recent work suggests that state agencies in a number of European countries and Australia have increased the participation of women's groups in the policy-making process (Stetson and Mazur 1995). Similarly, in her work on state feminism in The Netherlands, Outshoorn found that femocrats became firmly entrenched within the bureaucracy and that the majority who were recruited from the outside had experience with women's groups before entering the civil service (1994). The roles that the Women's Ministry in France and European political party quotas such as that adopted by the German Social Democratic Party have played in the recruitment of women need to be explored in greater detail, and their potential relevance for American politics considered.

❖ 3. Perceptions of Opportunity Structures and the Social Construction of Reality

As mentioned earlier there has been a great deal of research devoted to factors affecting the recruitment of women to electoral politics. The impact of family roles, professional credentials, socialization to gender role, and the recruitment practices of political parties have been studied extensively. Although this work shed a great deal of light on certain aspects of the political recruitment of women, a number of questions remain, one of the most crucial being: not whether opportunity structures in elective politics are open, but rather whether they are *perceived* as open. Men, both as a group and as individual politicians, may have different *perceptions* than women of how open the political arena is to women. The voting electorate may have still different *perceptions*. These differing views may well affect the political recruitment of women and their aspirations to run for higher office. Do women perceive a glass ceiling in the electoral arena? Do men also perceive a glass ceiling for women? Does the electorate? If so, what are the implications for women's recruitment to electoral politics? If there is the perception of a glass ceiling, are women more likely to choose "movement" politics? Do women or men or the voting public perceive an "ideal" quota for women in certain categories of public office? For example, is it permissible for a majority of an elected school board to be female, but not a county council or a state legislature? What are the implications of the traditional political gender-role orientation among college-educated, young men discussed by the Bennetts (1992) for women and the electorate's *perception* of open political opportunity structures for women? What are the *perceptions* of the extent to which "movement" politics is open to women?

Although the impact of opportunity structures on women's political recruitment has been explored in great detail, the research has concentrated on objective conditions that affect women's electoral success, not perceptions. Now *perceptions* about opportunity structures need the same close scrutiny. Are opportunity structures *perceived* as favorable or unfavorable to women's gaining public office a factor in the recruitment process? If women perceive opportunity structures as unfavorable, do they shun electoral politics and instead opt to participate in "movement" politics? Such questions should be addressed, for what we *think* is true is often as likely to determine our behavior as what actually is true.

❖ 4. Political Role Styles

Some of the early research on legislative behavior suggested that there were different roles an individual officeholder might choose to play (Wahlke, Eulau, et al. 1962; Barber 1965). According to Wahlke, Eulau, et al. the basis for assuming one of these roles was an individual's definition of himself or herself as an expert, or his or her desire to express the wishes of his or her constituency, or his or her desire to be politically effective. For Barber a legislator's role was expressed in varying degrees as a sense of commitment to the community or to one's own political advancement. Although there has been considerable attention directed to the agenda and priorities of women officeholders, research on women's roles and the extent to which they mirror or deviate from those suggested in the Wahlke, Eulau, et al. and Barber studies has been somewhat limited.

Work dealing with European women officeholders moved beyond the idea of a women's agenda and hinted at a somewhat different notion of role. It indicated that many of the women viewed their ongoing interaction with their constituents as very important. Women members of the Green Party in the European Parliament, for example, spoke at some length about the need for frequent, face-to-face contact with the people in their community.[9] Do American women in electoral politics feel similarly estranged from their reference group "politician" and their identity group "women"? Might it be that both voluntary and involuntary association with the identity, woman, coupled with their affiliation with the male-dominated and male-value-oriented reference group, politician, produce feelings of isolation for women in electoral politics? Is fear of isolation a factor in their recruitment to electoral politics? Research has indicated that students coming from economically deprived backgrounds often feel lonely and isolated in the middle- or upper-class environments of many of our best colleges and universities. Might not the same be true for women in electoral politics? Is their recruitment to "movement" politics where they can find a supportive group a preferable alternative to "electoral" politics? In short, the issue of women politicians' isolation requires systematic investigation.

The risky-shift hypothesis claims that a group is more willing to take risks than an individual. If women feel isolated in the political arena, does this affect their willingness to take risks? If so, this might make them feel uncomfortable in assuming leadership roles. It might also make their peers in the political arena and their constituents less likely to view them as leaders, thus discouraging their recruitment to electoral politics or inhibiting their ambition to seek higher office.

Then too, there is the male orientation of Wahlke's, Eulau's, et al., and Barber's role styles. The notion of "professional politician," with its emphasis on pragmatic bargaining, is akin to arguing over rules that Gilligan's research (1982) reported that girls dislike. Perhaps Cockburn's observation about British women's view of the House of Commons, mentioned earlier, is as much an expression of women's rejection of the male orientation of the political arena as the absence of an inclusive agenda. We need to look at whether or not women are deterred from entering electoral politics by the role style of professional politician. Is the less male gendered amateur role with its emphasis on policy more attractive to women? Finally are women more likely to be recruited to "movement" politics because they see it as affording them a better opportunity of realizing their agenda as well as being effective?

❖ 5. The Importance of Role Models

Much has been written about the importance of female role models and internship programs. Some programs, dating back twenty years, have been established at schools, colleges, and universities to provide young women with female role models in the conventional political arena. What has been the impact of these programs? Have they facilitated women's recruitment to "electoral" politics? Does the gender of the person with whom young women are interning make a difference? How important are internships in "movement" politics to the political recruitment of women? What is the starting point of the recruitment process for women? Does the process have stages? What are they? How crucial is the variable of gender at each stage of the process?

Similarly what is impact of role models on women working on campaigns or on the staff of public officials? Does it make a difference if the candidate or public official is a man? Or a woman? Are experiences such as these likely to encourage the political recruitment of women?

❖ CONCLUSION

To date, women's political recruitment has been studied primarily in terms of electoral politics, or social movements, or difference. As a consequence, only a partial picture of women's political recruitment exists. It is time to integrate the three patterns of participation and to examine the interplay among them. We need to understand the extent to which each is linked to and supports the others. Only then will we understand the dynamic and complex character of women's participation in and recruitment to politics.

In pursuing the research agenda suggested here we need:

(1) To emphasize comparative study. To understand the problems and prospects of women's recruitment to politics, it is necessary to look beyond patterns here in the United States. The experiences of women elsewhere provide an important dimension for understanding women and politics here.

As mentioned earlier, political parties have adopted quotas for women in a number of European countries, and quotas have been constitutionally mandated in Argentina. The impact of these quotas can tell us a great deal about the recruitment process and the factors that affect women's participation in electoral politics. The representation of women in Scandinavian parliaments, especially in Norway and Finland, also provides us with data about the significance of critical mass and its ramifications for women's political recruitment. Experiences of state feminism and their impact on women's recruitment would also be useful in assessing the opportunities for American women in electoral politics.

(2) To acknowledge both the diverse forms of women's political participation and recruitment and investigate the connection among them. To concentrate on electoral politics or on "movement" politics or on difference diminishes women's role in politics and distorts both its complexity and subtlety.

(3) To distinguish more carefully among the various meanings of recruitment and appreciate the different patterns of recruitment which men and women have experienced.

(4) To recognize more completely than we have in the past that recruitment is an ongoing process rather than an occurrence like signing up for the army. The relevance of gender at the various stages of the recruitment process must be scrutinized more carefully.

Adopting a research strategy that recognizes the multidimensional role of women in politics will benefit both those in the academy and practitioners. In the twenty-first century perhaps academics and practitioners together will be able to answer the question, why were they so few? Hopefully we will also be able to celebrate the changes that have taken place.

❖ Notes

1 See Githens and Prestage 1977. Several of the essays in this volume deal with the social class, educational, and religious background of women entering the arena of electoral politics. Several essays also attempt to contrast the backgrounds of men and women in electoral politics and distinguish politically active women from those who are less politicized.

2 Kirkpatrick (1974) mentions physiology as a constraint but quickly dismisses it as a reasonable explanation for the absence of women from public office. Of course, nineteenth-century scientists had claimed that biological difference, especially brain size, rendered women unsuitable for public positions of responsibility, and some work of twentieth-century sociobiologists has argued that a different investment in reproduction necessitates women's preoccupation with the domestic sphere. It is hard to accept the scientific bases of any of these assertions, however, with a straight face.

3 Bock and James (1992, 6) argue that it is wrong to equate the American notion of a separate sphere for women with the French and Italian concept of difference and gender separation. For the American position, a separate sphere is a domain of power for women, whereas for French and Italian feminists all areas of life, public and private, have been assimilated into a male perspective which hides behind a mask of gender neutrality in order to subordinate women.

4 There is an interesting discussion of the problems inherent in the concept of group identity, and an argument is made against group representation in Phillips 1992.

5 The concept of social movement is usually associated with far-reaching protests against the established order or dominant values and norms, but women's movements, like special interest groups, are sometimes concerned with more limited goals and objectives. The term, women's movement, as it is used here, represents an attempt to include women's organizations committed to broad scale social reform as well as those advocating more narrowly conceived demands for change.

6 Fowlkes (1984) has looked at this question, but her main focus was on categorizing white women activists' definitions of political. Reed (1977) looked at this phenomenon from the perspective of African American women activists at the community level in the 1960s, but in light of changes over the past 25 years, it might be useful now to reassess some of her conclusions.

7 According to the concept of critical mass, it is necessary for the percentage of women to reach a certain point, somewhere between 20% to $33\frac{1}{3}$%, for the culture of the legislature to change.

8 In Maryland, for example, a commission investigating the appointment of women to the bench of the district and circuit courts reported a pattern of open, undisguised hostility based on gender prejudice. Some have also suggested that sexual harassment is a means of discouraging women's aspirations. See "Report of the Special Joint Committee on Gender Bias in the Courts" 1989.

9 In January 1992 I was involved in a project which entailed interviewing a quarter of the women members of the European Parliament. Membership in the European Parliament imposes a greater degree of isolation than membership in national legislatures; MEPs must live in Belgium and France for three weeks out of every month that the Parliament is in session. Nevertheless, many of the women talked about the rewards of interacting with their constituents and claimed it was one of the primary factors that motivated them to enter politics.

❖ REFERENCES

Ackelsberg, Martha, and Irene Diamond. 1987. "Gender and Political Life: New Directions in Political Science." In *Analyzing Gender: A Handbook of Social Science Research*, ed. B. Hess and M. Ferree. Newbury Park: Sage Publications.

Barber, James, D. 1965. *The Lawmakers: Recruitment and Adaptation to Legislative Life.* New Haven: Yale University Press.

Beckwith, Karen. 1989. "Sneaking Women into Office: Alternative Access to Parliament in France and Italy." *Women & Politics* 9: 1–15.

Bennett, S. E., and L. M. Bennett. 1992. "From Traditional to Modern Conceptions of Gender Equality in Politics: Gradual Change and Lingering Doubts." *Western Political Quarterly* 45: 93–111.

Bock, Gisela, and Susan James. 1992. *Beyond Equality and Difference.* London: Routledge.

Boneparth, Ellen, ed. 1982. *Women, Power and Policy.* New York: Pergamon Press.

Bullock, Charles, and S. MacManus. 1991. "Municipal Electoral Structures." *Journal of Politics* 53: 75–89.

Burrell, Barbara. 1996. *A Woman's Place Is in the House: Campaigning for Congress in the Feminist Era.* Ann Arbor: University of Michigan Press.

Carroll, Susan. 1994. *Women as Candidates in American Politics.* 2nd ed. Bloomington: Indiana University Press.

——and Wendy S. Strimling. 1983. *Women's Routes to Elective Office.* New Brunswick: Center for the American Woman and Politics.

Carter, Cynthia, Gill Branston, and Stuart Allan, eds. 1998. *News, Gender, and Power.* London: Routledge.

Cavarero, Adriana. 1992. "Equality and Sexual Difference: Amnesia in Political Thought." In *Beyond Equality and Difference*, ed. Gisela Block and Susan James. London: Routledge.

Chodorow, Nancy. 1978. *The Reproduction of Mothering.* Berkeley: University of California Press.

Clark, Janet. 1991. "Getting There: Women in Public Office." *Annals of the American Academy of Political and Social Science* 515: 62–72.

——Charles Hadley, and Robert Darcy. 1989. "Political Ambition Among Men and Women State Party Leaders: Testing the Countersocialization Perspective." *American Politics Quarterly* 17: 194–207.

Cockburn, Cynthia. 1991. "Review: *Power and Prejudice: Women and Politics* by Anna Coote and Polly Pattullo." *Political Quarterly* 62: 141–43.

Cook, Beverly. 1980. "Political Culture and the Selection of Women Judges in Trial Courts." In *Women in Local Politics*, ed. Debra W. Stewart. Metuchen, NJ: Scarecrow Press.

——1984. "Women Judges: A Preface to Their History." *Golden Gate University Law Review* 14(3).

Dahlerup, Drude, ed. 1986. *The New Women's Movement*. Newbury Park: Sage Publications.

Darcy, Robert, Susan Welch, and Janet Clark. 1987. *Women, Elections and Representation*. New York: Longman.

Degan, Marie Louise. 1939. *The History of the Woman's Peace Party*. Baltimore: Johns Hopkins University Press.

Diamond, Irene. 1977. *Sex Roles in the State House*. New Haven: Yale University Press.

——ed. 1983. *Families, Politics and Public Policy*. New York: Longman.

Duerst-Lahti, Georgia, and Rita Mae Kelly, eds. 1995. *Gender Power, Leadership and Governance*. Ann Arbor: University of Michigan Press.

Duverger, Maurice. 1955. *The Political Role of Women*. Paris: UNESCO.

Eisenberg, A. 1994. "Voluntary Association and the Politics of Identity." Presented at the meeting of the International Political Science Association: Berlin.

Eisenstein, Zillah, ed. 1979. *Capitalist Patriarchy and the Case for Socialist Feminism*. New York: Monthly Review Press.

——1989. *The Female Body and the Law*. Berkeley: University of California Press.

Elshtain, Jean Bethke. 1981. *Public Man, Private Woman*. Princeton: Princeton University Press.

——1982. "Feminism, Family and Community." *Dissent*: 442–49.

Farah, Barbara. 1976. "Climbing the Political Ladder: The Aspirations and Expectations of Partisan Elites." In *New Research on Women and Sex Roles*, ed. D. McGuigan. Ann Arbor: University of Michigan Press.

Foerstel, Karen, and Herbert Foerstel. 1996. *Climbing the Hill: Gender Conflict in Congress*. Westport, Conn.: Praeger.

Fowlkes, Diane. 1984. "Concepts of the 'Political': White Activists in Atlanta." In *Political Women*, ed. Janet Flammang. Newbury Park: Sage.

Gilligan, Carol. 1982. *In a Different Voice*. Cambridge: Harvard University Press.

Githens, Marianne. 1977. "Spectators, Agitators, or Lawgivers: Women in State Legislatures." In *A Portrait of Marginality*, ed. Marianne Githens and Jewel Prestage. New York: David McKay.

——1995. "Getting Appointed to the State Court: The Gender Dimension." *Women & Politics* 15(4): 1–23.

——and Jewel Prestage, eds. 1977. *A Portrait of Marginality*. New York: David McKay.

——1979. "Styles and Priorities of Marginality." In *Race, Sex and Policy Problems*, ed. Marian Lief Palley and Michael B. Preston. Lexington: Lexington Books.

Gordon, Linda. 1990. *Women, the State and Welfare*. Madison, Wis.: University of Wisconsin Press.

Haavio-Mannila, E. 1985. *Unfinished Democracy: Women in Nordic Politics.* New York: Pergammon.

Iglitzin, Lynn. 1974. "The Making of the Apolitical Woman: Femininity and Sex Stereotyping in Girls." In *Women and Politics,* ed. Jane Jaquette. New York: John Wiley.

Johnson, Marilyn, and Susan Carroll. 1978. *Profile of Women Holding Office II.* New Brunswick: Center for the American Woman and Politics.

Kahn, K. 1994. "Does Gender Make a Difference? An Experimental Examination of Sex Stereotypes and Press Patterns in Statewide Campaigns." *American Journal of Political Science* 38: 162–95.

—— and Goldenberg, E. 1991. "Women Candidates in the News: An Examination of Gender Difference in the U.S. Senate Campaign Coverage." *Public Opinion Quarterly* 55: 180–99.

Katz, Richard, and Peter Mair, ed. 1994. *How Parties Organize: Change and Adaptation in Party Organizations in Western Democracies.* London: Sage.

Kelly Rita Mae, and Boutilier M. 1978. *The Making of the Political Woman: A Study of Socialization and Role Conflict.* Chicago: Nelson-Hall.

Kirkpatrick, Jeane J. 1974. *Political Woman.* New York: Basic Books.

Lane, Robert. 1959. *Political Life: Why People Get Involved in Politics.* Glencoe, Ill.: Free Press.

Lovenduski, Joni, and Pippa Norris, ed. 1993. *Gender and Party Politics.* London: Sage.

—— and Joyce Outshoorn, ed. 1986. *The New Politics of Abortion.* London: Sage Publications.

—— and Vicki Randall. 1993. *Contemporary Feminist Politics: Women and Power in Britain.* Oxford: Oxford University Press.

Modhadam, V., ed. 1994. *Identity Politics and Women.* Boulder, Colo.: Westview Press.

Norris, Pippa. 1994. "The Impact of the Electoral System on the Election of Women to National Legislatures." In *Different Roles, Different Voices,* ed. Marianne Githens, Pippa Norris, and Joni Lovenduski. New York: HarperCollins.

—— ed. 1997. *Women, Media, and Politics.* New York: Oxford University Press.

Orum, Anthony, Roberta Cohen, Sherri Grasmuck, and Amy Orum. 1977. "The Problems of Being a Minority: Sex, Socialization and Politics." In *A Portrait of Marginality,* ed. Marianne Githens and Jewel Prestage. New York: David McKay.

Outshoorn, Joyce. 1994. "Between Movement and Government: 'Femocrats' in the Netherlands." In *Yearbook of Swiss Political Science,* ed. Hanspter Kriesi. Berne, Switzerland: University of Berne.

Pascall, G. 1986. *Social Policy: A Feminist Analysis.* London: Tavistock Publications.

Pateman, Carole. 1988. *The Sexual Contract.* Palo Alto: Stanford University Press.

—— 1992. "Equality, Difference, Subordination: The Politics of Motherhood and Women's Citizenship." In *Beyond Equality and Difference,* ed. Gisela Bock and Susan James. London: Routledge.

Perkins, J., and Fowlkes, Diane. 1980. "Opinion Representation vs. Social Representation: Or Why Women Can't Run As Women and Win." *American Political Science Review* 74: 92–103.

Phillips, Anne. 1993. *Democracy and Difference.* Cambridge: Polity Press.

Piven, Frances. 1985. "Women and the State: Ideology, Power and the Welfare State." In *Life and Gender Course*, ed. Alice Rossi. Chicago: Adeline.

Prestage, Jewel. 1977. "Black Women State Legislators." In *A Portrait of Marginality: The Political Behavior of the American Woman*, ed. Marianne Githens and Jewel Prestage. New York: David McKay.

——— 1992. "In Quest of the African American Political Woman." *Annals of the American Academy of Political and Social Sciences* 515: 88–103.

Report of the Special Joint Committee on Gender Bias in the Courts. May 1989. Reporters Professor Kren Czpanskiy and Tricia O'Neill, Esquire. Administrative Office of the Courts. Annapolis, Md.

Rule, Wilma. 1981. "Why Women Don't Run." *Western Political Quarterly* 34: 60–77.

——— 1987. "Electoral Systems, Contextual Factors, and Women's Opportunity for Election to Parliament in Twenty-three Democracies." *Western Political Quarterly* 40: 477–98.

——— and Joseph Zimmerman. 1992. *United States Electoral Systems: Their Impact on Women and Minorities.* New York: Praeger.

Sainsbury, Diane, ed. 1994. *Gendering Welfare States.* London: Sage Publications.

Stetson, Dorothy, and Amy Mazur, eds. 1995. *Comparative State Feminisms.* Thousand Oaks, CA: Sage.

Stoper, Emily. 1977. "Wife and Politician: Role Strain Among Women in Public Office." In *A Portrait in Marginality*, ed. Marianne Githens and Jewel Prestage. New York: David McKay.

Studlar, Donley, and Ian McAllister. 1991. "Political Recruitment to the Australian Legislature: Toward an Explanation of Women's Electoral Disadvantage." *Western Political Quarterly* 44: 467–85.

——— and Susan Welch. 1991. "Does District Magnitude Matter? Women Candidates in London Local Elections." *Western Political Quarterly* 44: 457–65.

Thomas, Sue. 1994. *How Women Legislate.* New York: Oxford University Press.

Tolleson-Rinehart, Sue, and Jeanie R. Stanley. 1994. *Claytie and the Lady: Ann Richards, Gender, and Politics in Texas.* Austin: University of Texas Press.

Wahlke, John, Heinz Eulau, W. Buchanan, and L. Ferguson. 1962. *The Legislative System: Explorations in Legislative Behavior.* New York: Wiley.

Welch, Susan. 1978. "The Recruitment of Women to Public Office." *Western Political Quarterly* 31: 372–80.

2 ❖ Campaign Strategy

Joan E. McLean

With more women running for public office, developing a richer understanding of how gender affects campaign strategy is critical. Findings produced by research on this topic would be valuable not only to scholars studying women in politics, but also to practitioners working for women candidates. More systematic studies are needed that capture campaign dynamics from inside the campaign, that is, from the perspective of the candidate and her advisors. By exploring the internal dynamics of political campaigns, researchers can identify the extent to which various strategic and tactical moves are successful in overcoming a myriad of political obstacles that naturally emerge over the course of a campaign.

This chapter describes a possible research agenda for studying campaign strategy. The five topics explored are campaign decision-making, staffing patterns, media strategy, campaign fund raising, and voter targeting. For each topic, possible research questions are presented.

❖ CAMPAIGN DECISION-MAKING

Most of the research about women and political decision-making focuses on the way women make decisions once in office. These works suggest that women officeholders are more likely than their male counterparts to employ decision-making styles that are collegial rather than hierarchical or competitive in nature (Carroll, Dodson, and Mandel 1991; Flammang 1985; Johnson and Carroll 1978; Mezey 1978; Rossi 1983; Thomas 1994). Flammang found that when women became a majority on a local government board, they developed "a common understanding of power, not as force and domination, but as cooperation based on consensus and mutual respect, features of their homemaking and child-rearing experiences which challenge the practices of male politics as usual" (1985, 115). In the 1990s, women's inclusive style of "doing" politics was often promoted as a reason for electing more women to public office. Carroll,

Dodson, and Mandel (1991) suggested that this women's way of "doing" politics might be exactly what was needed to counter the growing cynicism about politicians and government in general.

Yet, findings from other studies suggested few significant differences in how women and men operated in the political arena (Kirkpatrick 1974; Schlozman 1990; Verba 1990). Although Verba acknowledged that there was some evidence that women employed a different style of politics than men, he was cautious about the long-term impact that these differences would have on political life:

> Women in the same political settings as men behave somewhat differently, but not radically so . . . Women, in general, have taken part in American life in ways that fit the traditional pattern of activity for American men . . . Women are educated in the same school system, read the same history, are exposed to the same media as men, and therefore, share a political culture that defines the norms of political behavior . . . they learn about the same politics that men learn about and receive no message that, if they do enter politics, they ought to act differently from men . . . if this is the case, one would expect, that over time, their similarity to men will increase in the political realm—as expectations increase that women can have an active professional career in politics similar to that of men . . . Principled communal politics flourishes in social movements outside mainstream politics . . . mainstream politics may demand another style. (1990, 566–67)

Scholzman studied 89 organizations representing women in Washington pressure politics and found little evidence of a "single characterization of a feminine style in government affairs (except) that women are more likely to play by the rules" (1990, 360). Echoing what Kirkpatrick (1974) observed about the behavior of women state legislators, Schlozman noted that in pressure politics women "act like the boys."

Given these contradictory findings, additional research is needed to clarify the extent to which women and men operate differently in the political world and whether these differences have any significant impact on their political careers. The campaign setting offers researchers a unique environment in which to conduct such an examination. For many candidates, the campaign is the political venue where they exert the most individual influence over both day-to-day and long-range decisions. Since candidates are the central figures in campaigns, it stands to reason that they would feel freer there than in any other political setting to employ the decision-making style with which they are most comfortable. If women and men do have a different way of "doing" politics, we would expect such differences to reveal themselves in how they operate in their campaigns.

There are several insightful books that provide anecdotal information about how individual female candidates have made decisions in their campaigns (Ferraro and Francke 1985; Fowler and McClure 1989; Kunin 1994; Lansing

1991; Mandel 1981; Morris 1992; Romney and Harrison 1988; Tolchin and Tolchin 1976; Witt, Paget, and Matthews 1994). In addition, there are systematic works that examine the decisions female candidates made regarding their campaign plans and organization (Carroll 1994; Darcy, Welch, and Clark 1987; Kirkpatrick 1974; McLean 1994). Added to this body of literature are findings from studies commissioned by various women's groups such as the National Women's Political Caucus, Women's Campaign Fund, and EMILY's List (Cooper and Secrest 1984; Lake 1989, 1991; Newman et al. 1984). Together these accounts reveal a tremendous amount of variation in the sophistication of the campaign plans, budget outlines, and staffing patterns used by female candidates. This variation is attributed to factors such as level of office sought, prior office-holding or electoral experience, gender, financial or party support, and the specifics of the races examined.

In general, these studies suggest that the higher the office sought and the more financial resources available, the more likely candidates are to have a well-developed campaign strategy. Because they need to raise large amounts of money in order to reach substantial numbers of voters, candidates running for higher office are more likely than candidates running for other offices to recognize the need for detailed campaign plans and professional campaign staff. In addition, those with previous office-holding or campaign experience are more likely to have more sophisticated campaign plans—especially in the area of fund raising—than those candidates running for the first time. Experienced candidates are more likely to understand not only the importance of raising sufficient amounts of campaign funds, but also the need for raising money early and spending it wisely. To accomplish each requires detailed plans and time lines.

Additional systematic research regarding campaign decision-making could identify the extent to which women and men employ different styles to run their campaigns and the impact these differences have on the decisions they reach. To further study decision-making, research designs could identify the degree to which candidates rely on various types of advisors or information in order to make both routine and crisis decisions.

Research designs focused on these topics could explore a number of practical questions. For instance, if women candidates are more likely than their male counterparts to employ collegial decision-making styles rather than hierarchical or competitive styles, then what impact does this stylistic difference have on their strategic and tactical campaign decisions? Are female candidates more likely to transmit information in a collegial setting in which a wide cross-section of staff exchange information? If so, does this "hands-on" style require women candidates to spend substantially more time making day-to-day tactical decisions? If this were the case, how do female candidates find the extra time to operate this way? Do they spend less time than their male counterparts discussing long-range strategic decisions, reacting to crises, and participating in other campaign activities such as fund raising, campaign appearances, or media interviews? Or does a collegial style of decision-making require female candidates to work more hours than male candidates in order to accomplish all the required tasks involved in running for public office? If the former, then what impact does spending less time on strategic activities and more time on routine campaign decisions have on women's campaigns? If the latter, then what toll does working extra hours have on the female candidate's stamina over the course of the campaign? Clearly, working extra hours may not be too high a price to pay for female candidates who believe that the process by which a campaign is run is as important as its outcome. But what are the practical trade-offs they must make to operate in such a way?

To reiterate, the major goals of research on how gender affects campaign decision-making are threefold. The first is to identify the extent to which female and male candidates employ different decision-making styles in their campaigns. Where gender differences are identified, the second goal is to determine the impact of these stylistic differences on strategic and tactical campaign decisions. The third goal is to determine the overall effect of decision-making styles on the campaign's outcome.

Written questionnaires or interviews with candidates and their staff could explore the processes candidates use to make decisions. Ideally such information should be gathered as the decisions are being made, or shortly thereafter. This "timing" issue could prove to be problematic for a variety of reasons. First, candidates and their staff may be reluctant to talk about sensitive decisions as they are being made and implemented. Second, even if campaigns open their decision-making process to researchers, it would be difficult for most researchers to spend enough time with one campaign to do an adequate single case study, let alone enough time with several candidates to do thorough multiple case studies. In dealing with these time constraints in the past, researchers have asked campaign participants to complete post- election questionnaires or to attend debriefing sessions. These methods are certainly workable and time-saving alternatives, but relying on "recall" data runs the risk of having campaign participants evaluate their decisions through the lens of "revisionist" history. In addition, the outcome of the election could affect campaign participants' analysis of the decision-making styles used in the campaign. So research designs that mix "real-time" case studies with post-election surveys would seem the practical solution.

❖ CAMPAIGN STAFFING PATTERNS

Along with making decisions about overall campaign strategy, candidates must determine who in their campaigns should be responsible for completing a variety of tasks. Campaigns often employ a staff consisting of paid workers, volunteers, and consultants. Clearly, the "mix" of staff employed in any one campaign is dependent upon the level of office sought, the availability of financial resources, and the choices candidates make about the division of labor. Because they need to reach fewer voters and generally raise less money, candidates for local office or seats in part-time state legislatures rely more on volunteers than paid staff to organize their campaigns (e.g., see Kunin 1994; Lansing 1991). In these campaigns, few distinctions are made about who does what. For the most part, whoever (and that includes the candidate) in the campaign has the time and talent to complete a task does so.

Candidates for local office in large urban areas or for full-time state legislative seats, as well as those who seek statewide or federal office, usually rely more on paid staff and consultants than volunteers to build their campaign organization. Paid staff are generally used to run the day-to-day operations. They fill such jobs as campaign manager, press secretary, fund raiser, scheduler, researcher, and volunteer coordinator. Consultants usually are employed to help develop overall strategy, devise media and fund raising plans, and conduct polls. Volunteers likely are used to supplement paid workers and consultants in such areas as staffing the campaign headquarters, coordinating direct mail and canvassing operations, traveling with the candidate, doing other candidate "care-and-feeding" activities, and organizing get-out-the-vote efforts.

Regardless of the staffing pattern used, candidates and staff in a well-run organization know "who needs to know what" and "what they need to do and when" at every stage of the campaign. In order for that to occur, the candidate along with a campaign manager or executive coordinating committee has to periodically set priorities and delegate responsibilities.

Anecdotal information suggests that female candidates are more likely than their male counterparts to have difficulty delegating responsibilities to others. Writing about her run for statewide office in Oregon, Jewell Lansing noted:

> One of the hardest things for me to adapt to was relying on other people to do things for me. As wife, mother, administrator, and president of organizations, I depended on my own resources and others relied on me . . . Now things were different . . . I had a finite number of hours and energy resources to spend. I was learning to ask others to do tasks for me. (Lansing 1991, 54)

If Lansing's experiences are typical, then women candidates running for higher office may put themselves at a distinct disadvantage. At the start of their campaigns, they may not hire the right mix of staff or, if they do, they may be reluctant to let them have enough autonomy to do their jobs. Without the right campaign staff in place and functioning efficiently, female candidates may be more likely than their male counterparts to find themselves overwhelmed by day-to-day operations, leaving them less time to campaign effectively. This problem may be especially difficult to solve for candidates who in previous campaigns for local office relied on family members, friends, and volunteers to staff their entire campaign operations. When such candidates run for higher office and find themselves in need of more professional help, they, along with their volunteer staff, often remain skeptical about hiring experienced campaign staff with whom they may not be very well acquainted. They may also resist suggestions from other interested parties—donors, party leaders, special interest groups—that they hire professionals to help their campaign. Even if female candidates eventually recognize they have a problem delegating campaign responsibilities, they may not have enough time left to change their operating style. Plus, they may not have the necessary staff in place to take over the campaign tasks they perform nor enough money to hire additional staff to do so.

Ultimately, we are interested in determining whether female candidates are less likely than their male counterparts to delegate responsibilities and to recognize the need for paid staff and consultants. If so, what effect do these actions have on the campaign's viability? Through focus groups and interviews with candidates and their staff, researchers could explore how gender affects campaign decisions regarding the mix between paid and volunteer staff, and the duties assigned to each. Researchers could also examine whether gender affects the degree to which candidates delegate campaign activities. In addition, they could determine how gender affects a candidate's ability to make staffing adjustments over the course of a campaign.

If, as suggested, we find that female candidates are more likely than their male colleagues to employ a "hands-on" management style, then we must determine the impact of this style on the overall success of the campaign. With such information, female candidates and their advisors would have a better understanding of the strengths and weaknesses associated with different operating styles. As a result, strategic campaign plans could be designed that capitalized on the strengths and compensated for the weaknesses of each style.

❖ MEDIA STRATEGY

A comprehensive media plan outlines how campaigns successfully transmit a variety of messages to targeted audiences. Some of the most important early messages a campaign must create are those aimed at convincing the media that their candidate is credible. These messages are especially critical for female candidates. Because of gender stereotyping, the media often are less likely to automatically assume that female candidates, as compared to their male counterparts, have the credentials to hold public office—especially executive and higher offices (Devitt 1999; Huddy and Terkildsen 1993; Kunin 1994; Williams 1994; Witt, Paget, and Matthews 1994; Kahn, this volume). Often in order to establish their credibility, female candidates must not only stress their formal credentials, but also explain how other relevant life experiences prepared them for public office (Kern and Edley 1994). Political analyst Charlie Cook observed that "when I meet with candidates, female candidates are more likely to tell me their story and male candidates are more likely to read me their resume . . . I think that this is actually a strength for women candidates as long as they do it in the correct way" (Women's Leadership Fund 1999).

Findings from previous systematic studies, experimental research designs, candidate interviews, and focus groups identify additional concerns female candidates face when making initial communication decisions. These findings suggest that candidates must work not only to get the media to accurately report their credentials for holding office but also to acknowledge their ability to mount viable campaigns. These are not easy tasks. Female candidates continue to report having difficulties attracting favorable coverage in the "horse race" stories that dominate early campaign coverage (Connolly 1994; Kahn 1994; but also see Devitt 1999). These stories often influence which candidates receive key endorsements and early campaign contributions. If additional systematic studies continue to confirm these observations, then several questions should be asked. First, to what extent does the coverage vary because of gender-related differences in the strategies candidates use to attract early campaign coverage? For instance, does gender affect whether or not candidates supply the media and other elites with polling results and campaign finance reports as a way of bolstering their claims of viability? Are male candidates more likely than female candidates to have well-developed plans for attracting media coverage of their formal announcement about running for office? In what ways does gender affect how aggressive candidates are about challenging the media when they think their opponents are receiving more extensive or more positive early campaign coverage? To what extent does gender affect whether key political and community figures try to help candidates reverse the media's lack of (or negative) campaign coverage?

Identifying the strategies campaigns employ when they believe their candidate's qualifications are not being accurately reported in the media would be invaluable. For instance, how effective is using others (party or elected officials, community leaders, co-workers, constituency leaders, family members) to challenge the media's portrayal compared with relying solely on the campaign to do it (see Hitchon and Chang 1995)? Under what circumstances do candidates request a meeting with reporters or editorial boards to discuss such coverage? At what point in the early stages of a race do campaigns use valuable funds to buy advertising to counter coverage that does not accurately portray their candidate's credentials or the campaign's viability?

Another way to examine gender's effect on candidate-media interactions is to identify to what extent female and male candidates and their staffs deal differently with the media. Because of differences in occupations and life experiences, women running for office may have less experience than their male colleagues in dealing directly with the mass media. If this is the case, what are the consequences? Are women more likely than men to wait for the media to contact them rather than to initiate the contact themselves? Does gender affect the degree to which candidates make themselves accessible to the media? If so, what effect do these patterns have on the coverage female candidates receive in the early stages of their campaigns?

Gender is related to media coverage in others ways as well. For instance, some studies have suggested that female reporters are more likely than their male colleagues—especially those over 50—to treat women candidates seriously (Kahn and Goldenberg 1991; Kahn 1992; Mills 1997; Kahn, this volume). A 1999 study conducted by the Women's Leadership Fund found that "female journalists covered the personal qualities of both male and female candidates more than men journalists did, and they covered the personal qualities of more women candidates than male candidates" (Women's Leadership Fund 1999). These observations suggest that campaigns should have a conscious strategy for dealing with specific types of reporters. But do they? If so, what are their strategies? How successful are campaigns in building working relationships with individual reporters or editorial boards that they know might be biased against them because of gender or age?

Another media-related concern for most candidates involves developing effective strategies for answering questions about their private lives (Ferraro and Francke 1985; Kunin 1994; Witt, Paget, and Matthews 1994). To adequately prepare for such inquires, candidates need to assess if there is anything in their private lives that has the potential of becoming a negative campaign issue. It is unclear to what extent candidates conduct such opposition research on their own campaigns. Interviews with or written questionnaires to candidates, campaign managers, or opposition research consultants could identify the factors that affect whether or not candidates do such critical research. For candidates who decide not to allocate important early money or other resources for this type of opposition research, what are the consequences? If opposition research is conducted and troublesome issues are found, then how does gender affect the strategies campaigns adopt to deal with those issues? Are there differences in the ways in which candidates who are women of color, or single, or lesbian deal with potentially controversial issues from their private lives?

One aspect of media coverage that has recently worked in favor of women candidates is the emphasis that the media have placed on stories about voters' desire for a change in the political line-up. In the 1990s, women running for office effectively used their "outsider" and "agents of change" images to capitalize on voters' anti-incumbency sentiment. Of course, at the same time female candidates were telling voters they were "outsiders," they were also trying to convince them that, if elected, they were capable of playing hard-ball, "insider's" politics. It would be helpful to future candidates if researchers could identify the campaign strategies that are successful in delivering these dual messages. Then in subsequent studies, researchers could explore how women who are elected as "outsiders" adapt their messages when they seek reelection as incumbents—the ultimate "insiders."

When dissecting various campaign media strategies, researchers must carefully examine the decisions candidates make about negative campaigning (Johnston and White 1994; Williams 1994). In previous studies women candidates have reported that although they were not as comfortable "going negative" as their male colleagues, there were times when they had to do so. When they felt compelled to use negative advertising, they preferred to use issue contrasts instead of personal attacks. Female candidates also felt more successful engaging in negative advertising if they first set the ground rules that they would run a "positive" campaign *unless* their opponent violated that agreement and forced them to resort to negative campaigning (Staton and Hughes 1992). Some female candidates also have used humor effectively to respond to negative attacks.

Although there has been a lot of discussion about negative advertising, there is limited scholarly research on this issue. There remain numerous strategic questions to examine. First, to what extent does gender affect the degree to which candidates initiate and respond to negative advertising? Next, under what conditions are male candidates more likely than their female counterparts to launch a "first strike" negative attack against their opponents? When are female candidates more likely than male candidates to issue a "warning" in regard to negative advertising: I won't go negative if you don't, but if you do, I will? When races involve only female candidates, are the types of negative attacks different than when the campaigns feature both female and male candidates? To what extent does having women of color in the race alter how they and their opponents use negative advertising? Finally, in what ways does gender affect how quickly candidates respond to their opponents' effective use of negative advertising or to their own campaign's ineffective use of negative advertising?

With a plethora of media formats from which to choose, campaigns must make strategic decisions not only about message content, but also about the appropriate media outlets to use to reach key voters. Effective and cost efficient media buys are especially critical to women candidates who often find themselves running against incumbents with large campaign war chests. Research designs based on case studies and content analysis could be used to explore a variety of questions in this area. First, to what extent does gender affect the mix of communication outlets that campaigns use to deliver their messages? Second, how does gender affect the styles candidates use to provide information in different forums? For instance, are men more comfortable with formal debate forums because they are more likely than their female counterparts to have professional training as lawyers and business executives and, as a result, more experience in making such presentations? Are women more effective in informal, town-meeting settings because of being socialized to excel at two-way, give-and-take conversations? In "talk show" formats, are women (again because of socialization) less likely than men to interrupt or talk over other participants to make a point? For the same reasons, are women more likely than men to "play by the rules" and answer only the questions posed and within the stated time limits? If such gender differences exist, what effect do they have on how the media evaluate candidate performances? Through interviews or written questionnaires with candidates, campaign staff, consultants, and members of the media, researchers could examine the extent to which gender affects the media outlets candidates use to communicate with voters. Additionally, researchers could examine the combined effect of gender and other interrelated factors (e.g., race, incumbency, level of office) on media-buying strategies.

Finally, with greater numbers of women candidates running as incumbents and as challengers, races featuring two or more woman as candidates will occur more frequently. To better understand the media dynamics in these races, researchers need to identify the strategies women candidates use to separate their messages from one another (Bragdon 1986). In addition, researchers could examine the types of messages campaigns avoid in order not to reinforce gender-based stereotypes that could be used against all the women candidates in the race.

❖ Campaign Fund Raising

There exists an expanding body of literature about the fund raising capabilities of female candidates (see Burrell, this volume). For the most part, studies conducted since the mid-1980s have concluded that female candidates raised as much money as their male counterparts in comparable races (Burrell 1994; Darcy, Welch, and Clark 1987; McLean 1994; Newman et al. 1984; but also see Donovan 1992; Green 1998; Koenen 1991). Still unclear is whether female and male candidates and their fund raising staff spend the same amount of campaign time and exert similar effort (calls, meetings, direct mail, appearances, events) to raise comparable campaign dollars. Given that the allocation of a candidate's time and her campaign's resources are such strategic decisions, it would be useful to know if gender significantly affects the ratio of time spent to dollar raised so that campaigns could plan accordingly. Interviews or questionnaires to candidates and their fund raisers, plus content analysis of campaign schedules, could be used to explore these topics. Additional issues that could be examined include the extent to which race, level of office sought, and prior office-holding experience affects the amount of time and effort candidates devote to fund raising activities to raise comparable levels of campaign contributions as other candidates in similarly situated races.

Another important campaign fund raising topic to explore is the timing of campaign contributions. Those involved with electing more women to office are keenly aware of how important raising early money is in establishing a campaign's viability. Recent studies have found that female candidates running for the U.S. House either matched or exceeded the amount of money that male candidates raised prior to the first Federal Election Commission (FEC) filing deadline (Burrell 1994). Because these findings were based on aggregate data, there is some concern that they did not accurately capture what individual female candidates actually experienced in their specific races (Green 1998; Herrick 1995). Additional studies are needed to further clarify this issue. Also it is important for researchers to determine what effect gender has on raising early money in campaigns for offices at local and statewide levels of office. These findings would be especially helpful to women candidates in states affected by term limits because they are likely to face contested primaries for vacated legislative seats and crowded fields for other offices as well.

An area in which gender continues to be significantly associated with campaign fund raising is the amount of personal or family money that candidates invest or are willing to invest in their own campaigns. Male politicians report they invested or were willing to invest more of their own money than their female counterparts (Mandel 1981; McLean 1994). Male candidates also appear to be more comfortable than female candidates authorizing expenditures for campaign activities before raising the funds to pay for them (Staton and Hughes 1993). Gender differences in these fund raising areas may be explained in two ways. First, compared to male candidates, female candidates may actually have less disposable personal or family income. As a result, they may be more prudent than their financially better-off male colleagues about tapping those resources to finance their campaigns. Second, female candidates may contribute less financially to their family's total income and, consequently, may not feel as free as their male counterparts to use family finances to pay for campaign debts (Carroll 1994; Mandel 1981).

If female candidates are more reluctant than male candidates to authorize expenditures for campaign activities before funds to cover those costs are actually raised, what strategic adjustments do women need to make in order to run successful campaigns? Interviews with candidates and their financial team could examine to what extent women are more likely than men to sacrifice making media buys or conducting field activities at critical points in their campaigns in order to avoid deficit financing. Such studies could identify the benefits and consequences associated with postponing non-critical and critical campaign activities in order for the campaign not to go into debt. Researchers could also explore whether female candidates are successful in holding to their "no debt" plan throughout the campaign or if there are key points at which candidates are more likely to abandon such a strategy. If a pattern emerges as to the circumstances under which a "no-debt" strategy is abandoned, then those charged with developing campaign plans could be alerted to such possibilities. Finally, researchers may find that female candidates who had "no debt" plans when they campaigned for local or state legislative offices are the ones most likely to insist on such plans in their campaigns for statewide or federal office. If this is so, then the impact of such a strategy needs to be discussed with these office-holders very early in the process of their thinking about running for higher office.

In general, both female and male candidates report a dislike for the enormous amount of time and emotional energy they devote to fund raising. Some studies suggest that fund raising takes a higher emotional toll on women because they are less likely than men to let go of the rejections that naturally come from constantly asking others for campaign contributions (Mandel 1981; Morris 1992; Staton and Hughes 1993; Tolchin and Tolchin 1976). As a result, raising the same amount of money as male candidates may take not only more of a female candidate's time but also more of her stamina. To confirm such speculation, researchers through focus groups, interviews, and mailed questionnaires could identify the extent to which gender affects the steps candidates take to make fund raising activities less time-consuming and emotionally draining. Such information would be valuable to women contemplating running for higher office or for any office that requires raising large sums of campaign dollars.

Finally, with more women seeking office, more races featuring either head-to-head or field races between two or more women candidates are likely. As the number of these races grows, it is important to identify the ways in which female candidates change their fund raising plans when more than one woman candidate is running or when all the candidates running are women. For strategic campaign planning reasons, it is especially important for candidates to have information about the effect that having more than one woman candidate in a race has on potential donors. In such races, are donors who are interested in supporting women candidates more likely to divide their contributions among all the women candidates? Or are donors more likely not to give to any of the women candidates? How does the mix among other relevant factors such as race, issue differences, partisanship, political experience, and electoral viability play out when gender is not an issue? Answers to these questions would help women candidates and those interested in providing them with financial backing better understand the fund raising dynamics in races featuring two or more women candidates.

✦ JOAN E. MCLEAN

❖ Voter Targeting

The ultimate goal of any campaign strategy is attracting enough votes to win. To achieve this goal, every campaign must engage in voter targeting. Although all campaigns must target voters based on the context of their specific race, women candidates in general have benefitted from an increasingly positive voter attitude about the need for more women in public office.

A 1992 poll conducted by *U.S. News and World Report* found that 80% of women under 30 wanted more women elected to public office. Results from a 1999 poll showed that 60% of all voters "agreed there are not enough women in public office" (Lake Snell Perry and American Viewpoint 1999). Data from that same survey revealed that voters by a huge margin believed that women, as compared to men, were more caring about people and more honest. In addition, "nearly half of those surveyed said female political leaders would bring the nation better governance, and govern better for families." Even when it came to whether or not voters would support a woman for U.S. president, the news was generally positive—75% of men and 82% of women responded they would vote for a woman running for president. Pollster Celinda Lake summed up these turn-of-the-century findings:

> Increasingly, men and women are welcoming women into non-traditional leadership roles . . . men and women agree on the issues which are most important to them, health care, education and values. And they view women as having qualities that better equip them to deal with these issues effectively. (Lake Snell Perry and American Viewpoint 1999)

Still several surveys conducted during the late 1980s and 1990s revealed several roadblocks standing in the way of women candidates running successfully for president or for higher office in general. Survey data asking voters whether a woman would do as well or better than a man as president suggested that women candidates—especially those running for executive offices—were less likely to receive support from voters who were older (60+), lived in urban areas, were southern white women, had less than a college education, or were working in non-white-collar occupations (Hickman–Maslin 1987). Other polling data found that young, white men were also less likely to support women candidates in general (Witt, Paget, and Matthews 1994, 172–73).

As for issues, Roper Starch Worldwide (1999) found that a majority of the voters surveyed thought a man would do a better job than a woman at handling a national crisis or making difficult decisions. In terms of specific issues, gender stereotypes continued to affect voters' perceptions. They gave the nod to a male president when it came to dealing with law and order, the economy, and foreign policy. A woman president was seen as more effective at handling moral questions and social issues such as education and poverty. Results from this poll also indicated that "one-third of the population—and even more Americans over the age of 55—still believe there are general characteristics about women that make them less qualified as president" (Roper Starch Worldwide 1999). A 1999 Gallup survey which asked, "everything else being equal, whom do you think would make the better president", found that "42% of Americans said a man, while 31% said a woman. Twenty-two percent said the gender of a president would not matter" (Gillespie 1999). The survey noted that male voters especially had a bias against women holding higher office. Women voters, on the other hand, had "roughly even levels of support for a president of either gender".

When it comes to the issue of female voters actually voting for women candidates, the data are mixed. Similar to male candidates, some female candidates can attribute their margin of victory to women's votes but most cannot (Burrell 1994, 31–32; Paolino 1995; Romney and Harrison 1988, 106–107; Seltzer, Newman, and Leighton 1997; Witt, Paget, and Matthews 1994, 153–55). As is typical with most large blocks of voters, the data suggest that in order to decide which female voters to target, campaigns must divide women voters not only into demographic sub-categories but also into groups according to other relevant political characteristics such as party identification, issue preferences, and turnout (Burrell 1994; Cook 1994; Dolan 1998; McDermott 1997; Plutzer and Zipp 1996).

Of course, it is especially important that voter targeting plans take into account the effect of gender on political party preferences (also see Norris, this volume). Survey data throughout the 1990s consistently showed that female voters were more likely to support Democratic candidates for President and Congress while men were more likely than women to support Republican candidates for these offices. In 1997, pollster Linda DiVall noted that this gap was a product of the difference between men's and women's views about the role of government in general. These views translated into issue preferences which revealed that women were more likely than men to favor government action for education, health care security, and the environment and to oppose government action when it came to gay rights and school prayer (Espo 1997). Such policies were more likely to be supported by Democratic than Republican candidates, hence a partial explanation for the gender gap (also see Kaufmann and Petrocik 1999). These trends continued in the 2000 elections. An EMILY's List Women's Monitor survey, conducted in March 2000, found women and men held different views in regard to the role government should play in such key campaign issues as education. The survey noted that "(w)hen assessing the two parties on the issue of education, women voters continue to give Democrats a significant advantage—by 42% to 26% they believe that Democrats would do better than Republicans on the issue" (EMILY's List 2000).

Clearly, findings from these national polls about voter preferences would be the most useful to those doing voter targeting for women candidates running for Congress or statewide offices. But the data can also help candidates for state legislative seats or local offices make some initial targeting decisions about likely supporters and swing voters.

With a growing body of information about which voters were most likely to support women candidates, we need more systematic research to determine how successful campaigns are in reaching key voters. Identifying the strategies that campaigns use to target and communicate with voters—especially swing voters—would provide female candidates in the future with vital information about how to mobilize their respective voter coalitions. Additional case studies, focus groups, interviews with campaign participants and voters, as well as content analysis of campaign plans and campaign literature, could be used to analyze the different approaches campaigns use in their targeted appeals. In races in which candidates have to pick up votes from independents or across party lines, how are messages crafted to do so without jeopardizing their partisan base? Researchers could also identify campaign strategies that are successful at appealing directly to targeted female voters without alienating targeted male voters. Also, more research is needed to identify the strategies campaigns use to target and mobilize voters in non-presidential election years when voter drop-off is the greatest—especially among non-college-educated women (EMILY's List 1998).

In regard to races featuring more than one female candidate, it would be helpful to those designing campaign plans to understand the strategies female candidates use to compete for the same targeted voters. Researchers and practitioners also would want to know how these strategies are modified when the female candidates in the race are all from the same party. It also would be important to know how strategies are changed when at least one of the female candidates in the race is a woman of color or when all the candidates are women of color.

More systematic research about how campaigns target various groups of voters may allow us to identify the strategies that are the most successful at mobilizing voters for women candidates at each stage of their electoral career: first-time candidates; incumbents running for reelection; and candidates for higher office. Such information might be especially helpful to those who must design campaign plans for women officeholders who originally appealed to voters because of their "outsider" or "agents of change" images but who, once elected, must seek reelection as incumbents.

❖ Conclusion

As increasing numbers of women run for public office, more of our attention is likely to focus on questions related to campaign strategy. The research agenda outlined in this chapter attempts to identify the information that would be the most helpful to both scholars studying women candidates and political practitioners helping women candidates run successful campaigns. Clearly election dynamics are constantly changing. What we learn about strategies used in previous campaigns may not always be useful in future ones. Yet, carefully collected and analyzed data are one way we can ensure that the combined wisdom of scholars and practitioners is available to women candidates in the twenty-first century.

❖ REFERENCES

Bragdon, Peter. 1986. "Nebraska's Primary Voters Break New Ground." *Congressional Quarterly Weekly Report* 44: 1123.

Burrell, Barbara. 1994. *A Woman's Place Is in the House.* Ann Arbor: University of Michigan.

Carroll, Susan J. 1994. *Women as Candidates in American Politics.* 2nd ed. Bloomington: Indiana University Press.

——Debra L. Dodson, and Ruth B. Mandel. 1991. "The Impact of Women in Public Office: An Overview." New Brunswick, NJ: Center for the American Woman and Politics, Rutgers University.

Connolly, Ceci. 1994. "Despite Public Ire, Insiders Still Having Winning Ways." *Congressional Quarterly Weekly Report* 52: 2274.

Cook, Elizabeth Adell. 1994. "Voter Responses to Women Senate Candidates." In *The Year of the Woman: Myths and Realities,* ed. Elizabeth Adell Cook, Sue Thomas, and Clyde Wilcox. Boulder, Colo.: Westview Press.

Cooper and Secrest Associates, Inc. 1984. "Women as Candidates in the 1984 Congressional Elections." Report commissioned by the National Women's Political Caucus. Washington, DC.

Darcy, R., Susan Welch, and Janet Clark. 1987. *Women, Elections, and Representation.* New York: Longman Press.

Devitt, James. 1999. "Framing Gender on the Campaign Trail: Women's Executive Leadership and the Press" New York: Women's Leadership Fund.
http://www.womensleadershipfund.org/programs/study.pdf

Dolan, Kathleen. 1998. "Voting for Women in the 'Year of the Woman.'" *American Journal of Political Science* 42: 272–93.

Donovan, Beth. 1992. "Women's Campaigns Fueled Mostly by Women's Checks." *Congressional Quarterly Weekly Report* 50: 3269–73.

EMILY's List. 1998. "Women Voter Fact Sheet." Washington, DC: EMILY's List.

——2000. "The Women's Vote and the 2000 Elections." *Women's Monitor,* 5 April.

Espo, David. 1997. "Poll: GOP Faces 'Gender Canyon,'" Associated Press, 28 October.

Ferraro, Geraldine A., and Linda Bird Francke. 1985. *Ferraro: My Story.* New York: Bantam Books.

Flammang, Janet A. 1985. "Female Officials in the Feminist Capital: The Case of Santa Clara County." *Western Political Quarterly* 38: 94–118.

Fowler, Linda L., and Robert D. McClure. 1989. *Political Ambition: Who Decides to Run for Congress.* New Haven: Yale University Press.

Green, Joanne Connor. 1998. "The Role of Gender in Open Seat Elections for the U.S. House of Representatives: A District Level Test for a Differential Value for Campaign Resources." *Women & Politics* 19: 33–55.

Gillespie, Mark. 1999. "Dole Dips Toe in Presidential Poll." Gallup News Service, 10 March. http//www.gallup.com/poll/releases/pr990310b.asp

Herrick, Rebekah. 1995. "A Reappraisal of the Quality of Women Candidates." *Women & Politics* 15: 25–38.

Hickman–Maslin Research. 1987. "The New Women Political Survey." Washington, DC: National Women's Political Caucus.

Hitchon, Jacqueline C., and Chingching Chan. 1995. "Effects of Gender Schematic Processing on the Reception of Political Commercials for Men and Women Candidates." *Communication Research* 22: 430–58.

Huddy, Leonie, and Nayda Terkildsen. 1993. "Gender Stereotypes and the Perception of Male and Female Candidates." *American Journal of Political Science* 37: 119–47.

Johnson, Marilyn, and Susan Carroll. 1978. "Profile of Women Holding Office, 1977." In *Women in Public Office: A Biographical Directory and Statistical Analysis.* Metuchen, NJ: The Scarecrow Press.

Johnston, Ane, and Anne Barton White. 1994. "Communication Styles and Female Candidates A Study of the Political Advertising During the 1986 State Elections." *Journalism Quarterly* 71: 321–29.

Kahn, Kim Fridkin. 1992. "Does Being Male Help: An Investigation of Gender and Media Effects in U.S. Senate Races." *Journal of Politics* 54: 497–517.

—— 1994. "Does Gender Make a Difference? An Experimental Examination of Sex Stereotypes and Press Patterns in Statewide Campaigns." *American Journal of Political Science* 38: 162–95.

—— and Edie N. Goldenberg. 1991. "Women Candidates in the News: An Examination of Gender Differences in U.S. Senate Campaigns." *Public Opinion Quarterly* 55: 180–99.

Kaufmann, Karen M., and John R. Petrocik. 1999. "The Changing Politics of American Men: Understanding the Sources of the Gender Gap." *American Journal of Political Science* 43: 864–87.

Kern, Montague, and Paige P. Edley. 1994. "Women Candidates Going Public: The 30-second Format." *Argumentation & Advocacy* 31: 80–95.

Kirkpatrick, Jeane J. 1974. *Political Woman.* New York: Basic Books.

Koenenn, Connie. 1991. "Setting Priorities for EMILY's List," *Los Angeles Times,* 9 October.

Kunin, Madeleine. 1994. *Living a Political Life.* New York: Knopf.

Lake, Celinda. 1989. "Campaigning in a Different Voice." Washington, DC: EMILY's List.

—— 1991. "Challenging the Credibility Gap." Washington, DC: EMILY's List.

Lake Snell Perry and American Viewpoint. 1999. Survey for Arthur Anderson and Ameritech Forum on "Women in Business, Politics and Power." http://www.womenconnect.com/LinkTo/10271999_wcna.htm

Lansing, Jewell. 1991. *Campaigning for Office: A Woman Runs.* Saratoga, Calif.: R&E Publishers.

Mandel, Ruth B. 1981. *In the Running: The New Woman Candidate.* New York: Ticknor and Fields.

McDermott, Monika L. 1997. "Voting Cues in Low-Information Elections: Candidate Gender as a Social Information Variable in Contemporary United States Elections." *American Journal of Political Science* 41: 270–83.

McLean, Joan E. 1994. "Strategic Choices: Career Decisions of Elected Women." Ph.D. dissertation. The Ohio State University.

Mezey, Susan Gluck. 1978. "Does Sex Make a Difference? A Case Study of Women in Politics." *Western Political Quarterly* 31: 492–501.

Mills, Kay. 1997. "What Differences Do Women Journalists Make?" In *Women, Media, and Politics*, ed. Pippa Norris. New York: Oxford University Press.

Morris, Celia. 1992. *Storming the Statehouse: Running for Governor with Ann Richards and Dianne Feinstein.* New York: Charles Scribner's Sons.

Newman, Jody, Carrie Costantin, Julie Goetz, and Amy Glosser. 1984. "Perception and Reality: A Study of Women Candidates and Fund Raising." Washington, DC: Women's Campaign Research Fund.

Paolino, Philip. 1995. "Group-Salient Issues and Group Representation: Support for Women Candidates in the 1992 Senate Election." *American Journal of Political Science* 39: 294–313.

Plutzer, Eric, and John Zipp. 1996. "Identity Politics, Partisanship, and Voting for Women Candidates." *Public Opinion Quarterly* 60: 30–57.

Romney, Ronna, and Beppie Harrison. 1988. *Momentum: Women in American Politics Now.* New York: Crown Publishers, Inc.

Roper Starch Worldwide. 1999. "Women in Elected Office." Survey commissioned by Deloitte & Touche. http://www.us.deloitte.com/us/news/ooJan/wilpoll.htm

Rossi, Alice. 1983. "Beyond the Gender Gap: Women's Bid for Political Power." *Social Science Quarterly* 64: 718–33.

Schlozman, Kay Lehman. 1990. "Representing Women in Washington: Sisterhood and Pressure Politics." In *Women, Politics and Change*, ed. Louise A. Tilly and Patricia Gurin. New York: Russell Sage Foundation.

Seltzer, Richard A., Jody Newman, and Melissa Voorhees Leighton. 1997. *Sex as a Political Variable: Women as Candidates and Voters in U.S. Elections.* London: Lynne Rienner Publishers.

Staton and Hughes. 1993. "To be Continued: Majority Council Summary." Washington, DC: EMILY's List.

Thomas, Sue. 1994. *How Women Legislate.* New York: Oxford University Press.

Tolchin, Susan, and Martin Tolchin. 1976. *Clout: Womanpower and Politics.* New York: G.P. Putnam's Sons.

U.S. News and World Report. 1992. "Will 1992 Be the Year of the Woman?" 21 April.

Verba, Sidney. 1990. "Women in American Politics." In *Women, Politics and Change*, ed. Louise A. Tilly and Patricia Gurin. New York: Russell Sage Foundation.

Williams, Leonard. 1994. "Political Advertising in the Year of the Woman: Did X Mark the Spot?" In *The Year of the Woman: Myths and Realities*, ed. Elizabeth Adell Cook, Sue Thomas, and Clyde Wilcox. Boulder, Colo.: Westview Press.

Witt, Linda, Karen M. Paget, and Glenna Matthews. 1994. *Running as a Woman.* New York: The Free Press.

❖ Joan E. McLean

Women's Leadership Fund. 1999. Press Conference: "Framing Gender on the Campaign Trail: Women's Executive Leadership and the Press" New York: Women's Leadership Fund, 25 November.
http://www.womenconnect.com/LinkTo/10291999_wcds.htm

3 ❖ Money and Women's Candidacies for Public Office

Barbara C. Burrell

You are thinking about running for public office. You have been active in your community, your political party, or other organizations. Perhaps you are concerned about a particular issue and want to be part of the policy-making process. You may feel that those who currently hold office could do much better than they are doing. You know that you could do better. Among the first questions you have to address as you decide whether to run are the following: What will others involved in the process ask as they consider the viability of your potential campaign, especially if it is for an office above the local level? How much money can you raise? How much are you willing to invest in the campaign? Can you contemplate raising millions of dollars for a seat in the U.S. Senate, over $500,000 for a U.S. House seat, or perhaps even tens of thousands of dollars for state legislative office?

Whether we like it or not, money plays a central role in campaigns for public office today. The ability to raise money is a major measure of electoral strength. The lack of money keeps many individuals from undertaking quests for public office. Thus, democracy loses an important element of what makes it the best type of political system: competition for leadership. Further, the quest for money keeps officeholders and would-be officeholders from spending time articulating issue positions and working with the voters. Once in office, campaign finance reform takes up the time and attention of lawmakers. It is a major issue at the national level and in many states.

❖ MONEY AND ELECTIONS

The basic questions concerning campaign finance have been: How is money raised? How much is raised and spent? When is it raised? And what effect does it have on the outcome of elections? A second set of questions explores the effect of money on the legislative process. Put most crudely, does money buy votes as lawmakers make public policy decisions? Thus, who contributes is important.

The linkage between money and gender is also critical to the study of the campaign process. Researchers of gender issues want to know: Do female candidates approach fund raising differently from male candidates? Do they have more difficulty raising money? Are the sources of their funds distinctive? What are the variations among female candidates in obtaining funds? And does money have a differential impact on the success of male and female candidates? If we were to change the ways campaigns can be run financially, how would that affect women's candidacies? The conventional wisdom has been that women are disadvantaged in raising money to finance their campaigns and that this disadvantage, perhaps above all others, has kept women from winning a larger number of public offices.

How well candidates perform on election day is a direct function of how much money they raise and spend (Jacobson 1987). In campaigns against incumbents, the more challengers spend, the more votes they receive, and the more likely they are to win (Jacobson 1990). For challengers, however, it has become increasingly difficult to raise the money needed to be competitive. Challengers have difficulty raising funds because they are not viewed as competitive. Incumbents are seen as overwhelmingly advantaged. The gap in spending between incumbents and challengers has grown over time (Makinson 1989).

A negative relationship exists between spending and votes for incumbents. The more incumbents spend, the lower their percentage of the vote and the greater their chances of losing. This is the case because incumbents spend more money the stronger the challenge they face. Incumbents also tend to keep a large treasury to scare off potential challengers. Thus, the more money an incumbent has at the beginning of the campaign season, the weaker will be any challenge. Strong challengers usually opt not to take the risk when faced with an incumbent with a substantial treasury to bankroll his or her re-election. At the same time, open seat races are the most expensive contests of all.

In the 2000 election cycle, congressional campaigns cost over $1 billion, an increase of 34% over the 1998 election cycle, and spent over $1 billion. According to Federal Election Commission records, Democratic House incumbents raised a median $669,000 and Republican incumbents raised a median $782,000; Democratic and Republican challengers raised a median $70,000 and $36,000, respectively, while Democratic open-seat candidates raised $837,000 and Republican open-seat candidates raised $1,111,000 (Federal Election Commission 2001a). In current elections, a candidate for the U.S. House of Representatives must expect to raise at least a half million dollars to run a viable campaign.

Political Action Committees (PACs) contributed nearly $260 million in the

2000 election cycle. Incumbents received $195 million or 75% of that total (Federal Election Commission 2001*b*). The role of PAC contributions has been a central focus of campaign finance reform legislation because they are believed to have a negative impact on the democratic process.

Campaign finance research has investigated the nature of individual contributions, personal financing of campaigns by candidates, PAC donations, and political party support (Sorauf 1992). Scholars of gender and politics have focused on the related question: Do these sources of funding differ for male and female candidates?

Researchers have also examined the timing of giving. Political professionals often emphasize that early money improves later fund raising. Recent research has shown that a dollar of seed money helps a challenger raise an additional two dollars later in the campaign, and challengers with previous elective experience raised significantly more early money than their less experienced counterparts, as did those challenging incumbents who had won narrowly in the previous election (Biersack, Herrnson, and Wilcox 1993). The role of early money has been of particular concern in the financing of women's campaigns as will become clear below.

❖ WOMEN CANDIDATES AND CAMPAIGN FINANCE

Given all the scholarly attention to questions about the role of money in elections and the emphasis the media and activists have put on the importance of fund raising to women's campaigns, it is surprising that only a small amount of research has empirically tested the relationship of gender to the financing of campaigns for public office, The conventional wisdom has been that women candidates have greater difficulty raising money than their male counterparts, and this difficulty is viewed as a major reason why more women are not in elective office. Women have faced a greater burden, it is believed, because they have lacked access to major types of contributors, they have lacked confidence in asking for money, and donors have discriminated against them. Researchers have now tested hypotheses to confirm or reject these conventional notions about women's disadvantages in raising money to finance campaigns for elective office (Newman et al. 1984; Burrell 1985; Theilmann and Wilhite 1991; Ingalls and Arrington 1991; Burrell 1994, 1998; Werner 1998).

Ingalls and Arrington (1991) have succinctly put forth a number of major research questions and anticipated answers regarding the role of gender in campaign financing. The questions and expectations in their own words are:

(1) Are there differences between the amount of money that men and women candidates spend? We expect that women can raise less and consequently spend less than their male counterparts.

(2) Do men and women candidates receive their money from different

sources? We expect women candidates to get money from different sources and in smaller average amounts than men.

(3) What are the characteristics of those who contribute to female and male candidates? Are there differences in partisanship, gender, and race? We expect gender to be an important element linking candidate and contributor; we expect women to contribute to women and men to contribute to men.

Items 1 and 2 from Ingalls and Arrington's list deal with *outcomes* of fund raising efforts, and all three items emphasize the importance of systematically comparing women's campaigns to men's to address questions and issues involving fund raising, primarily using quantitative methodologies. Traditional research approaches, such as the one they suggest, establish an implicit model of the campaign finance process that is masculine in nature, According to this model, if women are equal to men, then the system is working.

While studying outcomes and making quantitative comparisons is important and necessary in exploring gender issues in campaigns, examining the *process* of fund raising, and employing qualitative approaches that ask whether a gendered approach to campaigning exists that encompasses its fund raising aspects, would also contribute to our understanding of the role of gender in raising money and financing campaigns. Women may view and approach the acquisition of a campaign treasury in a distinctive manner, Women's ways of raising and spending money may affect the financing of political campaigns.

For example, EMILY's List pioneered the "bundling method" of raising funds, giving somewhat smaller donations greater political clout in elections. Bundling allows individuals to write a check to a candidate, but rather than sending it directly to the candidate, contributors send their checks to a fund raising organization, such as EMILY's List, that bundles all of the individual checks together and delivers them to the candidate. A bundle of $100 checks is more impressive than the same number of checks received individually. Also, the organizing efforts of the group may well increase the chance that a check will be written in the first place. EMILY's List started as the "ultimate Tupperware party," bringing women together with their checkbooks, as one of its founders described its early operation (Toner 1986).

In addition to reflecting on the gendered nature of campaign finance, other aspects of the process may be understood by undertaking a research strategy using either a quantitative or a qualitative analysis, that focuses more intensively on women's campaigns without the lens of traditional masculine ways of doing things. For example, research might explore whether women have a distinctive approach to raising funds. We do not know the extent to which women candidates have altered the nature of fund raising. How do women feel about asking for financial support, and how do they ask for money? How much of their campaign is devoted to fund raising? Do they tend to rely on men or women as treasurers and major fund raisers for their campaigns? Do women approach fund raising with a different intensity than men? Do women candidates work harder, as Fox found campaign managers reported that they do (2000), to raise the same amount of money? Are they less likely to mortgage their homes or take other financial risks?

❖ WOMEN'S CANDIDACIES AND WOMEN'S CAMPAIGN ORGANIZATIONS

In addition to focusing on the nature of individual women's campaigns, the connection between women's campaign organizations and women's candidacies deserves more attention. We would expect that these organizations help make women candidates more competitive by expanding sources of funds and increasing the financial involvement of women in the campaign process. But does women's giving merely compensate for disadvantages women candidates face in obtaining funds from traditional sources? Or does the support of the women's community supplement the giving of traditional contributors, thereby providing women candidates with an advantage?

Women's PACs have provided not only financial contributions to women candidates, but also training, consultation, and workers. How does the training and expertise women's PACs provide affect the nature of women's campaigns? Does their training provide women candidates with models of campaigning different from those that men traditionally have employed? Or have women's PACs principally taught women how to campaign in a fashion similar to that of men, thereby homogenizing the way in which women and men raise money to finance their campaigns? We know that one function women's organizations, like parties, have undertaken has been to teach women how to operate in the world of PACs. They have served as facilitators between women candidates and the political action community.

❖ DIVERSITY AMONG WOMEN CANDIDATES

The primary focus of activists and researchers concerned with gender and campaign finance has been on comparisons between women candidates as a group and men candidates as a group. Needless to say, racial and ethnic diversity also exists among women candidates, and it is certainly possible that minority women running for public office raise money and obtain other campaign resources in ways different from those of white women.

Do minority women have equal access to the same sources of funding? Are the traditional sources of financial resources and women's PACs less receptive to minority women candidates than to white women candidates or male candidates? Or have women's groups and other funders come to be more likely to support minority women's candidacies, either out of a belief that their representation is especially needed in elective office or from a sense that it is the right thing to do?

Support for minority women's candidacies within their communities may also be distinctive. Past research has stressed the importance of church life to women of color in developing a sense of community (Baxter and Lansing 1981). Churches and other community institutions may be a greater source of resources for minority women than for white women, thereby expanding minority women's sources of financial support in electoral politics.

❖ MALE AND FEMALE CANDIDATES AND CAMPAIGN RECEIPTS

A fair amount of research has been conducted on the amounts and sources of money raised by male and female candidates for legislative office. Based on its analysis of the financial aspects of three female U.S. Senate campaigns in 1992 (Carol Moseley-Braun, Lynn Yeakel, and Barbara Mikulski), *Congressional Quarterly Weekly Report* concluded that:

(1) Women candidates are dependent on women donors for financial viability.
(2) Women candidates are considerably more dependent upon small contributions than men.
(3) Women candidates win support from men only as the odds of their election increase to near certainty (Donovan 1992).

If *Congressional Quarterly's* findings were generalizable, then women candidates would be at a very serious financial disadvantage compared with men candidates. There are, however, serious defects in *Congressional Quarterly's* conclusions. For example, only one of the three candidates, Lynn Yeakel, drew financial support disproportionately from women. One candidate, Barbara Mikulski, showed a distribution of support typical of an incumbent. She greatly outpaced her male opponent obtaining, for instance, 32% of her contributions from PACs compared with 3% for challenger Alan Keyes. Further, all of these women were Democrats, so party differences have not been taken into account in explaining the outcome of their fund raising efforts.

If we wish to understand the relationship of money to gender in political campaigns, we need to compare the receipts and expenditures of male and female candidates in similar situations. We have to compare Democratic men with Democratic women and Republican men with Republican women. We have to compare female challengers with male challengers and female open-seat contenders with male open-seat contenders at each level of office-seeking.[1] If the proper type of analyses were undertaken, we might find that results attributed to gender are the effect of systematic factors, characteristic of the campaigns of both male and female candidates. Only with such a comprehensive and careful analysis can we confirm or disconfirm the conventional wisdom that women have more difficulty raising money than men.

This type of analysis has been conducted for campaigns for the U.S. House of Representatives and for some state legislatures. I have compared the amounts of money raised and spent by male and female candidates for the U.S. House of Representatives from 1972 through 1994 using Federal Election Commission records. The Federal Election Campaign Act of 1971 and subsequent amendments to it have mandated that candidates for federal office report their total receipts and expenditures on a quarterly basis during a campaign season. They must report all individual contributions of $500 or more as well as all political action committee and party contributions.

Comparing total receipts and expenditures for each of the elections from 1972 through 1994, I found the following results:

❖ *Major Party Female and Nominees for Congress Raise and Spend Equivalent Amounts of Money*

In *A Woman's Place Is in the House: Campaigning for Congress in the Feminist Era*, I compared the spending of male and female major party nominees for the U.S. House from 1972 through 1992. The small group of female major party nominees (32 candidates) in 1972 began the era raising and spending nearly equivalent amounts of money to that of male nominees in contested races. As their presence expanded through the 1974–80 elections, female nominees raised and spent approximately three-quarters of what male contenders acquired. In the 1982–86 period, women achieved near equality (and actually expended an average amount equal to that of male nominees if median figures are examined). In the 1988 election, a major breakthrough occurred when female nominees raised and spent greater average amounts of money than male nominees. Equality continued in subsequent elections:

In 1988, women raised 119% of what male candidates raised.

In 1990, women raised 97% of what male candidates obtained and spent 102% of what men spent.

In 1992, women raised 111% and spent 108% of what men raised and spent, and in 1994 they raised 101% (Burrell 1998).

Above, I pointed out the importance of taking into account party and candidate status when analyzing the relationship of gender and money. When I examined separately the receipts of candidate groups within the Democratic and Republican parties, I obtained the following findings for the 1972 through 1992 period for the U.S. House of Representatives:

(1) Female incumbents tended to raise less than their male counterparts in the early part of this period but have equaled or surpassed them in recent elections (Burrell 1994).

❖ Barbara C. Burrell

(2) Challengers, in general, operate at a great disadvantage in acquiring a campaign treasury. Since women have disproportionately been challengers, they have had difficulty attracting contributors. But they have not been particularly disadvantaged vis-à-vis male challengers. Women challengers have raised amounts similar to those of male challengers of the same party.

(3) Open seat races, where incumbency is not a factor, are crucial for increasing the number of women in the national legislature. If female candidates are disadvantaged in campaign financing in these races, then little progress will be made in achieving numerical equality in the U.S. House no matter how well women do as incumbents.

But female open-seat nominees have not been disadvantaged in fund raising. In recent elections especially, they have been formidable fund raisers compared to their male counterparts. In each of the election cycles beginning with 1984, female Democratic open-seat nominees raised more than male Democratic contenders in open-seat races. Female Republican open-seat nominees similarly have not been disadvantaged in the financing of their campaigns, but they have been so few in number that systematic comparisons are difficult.

In addition to my own research, a number of other studies confirm this equality in the financing of men's and women's campaigns for public office in recent elections. The Center for the American Woman and Politics' report on the 1994 U.S. House and Senate elections showed no disadvantage for women candidates (McCormick and Baruch 1994, 16–17). Fox reports that female candidates for the U.S. House of Representatives in California in 1992 and 1994 "raised considerably more money than their male counterparts" (1997, 112). At the state legislative level, Werner has found that "women candidates were able to raise as much and sometimes significantly more than men" in the three states that he studied (1998, 95).

❖ Female Nominees Have Tapped the PAC Community Almost as Effectively as Men Who Have Run for National Office

Only a modest "PAC"[2] gap has been present in the financial structure of male and female nominees' campaigns for the U.S. House, and in one election, 1988, the gap was in women's favor. But we know that PAC money flows disproportionately to incumbents in House elections and that incumbents have tended to be men; thus any gap in men's favor should not be surprising. Moreover, after controlling for incumbency and party, any female disadvantage disappeared. In each of the elections from 1980 through 1992, women tended to acquire larger amounts of funds from PACs than their male counterparts, ranging from $2,000 to over $22,000 (Burrell 1994).

❖ *Female Nominees Can Match Their Male Counterparts in Acquiring Large Donations for Their Campaigns*

Large donations are defined as donations of $500 or more from individual contributors. Since 1980 the Federal Election Commission has compiled data on the total amount of contributions of $500 or more and the number of donors who have given such amounts. In three of the elections between 1980 and 1990, women did slightly worse than their male counterparts, raising from $1,500 to over $9,000 less in contributions of $500 or more. But in three of the elections, they acquired more in large donations ranging from $200 to over $17,000.

Political parties are the final major source of campaign financing. The Federal Election Campaign Act allows national, congressional, and state party organizations to give a maximum contribution of $5,000 to general election candidates for the U.S. House of Representative. Party organizations can give another $5,000 to candidates in primary elections, but they seldom enter primary elections with financial support. State and national party committees can also make limited expenditures in coordination with congressional candidates' campaigns. Originally set at $10,000 per committee, the limits for coordinated expenditures for U.S. House candidates reached $27,620 each per national and state party committee in 1992 after being adjusted for inflation (Biersack and Herrnson 1994).

In each of the elections between 1980 and 1990, Republican party committees contributed a larger average amount to their female candidates than to their male nominees. In four of the six elections, they were also more generous to their female nominees in their coordinated expenditures. Democratic female nominees also did better than Democratic male nominees in acquiring direct contributions and coordinated expenditures from their party in four of the six elections. (See Burrell 1994.) According to the research of Biersack and Herrnson:

> National party organizations did not give special consideration to women in 1992, but their gender did not hurt their ability to get party financial support. After controlling for the effects of candidate experience and marginality of the district, there was no significant difference in party financial support between men and women of either party. Candidate quality and closeness of the election were, however, very important predictors of party financial support for both Democrats and Republicans. Candidates in both parties involved in close races received more party money than those whose victory or defeat seemed certain . . . Both parties also directed more monies to candidates with prior experience in elected office. (1994, 172–73)

Thus, it would appear that Democratic and Republican party organizations are not sources of financial discrimination against women party nominees.

❖ BARBARA C. BURRELL

On occasion the parties have even established extra sources for funding for their female candidates. However, these funds have waxed and waned mainly contingent on the interests of the heads of the various party committees. (See Burrell 1994 for an overview of these efforts.) The parties have come to view it as advantageous to promote the candidacies of their female would-be officeholders.

Comparisons of the financial structure of their campaigns have failed to find evidence to support the notion that women suffer financial disadvantages relative to male candidates in seeking public office, at least at the national level and at least as major party nominees.

❖ EARLY MONEY

Research on questions about the relationship between gender and money needs to go beyond a focus on nominees. The financial problems for women candidates may not be as nominees of their party, but may be at the crucial stage of obtaining good nominations—in primary elections and especially in open seat contests. The belief that lack of early money is a major obstacle to increasing women's numerical representation in Congress served as a catalyst for the founding of EMILY's List for Democratic female candidates and more recently the WISH List on the Republican side.

Does evidence suggest that early money flows disproportionately to male candidates? An analysis of the financial reports of the first and second reporting periods of the election cycles between 1988 and 1992 failed to show that women candidates in open seat races for the U.S. House of Representatives were disadvantaged. Table 3.1 shows female contenders doing better than their male

Table 3.1 Average receipts (dollars) of male and female open seat primary contenders, first and second reporting periods

Year	First Period		Second Period	
	Men	Women	Men	Women
1988	42,475	45,942	97,160	103,864
	(164)	(17)	(164)	(17)
1990	37,607	43,910	79,004	132,552
	(145)	(20)	(145)	(20)
1992	29,228	35,854	78,350	104,396
	(418)	(82)	(418)	(82)

counterparts in the early part of the campaign season. In each election a larger percentage of female than male candidates reported having raised funds at the end of the first reporting period and having accumulated larger average campaign treasuries in the early stages of the election cycle. Women's success in raising funds may at least in part be attributed to support, especially early support, from women's PACs.

❖ SHIFTING THE FOCUS: ARE WOMEN ADVANTAGED AND WHY?

We have searched in vain to find empirical evidence to support the idea that women candidates as a group suffer from a financial disadvantage. What they raise, how they raise it, and when they raise it, at least as candidates for the U.S. Congress, support a contrary vision of the fund raising ability of women. Perhaps we should begin asking whether women have become advantaged as candidates when it comes to accumulating campaign treasuries.

Note that the top fund raiser in 1992 U.S. Senate contests was Barbara Boxer who raised $10,349,048; number two was Dianne Feinstein who raised over $8 million. Among open seat candidates for the U.S. House in 1992, the number one fund raiser was Jane Harman in California who raised $2.3 million. Women were four of the top ten open-seat fund raisers in U.S. House elections that year. They were five of the ten top open-seat fund raisers in obtaining PAC funds.

In the 1997–1998 election cycle, of candidates for the U.S. House of Representatives the top 50 in fund raising had receipts of over $1,350,000. Ten of those top 50 were women candidates. In the 1999–2000 election, 11 of the top 50 House recipients were women. If we look only at receipts from individuals, women were 18 of the top 50 House recipients in the 2000 election cycle.

Women made up only 22% of the first term members of the U.S. House in the 103rd Congress (1993–1994), but they constituted 40% of those who took in more than $200,000 in PAC money in the 1992 election cycle. On average, women candidates received $54,000 more than men who took PAC money (Donovan 1993).

What is the explanation for women's fund raising success? At least part of the answer must lie in the women's community. According to Federal Election Commission records, women's PACs at the national level contributed over $7 million in 1992. Nevertheless, giving by women to women and trends in the size and extent of female contributions to political campaigns remain an essentially unexplored area of campaign finance research. One of the questions we should ask is about the extent to which women's candidacies have stimulated women to give as individual contributors. Expanding the sources of funds and stimulating more individuals to become involved in the political process enhances the democratic nature of our campaigns.

❖ BARBARA C. BURRELL

❖ MORE QUESTIONS FOR FUTURE RESEARCH

Are findings at the national level generalizable to the state and local levels? If women have gained equality at the national level where large sums of money are necessary to run a viable campaign, then perhaps the financing of campaigns for the state legislature, for example, should be no more difficult for women than for men. My research (1990) in Massachusetts in the 1980s replicated the findings at the congressional level, with women doing as well as men in similar situations. Ingalls and Arrington (1991) found women raised similar amounts as male candidates in state legislative races in North Carolina, and Werner (1998) expanded the research to three other states with similar results. Beyond this limited research, however, possible gender differences in campaign finance at the state level have not been examined. Clearly, more research is needed at this level. In addition, the role of money in women's campaigns for executive-level offices, including the presidency, needs to be examined.

Future research might also examine whether political scientists are operating under an outmoded premise. Fox, for example, notes that "an examination of the more nuanced experiences of men and women candidates suggest that the electoral environment still treats women and men differently. These differences in most instances tend to work against the interests of women candidates" (2000, 252). Perhaps the conventional wisdom has changed within the political community. Do women candidates and activists within the campaign process still view female contenders as disadvantaged raising funds to support their campaigns? Do they believe that "many traditional sources such as the trade associations and large donors . . . do not treat women as they might men" as was stated in the *Washington Post* (Melton 1994)?

What is the contemporary wisdom about the relationship between gender and money? Have women candidates' perceptions about their ability to raise funds changed? If so, this change should have an effect on the supply of female candidates because women who believe they can compete on a level playing field with men will be more likely to get into the game. When we perpetuate the conventional wisdom that women are less successful fund raisers than men, we discourage women from running.

Future research also needs to examine the *process* of raising money (and obtaining other campaign resources) as well as the outcomes of fund raising and to focus on diversity in financing campaigns with a wider-angle lens than the traditional masculine one of generating dollars.

Encompassing all of the discussion of the relationship between money and gender in campaigns for public office is the manner in which we finance campaigns in the United States through reliance on private money, without limits on how much one can raise and spend, and with groups (i.e., PACs) playing a major role. Women collectively have an important interest in issues surrounding campaign finance reform. Since women are more likely to be challengers or competitors for open seats than incumbents, public financing of campaigns should work to their advantage, helping to equalize financial resources that now very much provide an advantage for incumbents.

The question of PAC contributions is a difficult one from the perspective of women's interests. Women have learned both to use traditional PACs and also to develop their own to supplement reliance on individual contributions. If a change in the financing system were to make it harder for women to organize as a group to influence the campaign process, it would hurt individual women's ability to compete. Questions about how alternative campaign finance reform proposals would affect women's candidacies need more attention from researchers.

Let us finally then return to a very important question for future research: what is the effect of spending on electoral success, and does it differ for men and women? Do women get more votes, fewer votes, or the same amount of votes as men for every dollar spent in primaries and general elections? Given that women are viewed distinctively (and in recent elections that has been seen as a plus), must they raise and spend as much money as men to obtain the same amount of votes? Do they use their funds as efficiently? Is the pattern similar across many types of elections?

Since money is so crucial to the campaign process, perceptions about it and the empirical reality behind fund raising for male and female candidates must be ascertained as we consider the representation of women in public office and the democratic nature of our elections.

❖ NOTES

1 It has been suggested that in order to test hypotheses about the relationship between gender and campaign financing, one should compare the amount of money raised by a female candidate and her opponent. Do women candidates tend to be out-spent disproportionately by their male opponents? However, if we used this research approach and found that women candidates were outspent on the average by their male opponents, we would still be left with the question of whether that was because of their gender or because they tended disproportionately to be members of the party (e.g., Democrats) whose candidates tended to raise less money than candidates of the other party (e.g., Republicans). Because fund raising capacity is not evenly distributed across the parties, we have to make within-party comparisons.

2 Candidates for federal office are required to submit four financial reports to the FEC during the course of the election cycle. The first report is due March 31, and the second is due June 30. Analyses of the timing of fund raising are limited to studies of fund raising within these time periods. Consequently, we cannot be more flexible in our analyses, making them correspond more closely to the timing of primary elections.

❖ BARBARA C. BURRELL

❖ REFERENCES

Baxter, Sandra, and Marjorie Lansing. 1981. *Women and Politics: The Invisible Majority.* University of Michigan Press.

Biersack, Robert, Paul Herrnson, and Clyde Wilcox. 1993. "Seed for Success: Early Money in Congressional Elections." *Legislative Studies Quarterly* 18: 535–52.

——and Paul Herrnson. 1994. "Political Parties and the Year of the Woman." In *The Year of the Woman: Myths and Realities,* ed. Elizabeth Adell Cox, Sue Thomas, and Clyde Wilcox. Boulder, Colo.: Westview Press.

Burrell, Barbara. 1985. "Women's and Men's Campaigns for the U.S. House of Representatives, 1972–1982: A Finance Gap?" *American Politics Quarterly* 13: 251–72.

——1990. "The Presence of Women Candidates and the Role of Gender in Campaigns for the State Legislature in an Urban Setting." *Women and Politics* 3: 85–102.

——1994. *A Woman's Place Is in the House: Campaigning for Congress in the Feminist Era.* Ann Arbor: University of Michigan Press.

——1998. "Campaign Finance: Women's Experience in the Modern Era." In *Women and Elective Office: Past, Present, & Future,* ed. Sue Thomas and Clyde Wilcox, New York: Oxford University Press.

Donovan, Beth. 1992. "Women's Campaigns Fueled Mostly by Women's Checks." *Congressional Quarterly Weekly Report* 50: 3269–73.

——1993. "Freshmen Got to Washington with Help of PAC Funds." *Congressional Quarterly Weekly Report* 51: 723–27.

Federal Election Commission, Press Release, May 15, 2001*a*.

Federal Election Commission, Press Release, May 31, 2001*b*.

Fox, Richard Logan. 1997. *Gender Dynamics in Congressional Elections.* Thousand Oaks, Calif.: Sage Publications.

——2000. "Gender and Congressional Elections." In *Gender and American Politics,* ed. Sue Tolleson-Rinehart and Jyl Josephson. Armonk, NY: M. E. Sharpe.

Ingalls, Gerald, and Theodore Arrington. 1991. "The Role of Gender in Local Campaign Financing: The Case of Charlotte, North Carolina." *Women & Politics* 11: 61–90.

Jacobson, Gary. 1987. "The Marginals Never Vanished: Incumbency and Competition in Elections to the U.S. House of Representatives." *American Journal of Political Science* 31: 125–41.

——1990. *The Electoral Origins of Divided Government.* Boulder, Colo.: Westview Press.

Makinson, Larry. 1989. *The Price of Admission.* Washington, DC: Center for Responsive Politics.

McCormick, Katheryne, and Lucy Baruch. 1994. "Women Show Strength as Campaign Fundraisers." *CAWP News & Notes* 10.

Melton, R. H. 1994. "Women Seek Star Roles on Area Political Stages," *Washington Post,* 24 March, sec. Al.

Newman, Jody, Carrie Constantin, Julie Goertz, and Amy Glosser. 1984. *Perception and Reality: A Study of Women Candidates and Fundraising.* Washington, DC: The Women's Campaign Fund.

Sorauf, Frank. 1992. *Inside Campaign Finance.* New Haven: Yale University Press.

Theilman, John, and Al Wilhite. 1991. *Discrimination and Congressional Campaign Contributions.* New York: Praeger.

Toner, Robin. 1986. "Female Candidates Are No Longer Cash Poor," *New York Times*, 15 June, Sec. 4.

Werner, Brian L. 1998. "Financing the Campaigns of Women Candidates and Their Opponents: Evidence from Three States, 1982–1990." *Women & Politics* 18: 81–97.

❖ **Part II**

Other Aspects of
Women's Participation in
Electoral Politics

4 ❖ The Impact of Women In Political Leadership Positions

Sue Thomas

After approximately thirty years of studying women in formal and informal political leadership positions, scholars have learned a great deal about them—their career paths, attitudes, styles, behaviors, and impact—as well as the institutions they inhabit and seek to influence. This chapter gives a brief overview of what we have learned so far and explores where we need to go. Even in light of the substantial progress to date, there is much left to accomplish. As illuminated below, any brakes on our progress have not been due to a lack of what former President George Bush referred to as "the vision thing." Rather, they have been related to limited research funding, time frames for study, data collection, and, most importantly, the numbers of women holding political power.

❖ LEADERSHIP DEFINED

There is little agreement in the literatures of political science, psychology, or sociology about precisely what constitutes leadership. One thing is clear, however. As George Edwards III notes about presidential leadership over Congress, "it remains an elusive concept" (1989, 2).

In spite of the difficulty of pinning down a widely accepted definition, many authors have concentrated on leadership traits and areas in which leadership can be exerted. Perhaps the most common element in definitions is that leadership involves influence over followers, tasks, or culture. Additionally, leadership can be exerted in a wide variety of ways, informally and formally, and in a multiple milieus. One need not be an elective or appointive officeholder, for example, to be a leader, and many authors point to instances in which informal community leaders play large public sphere and political roles. The milieu itself, in conjunction with the individuals who inhabit leadership roles, shapes the models of leadership employed in a given situation and ranges from the single great leader style to the shared model of leadership (see Denmark 1977, 1993; Duerst-Lahti and Kelly 1995; Kelly, Saint-Germain, and Horn 1991).

Another aspect of leadership receiving increasing attention in the literature is the notion that leadership itself may very well be a gendered concept. As Georgia Duerst-Lahti and Rita Mae Kelly (1995) argue, because the concepts and styles of leadership, particularly political leadership, have developed in male-defined and dominated environments, whoever takes on those roles has been socialized into male norms of what constitutes leadership and is expected to act in ways consonant with those norms. In short, "masculinity permeates understandings of political leadership." As will be explored later in this chapter, the concept of masculinization of leadership has myriad implications for the possibilities and constraints on women in both achieving leadership positions and the ways they act once those positions are gained.

One last matter is relevant to the substance of this chapter—how the concept of women's political leadership is defined. Boundaries on the definition can be unnecessarily limiting and exclusive. Having no definitional boundaries, however, renders analysis impossible. A narrow definition of women leaders might be limited to those who hold formal political leadership titles (such as Speaker of the House or committee chairperson), or possibly those in executive positions (such as governors and mayors). In this chapter, however, I will speak of all women who hold formal political office, elective or appointive; women who serve in other sorts of political positions such as lobbyists and staff assistants; and women whose leadership positions (formal and informal) in civic, community, business, and church organizations make regular contact with and seek to influence the political sphere.

❖ A Constrained Research Agenda: The Tyranny of the Minority

Until rather recently, studying women in political leadership positions in ways that yielded generalizable results has been difficult. This is attributable to the dearth of women who held formal or informal leadership roles over time. Apart from overall totals, there has seldom been a concentration of women in particular types of positions so that meaningful comparison among women or between women and men could be conducted. Although there have been some wonderful cases studies and autobiographies (Kunin 1994; Margolies-Mezvinsky 1994; Boxer 1994; Tolleson-Rinehart and Stanley 1994), without comparison across women in similar positions at one time period, generalizability of findings is limited. Put simply, studying women as a group means that a group has to be present in the first place.

For those interested in elective office, one consequence of a limited universe has been that much extant research has focused on women in legislative office, more often than not, state legislative office. Because there have been so few women in Congress (even as recently as early 2002, only 13% of the U.S. Congress was female), and because data collection efforts on women in local level offices has been so difficult (there are hundreds of school boards, city councils, and board of supervisors across the nation), state legislatures, with their relatively high proportion of women and only 50 data sites, became attractive arenas for study. In contrast, women executives, governors, or mayors have been startlingly few over time. For example, only five women at a time have ever held gubernatorial positions (Center for American Women and Politics 2001). And, while numbers of women who hold statewide office are growing, we still have not seen sufficient numbers in similar positions across enough states for valid generalizations to be developed.

One way to illustrate this general claim concerns the rate at which women offer themselves as candidates for electoral office. In the 2000 elections, for example, a total of 14 women filed as candidates in U.S. Senate races; six won their primaries and all six won the general election. For the U.S. House, 168 women filed their candidacies, 122 won their primaries, and 59 won the general election (Center for American Women and Politics 2000). There is a long way to go until parity is reached.

Related problems have existed for those interested in studying women appointed to political office. If one's sights were set on the federal level, women were scarce. Whether the focus was on Cabinet officers or women in the Senior Executive Service, there have been so few women at any given point in time that a reliable and valid study has been problematic. For research on high-level appointees in state and local government, the numbers problem has been compounded by the multiplicity of data sites. Only a few researchers overcame these difficulties to some extent, and consequently, we have less knowledge of women in appointive positions than women in elective ones (for exceptions, see Carroll and Geiger-Parker 1983a, 1983b, Carroll 1989; Martin 1997; Meyer 1986; Havens and Healy 1991; Duerst-Lahti and Johnson 1990; Kelly, Saint-Germain, and Horn 1991; Guy 1992; Borrelli and Martin 1997).

The same issues arise when examining women's political leadership in grassroots organizations and informal community networks. Scholarship by Takash (1990) and Hardy-Fanta (1993) suggests much about Latin women's leadership styles and foci that differ from Latin men's, particularly related to notions of participatory democracy. Latinas embrace a "politics of connectedness" in which they mobilize a broad array of members of their community on economic and social issues by relying on interpersonal relationships. They are, in short, more broadly inclusive than Latino leaders. However, since the Takash study was performed in California and the Hardy-Fanta study in Boston, it is not clear how the inclusion of additional sites would temper, enhance, or mediate their findings.

Relatedly, the problem of small numbers of women holding political power is compounded when a scholar's focus rests on a subset of women leaders. Because the number of minority women in politics has been small, scholars who have studied women in office, for example, have focused mainly on white women (although see, for example, Githens and Prestage 1977; Barrett 1995 and 2001; Takash 1990, 1993; Thomas 1992; Darling 1998; Friedman 1993; and for comparative information with white women, see Johnson and Stanwick 1976; Johnson and Carroll 1978; Carroll and Strimling 1983; Dodson and Carroll 1991).

What all of this adds up to is that those who have concentrated on women political leaders to date, while accumulating much knowledge and insight, have also been constrained in terms of research development. For example, one study of a local city council or one county board of supervisors is useful to obtain preliminary findings and to perfect research questions and approaches. By itself, however, it cannot tell us a great deal about how women serving in different locales or at different levels of office tend to behave or how the level on which they work conditions their impact. Similarly, a study of community organizing among one group of actors in one locale brings a richness of context and a detail usually lacking in larger survey projects. Yet, whether and how a changing context will alter or reverse those findings is still largely unknown. At present, few comprehensive studies have been conducted and research performed on individual sites should be, where possible, supplemented with more comprehensive studies exploring women's leadership potential, barriers, styles, goals, and conduct across levels of government, type of organization, geographical location, and other contextual features of relevance.

❖ DREAMS AND DESIGNS: THE BEST OF ALL POSSIBLE RESEARCH WORLDS

❖ Building on a Slice of the Past: Studies of Women Officeholders

Because my own research background concerns the study of women officeholders, I use teachings from this area as a springboard for future research efforts.

To date, three broad questions have fueled research on women in elective and appointive office. Scholars have been interested in women's paths to power, their attitudes toward their professional roles and toward politics and political issues, and their behaviors in office and collective impact.

The first area of research has been sociological and has focused on participation patterns of women in office and how those have compared to the patterns of men. We learned, for example, that women have tended to enter politics from a civic worker or community volunteer background. Men, on the other hand, have tended to enter politics from a professional base, usually some sort of business career. Additionally, women often have entered politics later in life than their male counterparts because women fulfilled responsibilities as wives and mothers before entering the political realm (Kirkpatrick 1974; Diamond 1977; Gertzog 1995; Johnson and Stanwick 1976; Johnson and Carroll 1978; Mezey 1978c; Antolini 1984; Stewart 1980; Werner 1966, 1968; Cook 1980, 1984; Carroll and Geiger-Parker 1983a, 1983b; Dolan and Ford 1998).

The second area of research has provided insight into, among other things, women's attitudes about their roles in the political world, their attitudes toward a variety of issues, and their voting records. Women officeholders have tended to perceive themselves as hardworking and responsible contributors to the process, but also as people who often have had a harder time proving themselves as capable contributors. Women representatives also have had somewhat different issue positions than their male colleagues: they have been both more liberal and more supportive of women's issues regardless of party (Gehlen 1977; Leader 1977; Hill 1984; Frankovic 1977; Welch 1985; Boles, 1991; Norris, 1986; Mezey 1978a, 1978b; Stewart 1980; Antolini 1984; Cook 1980, 1984; Carroll and Geiger-Parker 1983a, 1983b; Vega and Firestone 1995; Tamerius 1995; Swers 1998; Clark 1998; Carey, Niemi, and Powell 1998).

The third area of research on women officeholders concentrates on women's contributions to the political realm and their impact. In other words, what difference does it make that women hold these positions? Women in office do indeed make distinctive contributions that transcend their symbolic function of diversifying politics. Perhaps the most dramatic of their contributions has been the distinctive policy priorities women elective and appointive officeholders have pursued. Women have concentrated, far more than men, on issues of women, children, and the family (Thomas 1994; Thomas and Welch 1991; Kathlene, Clarke, and Fox 1991; Reingold 1992; Boles 1991; Dodson 1991; Dodson and Carroll 1991; Havens and Healy 1991; Carroll 1990; Carroll and Taylor 1989a, 1989b; Martin 1991; Swers 1998). This does not mean that women have focused solely on these areas; it simply means that they have consistently give such issues higher priority. This line of research further indicates that women's priorities related to women, children, and family are ones at which they have been successful. For example, women legislators have achieved passage of legislation in these areas at a greater rate than men (Thomas 1994; Kathlene, Clarke, and Fox 1991; Dodson 1991; Dodson and Carroll 1991).

Another strain of this emergent research indicates that in addition to focusing on distinctive issues, women officeholders may bring a new dimension to the political decision-making process itself. Female politicians are more likely than their male counterparts to conceptualize public policy problems more broadly and, as a result, seek different types of solutions. In the field of criminal legislation, for example, whereas male officeholders tend to view a problem as one of individual flouting of legal mandates, female representatives are more likely to search for societal antecedents of criminal activity. One consequence of this wider perspective is that women's legislation is more likely than men's to address the roots of the problem rather than its most recent symptoms. Hence, it is often comprehensive and non-incremental in nature (Kathlene 1989).

Most recently, with the increase of women in formal leadership positions on the state legislative level, scholars have been able to address how women chairpersons approach their jobs. Following evidence in other disciplines indicating that women exercise a different type of leadership from men—one that relies more on cooperation than conflict, inclusion than exclusion, consensus rather than hierarchical, controlled decision-making (Rosener 1990; Eagly and Johnson 1990)—and preliminary political science evidence along similar lines (Tolleson-Rinehart 1991; Beck 1991), recent scholarship concludes that political leadership is gendered. Whicker and Jewell (1998) found that women at all levels of state legislative leadership, more than men, exhibit a consensus rather than a command and control style. Furthermore, despite the gender differences, it is the consensus style that is prevalent in legislatures across the country. Rosenthal (1998) reports that women chairs, more than men, place emphasis on getting the job done and doing it in a team-oriented way rather than relying upon positional authority or raw power. Together, these studies indicate that women in leadership positions may contribute to not only policy differences in legislatures, but also process differences.

✢ Future Research Directions: A Range of Political Women

As noted, the scholarship performed over the last thirty years suggests that as women have entered the political arena, they have brought with them much that is distinctive. With ever-growing numbers in all types of political leadership positions, it is quite likely that their contributions and impact will increase. Hence, one key element of a research agenda for the twenty-first century is a renewed and expanded focus on the range and diversity of political women. What follows is a discussion of the areas I believe deserve increased attention in our studies.

Women in elective and appointive office (including local, state, and national legislators; appointees at all levels and in the full range of positions; women in statewide elective office; chief executives at all three levels of government; and those in party offices) are in need of additional research. Additionally, earlier, I mentioned that past constraints on research in this area meant that scholars focused too little on minority women in office. This almost exclusive focus on white women officeholders must be surmounted and women of color in the full range of political leadership roles must be made the emergent focus (see Githens and Prestage 1977; Barrett 1995, 2001; Thomas 1992; Hardy-Fanta 1993; Takash 1993; Darling 1998; Jennings 1991; Friedman 1993 for existing scholarship on women of color in political leadership).

Scholarship must also continue to include women in the federal and state judiciaries. As is widely known, two women sit on the United States Supreme Court, Sandra Day O'Connor and Ruth Bader Ginsburg. President Johnson appointed 3 female federal judges, Nixon 1, Ford 1, Carter 40 (or 16% of his appointments during his one term), Reagan 28 (or .08% of his many appointments over two terms), Bush 36 (or 19% of his appointments during his one term) (*Congressional Quarterly Weekly Report* 1997, 369). President Bill Clinton's percentage was 28.5 (Crowley 2001). Over time, women are making up an increasing proportion of the federal and state judiciaries, making them good targets for the attention of scholars.

While newly developed studies have begun to address issues of formal legislative leadership at the state level, there is little systematic attention to women in the federal legislatures. Although the numbers are still very small, women are piercing these barriers as well. In the U.S. Congress, for example, the House in early 2002 has five women in leadership positions. The Republican Conference Vice Chairman is Deborah Pryce (OH) and the Conference Secretary is Barbara Cubin (WY). The Congressional Black Caucus is headed by Democrat Eddie Bernice Johnson (TX), and the head of the Democratic Congressional Campaign Committee (DCCC)is Nita Lowey (NY). But the best news is that Rep. Nancy Pelosi (D-CA) has risen to the House Minority Whip position, a critical one on the leadership ladder. This is the highest leadership position ever held by a woman in Congress and indicates that women are in a position to shatter the glass ceiling in the federal legislature. In the Senate in early 2002, Kay Bailey Hutchison (TX) is the Republican Conference Secretary. For the Democrats, Barbara Milkulski (MD) is the Conference Secretary and Patty Murray (WA) is the Democratic Senatorial Campaign Committee (DSCC) Chair. The fact that the heads of the Democratic fund raising operations for the House and Senate (the DCCC and the DSCC) are women suggests that women have well demonstrated their ability to raise money as effectively as men. The sources of this expertise are discussed later in the chapter. Styles of leadership, priorities of leaders, and paths to power on the federal level are among the areas awaiting attention.

I also want to urge political scientists and others interested in women as political leaders to devote increased attention to feeder institutions. There are many arenas in which women's participation and leadership is growing quite rapidly, and these are important both in themselves and because they serve as recruitment pools for elective and appointive political office. First, women are more represented than ever before among the legions of lobbyists, chiefs of staff

96

of legislative offices or committees, party activists, leaders of political action committees, and political consultants on all levels. If we are to expand our understanding of the impact of women in politics and their leadership potentials, styles, and goals, these types of roles cannot be overlooked (See Jennings 1992; Johannes 1984; Knoke 1992; Schlozman 1992; Gierzynski and Burdreck 1995; Van Assendelft and O'Connor 1994; Friedman and Nakamura 1991 for preliminary research on these topics).

The military is another area where women have long been excluded but where recent inroads have been made. As women rise to leadership positions in the uniformed services, their political impact will be heightened. Granted, this area will probably be the slowest to admit women to its leadership positions (see Stiehm 1989; McGlen and Sarkees 1991), but with time, the barriers will almost certainly begin to fall.

Grassroots organizations are also important to explore, including the National Women's Political Caucus, the NAACP, the Sierra Club, the Southern Christian Leadership Conference, the National Gay and Lesbian Task Force, the National Coalition on Black Voter Participation, and the National Council of LaRaza. In particular, the groups for which the advancement of women in society and politics is the major goal can yield interesting studies of women's leadership patterns and the extent to which leadership as a concept is a masculinized one.

Organizations with primary goals that are not directly political, but have political impact, are also fertile areas for studies of women's leadership but have been, with some exceptions, neglected. Community groups such as rape crisis centers, shelters, neighborhood watches, local chapters of Big Brothers/Big Sisters, Bread for the City, legal aid societies, and Parents and Friends of Lesbians and Gays are increasingly led by women. Similarly, civic and business organizations such as Chambers of Commerce, Bar Associations, local chapters of the National Association of Hispanic Journalists, Rotary Clubs, and United Ways are augmenting their proportions of women leaders.

Another arena in which women leaders can be studied are church and church-related charitable groups. Increasingly, churches are open to women in powerful positions up to and including clergy members, and despite the constitutional strictures demanding separation of church and state, much activity to involve parishioners in politics occurs. While the Christian Right gets a great deal of press attention for political involvement, we cannot overlook the fact that in many minority communities, particularly the African American community, church activity is an important connection to politics. Further, since women tend to have higher levels of church-related participation than do men (see Wuthnow and Lehrman 1992), their possibilities for leadership, both informal and formal, are rising.

❖ SUE THOMAS

❖ Substantive Questions of Interest

Future research on women political leaders of all types should focus on the next stage of discovery of their policy and process interests and their impact broadly defined, how they attain and perform their roles, and the factors that account for their staying power. Women elective and appointive officeholders will be used below as an example of how this research agenda may be implemented.

❖ Matters of Policy

One of the next steps for those interested in the impact of women public officials should be to analyze their contribution to and impact on policy issues. This means we need to test whether women bring anything new to the table on issues of mass transportation, agriculture, defense policy, economic development, tort law, international trade, nuclear proliferation, human rights, and more. Some recent work gets to the essence of how women approach all issues including those not explicitly gendered. Kathlene (1992) explored how women officeholders identify problems, the ways in which they perceive causes, and how they shape solutions. Her data-gathering efforts have focused on the range of information requested on an issue, from whom information has been requested, and what sort of compromises have been sought to achieve the passage of bills. Extending this type of effort will allow us to delineate ways in which women contribute to policy identification and development across-the-board and to detect general patterns as well as issue area distinctions. Additionally, answers to such questions will provide insights into how women officeholders relate to women activists and women voters and how each set of actors reinforces and supports the others.

Such an approach might be profitable in areas in which women are only now present in other than token roles. The presidential cabinet and cabinets of selected states, for example, might be especially illuminating sites for studying gendered policy development and decision-making (see Borrelli and Martin 1997). Since these environments are quite different from the legislative arena, and since allegiance to a president or a governor and the dynamics of cabinet operations determine much of what can be done, it is important to study the extent to which women can and may contribute. Cabinet dynamics are especially influenced by the masculinization of leadership, and inquiry into its effects could be fruitful.

Another aspect of policy-making that has only begun to be studied relates to the question of critical mass. The proportion of women in a given political environment, and whether differing levels have an effect on the types of policies that women and men pursue or their approach to policy, are key to understanding the conditions under which impact can be accelerated or attenuated. Some of the work done suggests, for example, that a high level (in the relative sense) of women in legislatures contributes to the pursuit and success of women's distinctive policy priorities (Thomas 1991, 1994; Saint-Germain 1989; Berkman and O'Connor 1993). Additionally, the presence of a unified group, such as a women's caucus, also has the potential for affecting women's impact on political outcomes. In one study, the states in which women's distinctive agendas were most evident were those with high (in the relative sense) proportions of women in office or a formal women's legislative caucus (Thomas 1994). What increasing numbers of women in office or a unified legislative caucus do is create power blocks and voting units useful for pursuing negotiation and outcome alteration.

Among the most important questions in this area are: When women's representation reaches balance with men's, do unified interests take a back seat to factional interests? At what percentage of women does this occur? Are there situations in which women are so numerous that they feel comfortable focusing their attention elsewhere? What are the dynamics of this? Does critical mass affect Republican and Democratic women differently? For example, will a larger proportion of Republican women in legislatures free them to deviate from party dictates if those dictates are contrary to women's policy priorities? How do the interests of women of color interact with the interests of white political women, particularly when those interests are articulated by legislative caucuses and other groups? More broadly, under what conditions do white women and women of color work jointly on issues and under what conditions is unified action hindered? What about other political locations? Research on women serving in the State and Defense Departments (McGlen and Sarkees 1991) and local offices across the nation (Tolleson-Rinehart 1991 on women mayors; and Beck 1991 on female local council members) indicates that certain types of institutional environments and policy agendas are less conducive to the emergence of women's distinctive priorities, styles, and approaches. Blair and Stanley's (1991) work also suggests that this may be so. They found that women legislators in the individualistic political cultures of Texas and Arkansas were seen by men as less effective than objective measures suggested. Whether this is true to a greater, lesser, or equal extent elsewhere is a subject for additional investigation as are the types of political environments most and least conducive to the expression of women's distinctiveness.

On the other hand, is it possible that as political bodies reach a balance, a backlash will develop? Research suggests that just such a phenomenon exists on state legislative committees (see Kathlene 1994). When women meet or exceed the proportions of men on legislative committees, men's verbal behavior becomes more aggressive and hence serves to silence women. To say that women's unique contribution to policy is likely to be diminished in such situations would be an understatement.

In related research, Kathlene (1992) discovered that variables such as strict hierarchical procedures and distancing techniques (such as where legislators sit and in what configurations relative to each other, witnesses, and other politically relevant actors) all have an effect on women's contribution level and impact. Hence, even the physical structure of political environments and the behavioral cues common to these arenas may influence the extent to which non-mainstream political actors are participatory and valued. We need to learn much more about how factors such as these may affect the input that women political leaders have on policy—especially when those leaders are not the formal variety—and where power disadvantages are particularly pronounced.

Legislative bodies are especially attractive targets for queries related to proportionality and group effects, although they are not the only arenas in which they are relevant. Federal and state cabinets are ripe for this type of study as are judicial conferences. Each would make an excellent research laboratory for studying issues of critical mass, threshold effects, and how proportionality releases or constrains behavior. Certainly, civic, business, and grassroots organizations also provide opportunities to test the effects of critical mass on women's leadership potential and pursuit.

A note about context is important. The ways in which women's distinctive impact is enhanced, constrained, or mediated must be explored in each setting. Variables such as institutional norms, party control, and whether one holds an advisory position (such as a cabinet officer) or whether one represents a constituency (and, if so, the type of constituency represented including the party identification, ideology, and major economic and social interests of one's constituents) are all contextual factors that influence impact and need to be included to the greatest extent possible in future research designs.

❖ Matters of Process

The previous discussion of policy-making distinctiveness of women relates naturally to questions of process. Do women desire or work to bring about changes in the ways in which political business is conducted? Beyond the ways in which they identify policy issues and possible solutions—whether in the legislature, the executive branch, community groups, or other arenas—do women have an effect on the rules of the game itself?

Available preliminary inquiries into these questions provide no evidence that women legislators have worked collectively to change the rules or processes by which legislative work is conducted despite some preliminary evidence that they are uncomfortable with the status quo (see Thomas 1991, 1994; Dodson and Carroll 1991; Johnson and Carroll 1978; CAWP 1985). Perhaps due to the multiple obstacles in the path of widespread systematic change (including women's ongoing, although gradually diminishing, minority status in political entities, the timeframe, compromises, and organizing efforts necessary for even modest system change), attempts at systematic reform have not been pursued.

However, changing process does not come about merely as a result of organized, collective efforts. Women leaders may also change processes through individual choices about the styles they use to pursue their political roles. Research done by the Center for American Women and Politics (Dodson and Carroll, 1991) suggests that women bring actors into the process who may not have had a voice previously and enhance the roles of those who have been marginalized in the past. Kathlene's (1989) work on women legislators in Colorado also suggests that females are more likely than their male counterparts to pursue issues by including a wider array of voices and viewpoints.

On the other hand, Paule Cruz Takash (1993) concludes that while Latina community organizers engage in a high degree of participatory leadership on issues, this type of leadership does not necessarily transfer into elective political office. Additional research needs to investigate that transition and the factors that encourage and support women in taking their skills and styles into office with them. The interaction of race and gender is an area that requires a great deal more investigation.

One way to pursue investigations of women's distinctive leadership styles and the conditions under which they are most and least prevalent is to study smaller political and quasi-political bodies, perhaps county boards of supervisors, local school boards, or civic organizations. Studying organizations that go from predominantly male to predominantly female might be useful. So would studying organizations in adjoining jurisdictions that vary according to the proportions of women and men and the proportions of women and men of color. Researchers could examine, among other questions, whether any procedure or rules changes are found among the comparison groups or whether informal methods of operation have been adopted or have evolved.

In the areas of both organized, collective attempts to change the process and informal, individual contributions to that end, it is important for future researchers to investigate the extent to which women leaders are dissatisfied with traditional political practices and, what, if anything, women think should be done to reform political and quasi-political environments. In part this entails examining the socio-cultural obstacles women leaders see before them (including variables such as implicit or explicit acceptance of masculinized views of political process), the compromises they feel they need to make, the extent to which they are willing to pursue change, and the chances women see for eventual success, both individual and collective.

Beyond socio-cultural barriers, but related to them, are psychological barriers. One clue from political science research that psychological barriers impede women's political progress is found in the work on ambition levels among women in politics. The work of Costantini (1990) on political party activists and Bledsoe and Herring's (1990) work on women officeholders suggest that women harbor constrained perceptions of political possibilities and their own political strength. Hence, questions important to extend these studies include: How do women's confidence levels affect their determination of whether they should collectively attempt reform? What other psychological obstacles inhibit their vision?

One last matter, loosely related to process questions, concerns the people female politicians bring into the political arena. I observed earlier that women leaders reach out widely to include the voices of those with policy input. Here, I am referring to how elective or appointive officeholders or civic and community leaders recruit and hire staff or volunteers and have an influence on who gets paid and unpaid jobs throughout their respective organizations. Related research, especially studies of the impact of minority politicians on the local level, indicates that diversity in political office begets diversity among those who surround officeholders (Mladenka 1989). Given that employees and volunteers contribute to policy development and decisions as well as to the ways in which policy is effectuated, it is imperative to investigate the people women politicians bring to the arena. Such queries are also important because they affect diversity among the politicians of the future. One question to ask about the impact of women leaders on those with whom they work is whether the more women in office, the more women staffers get hired? Similarly, the interaction of race and gender might yield the expectation that the more women of color in office, the more minorities will be hired and relied upon as important political actors.

❖ Obtaining and Staying in Power: The Psychology of Success

One last element of a research agenda for the future relates to the psychological tools women leaders use to negotiate, pursue, retain, and extend their places in the political world. Political psychology has offered much insight into the attitudes and behaviors of mass-level women, especially the nature of group consciousness, and the correlates of the gender gap (Burns, Scholzman, and Verba 1997; Scholzman, Burns, and Verba 1994, 1999; and Verba, Schlozman, and Burns 1997). But studies have not yet focused enough on how mass-level, politically interested women perceive their own opportunities for further contributions. For example, the National Women's Political Caucus conducted a national poll of voters supplemented by in-depth interviews of voters in occupations that have traditionally been pipelines to politics. The pollsters found that women are less likely (by half) to consider running for political office. Citizens believe that women have a harder time than men winning office. Women, more than men, are concerned about their own qualifications levels. And, women, more than men, tend to lack confidence without substantial levels of candidate training. Much more research is needed about the extent to which role models, mentors, candidate recruitment, and training affects women's desire to contribute politically (National Women's Political Caucus 1994).

A number of related questions remain about those who already hold office. The scholarship of Cantor and Bernay (1992) examined the kinds of psychological backgrounds shared by women who won U.S. Senate, U.S. House, mayoral, and gubernatorial races, but they did little to illuminate women's present strategies for coping in office. Cantor's and Bernay's work spurs visions of further investigations into what impelled women officials to join what has, heretofore, been an overwhelmingly male-dominated environment, what sustains them when they run into obstacles (either gender-related or otherwise), what women's support systems look like, and what connection, debt, or obligation female politicians feel toward other women aspiring to or winning political office. (For discussion of some of these issues, see Gierzynski and Burdreck 1995; Thomas 1997, 1998). The concepts here, while related to women in elective political office, are not limited to just this group. Women leaders across the spectrum face these issues, and research that compares the perceptions of different types of women political leaders is needed.

❖ Concerns of Research Design and Theory

Not only does the focus of our research need expansion, so too do the designs and approaches we use. Although there have been exceptions, principally the work on women candidates and officeholders at the state level done by the Center for American Women and Politics, much previous scholarship has relied upon a single research site or level and concentrated on one or two aspects of attitude or behavior. Although limited budgets, time, and personnel dictated this approach, the generalizability and scope of our findings have been constrained because of it. As a final task for this chapter, I will offer suggestions for expanded empirical and theoretical research tasks.

❖ The Empirical Focus

If I were asked, "What is your ideal in terms of research on current and future women leaders?" my answer would be the following. The first step entails the development of a large-scale research design to be administered in a variety of sites across levels of government and including non-governmental organizations. Scholars active in the study of women leaders would be given the opportunity to work together to develop common, comprehensive protocols and to train researchers (political scientists as well as specialists in other areas) from universities across the country in their implementation. In this way, gaps in the literature would be addressed in a coordinated fashion.

❖ SUE THOMAS

Coordinated studies of this sort avoid the limitations of one-shot studies. For example, variables such as diversity of region, level, competitiveness of parties, political culture, the proportion of women in the political or community environment, the decision-making rules and procedures, the scope and range of responsibilities accorded to the organization in question, and the full- or part-time nature of the organization can be explored and the effects explained. Additionally, the possibility of investigating multiple levels of analysis of the attitudes, behaviors, and impact of women leaders is enhanced. Individual, group, institutional, and societal influences can be studied simultaneously so that the effects of each can be accounted for in an interactive fashion. Finally, data on the perceptions of leaders as well as objective measures of their behavior could be collected. All these benefits would dramatically increase the likelihood that definitive results could emerge.

A large-scale, coordinated study could also expand the range of research instruments used by scholars and make their simultaneous use possible. To date, most scholars have relied upon mail, telephone, or in-person survey instruments. While these tools are invaluable and should continue to be used, additional methodological instruments need to be included in future research. In particular, studies of women leaders are well suited to participant-observation, recording of public sessions, focus groups, and one-on-one inter-views. Additionally, data could be collected not only from the women leaders, but also from those with whom they work most closely, such as other community activists, lobbyists, campaign workers, fund raisers, office staff members, media representatives, and other associates. This would allow for a well-rounded picture of the interactions among women leaders and relevant players in the process, the ways in which women leaders make decisions, and the sources of information and advice upon which they rely. While resource inten-sive, the full range of methodologies would allow researchers to investigate the motivations for and the influences on actions of women leaders in addition to behavioral outcomes.

Ideals are rarely achieved, but should never be ignored. Since funding for such coordinated efforts is unlikely, I urge scholars to collaborate to the extent possible, share resources, and include as many comparative elements in their studies as possible.

❖ *Theoretical Considerations*

New and expanded research designs about women leaders, whether in ideal form or in pieces, must also be guided by solid theoretical exploration. Extant research has relied on a variety of theoretical perspectives, some mutually exclu-sive, some not. Most of the current work has relied on implicit assumptions about whether women will behave either differently from or similarly to their male counterparts. Beyond that surface level, however, disagreement rests on variations of essentialist or social construction explanations (for further elaboration, see Thomas 1994, ch. 1). Because each new study has not necessarily been explicit about its expectations and how they are linked to the expectations and findings of earlier literature, theoretical development has suffered. Until we develop, explicitly acknowledge, and test competing hypotheses related to how women behave politically, we will do little more than catalog that behavior. Because the role of social scientists is to explain and predict as well as to describe, it is imperative that, in addition to coordinating and diversifying site selection, protocols, methodologies, and instruments to the extent possible, the underlying assumptions be made explicit and the testing of competing hypotheses be included in new research efforts.

❖ Toward the New World

The preceding discussion is intended to make clear the view that while the increasingly sophisticated study of women political leaders has yielded a great deal of vital knowledge to date, there is much more work to be done to keep scholars busy well into the twenty-first century. Whether or not the ideal vision of a large, coordinated research project ever comes to fruition, there are numerous individual and collaborative projects that will extend our knowledge of female political leaders.

❖ References

Antolini, Denise. 1984. "Women in Local Government: An Overview." In *Political Women: Current Roles in State and Local Government*, ed. Janet A. Flammang. Beverly Hills: Sage.

Barrett, Edith J. 1995. "The Policy Priorities of African American Women in State Legislatures." *Legislative Studies Quarterly* 20: 223–47.

——— 2001. "Black Women in State Legislatures: The Relationship of Race and Gender to the Legislative Experience." In *The Impact of Women in Public Office*, ed. Susan J. Carroll. Bloomington: Indiana University Press.

Beck, Susan Abrams. 1991. "Rethinking Municipal Governance: Gender Distinctions on Local Councils." In *Gender and Policymaking: Studies of Women in Office*, ed. Debra L. Dodson. New Brunswick, NJ: Center for the American Woman and Politics.

Berkman, Michael B., and Robert E. O'Connor. 1993. "Do Women Legislators Matter? Female Legislators and State Abortion Policy." *American Politics Quarterly* 21: 102–24.

Blair, Diane D., and Jeanie R. Stanley. 1991. "Gender Differences in Legislative Effectiveness: The Impact of the Legislative Environment." In *Gender and Policymaking: Studies of Women in Office*, ed. Debra L. Dodson. New Brunswick, NJ: Center for the American Woman and Politics.

Bledsoe, Timothy, and Mary Herring. 1990. "Victims of Circumstances: Women in Pursuit of Political Office in America." *American Political Science Review* 84: 213–24.

Boles, Janet K. 1991. "Advancing the Women's Agenda Within Local Legislatures: The Role of Female Elected Officials." In *Gender and Policymaking: Studies of Women in Office,* ed. Debra L. Dodson. New Brunswick, NJ: Center for the American Woman and Politics.

Borrelli, MaryAnne, and Janet M. Martin, eds. 1997. *The Other Elites: Women, Politics, and Power in the Executive Branch.* Boulder, Colo.: Lynne Rienner Publishers.

Boxer, Barbara. 1994. *Strangers in the Senate: Politics and the New Revolution of Women in America.* Washington, DC: National Press Books.

Burns, Nancy E., Kay Lehman Schlozman, and Sidney Verba. 1997. "The Public Consequences of Private Inequality: Family Life and Citizen Participation." *American Political Science Review* 91: 373–89.

Cantor, Dorothy W., and Toni Bernay. 1992. *Women in Power: The Secrets of Leadership.* Boston: Houghton Mifflin Company.

Carey, John M., Richard G. Niemi, and Lynda W. Powell. 1998. "Are Women State Legislators Different?" In *Women and Elective Office: Past, Present, and Future,* ed. Sue Thomas and Clyde Wilcox. New York: Oxford University Press.

Carroll, Susan J. 1989. "The Personal is Political: The Intersection of Private Lives and Public Roles Among Women and Men in Elective and Appointive Office." *Women & Politics* 9: 51–67.

—— 1990. "Looking Back at the 1980s and Forward to the 1990s." *CAWP News & Notes.* New Brunswick, NJ: Center for the American Woman and Politics 7: 9–12.

—— and Barbara Geiger-Parker. 1983*a*. *Women Appointed to the Carter Administration: A Comparison with Men.* New Brunswick, NJ: Center for the American Woman and Politics.

—— and Barbara Geiger-Parker. 1983*b*. *Women Appointed to State Government: A Comparison with All State Appointees.* New Brunswick, NJ: Center for the American Woman and Politics.

—— and Wendy S. Strimling. 1983. *Women's Routes to Public Office: A Comparison with Men's.* New Brunswick, NJ: Center for American Women and Politics, 1983.

—— and Ella Taylor. 1989*a*. "Gender Differences in the Committee Assignments of State Legislators: Preferences or Discrimination?" Paper presented at the annual meeting of the Midwest Political Science Association, Chicago.

—— and Ella Taylor. 1989*b*. "Gender Differences in Policy Priorities of U.S. State Legislators." Paper presented at the annual meeting of the American Political Science Association, Atlanta.

Center for the American Woman and Politics. 1985. *Women in Legislative Leadership: Report From a Conference.* New Brunswick, NJ: Center for the American Woman and Politics.

—— 2000. "Names of Women Candidates in 2000 Listed by State." Fact Sheet. New Brunswick, NJ: Center for American Women and Politics.

—— 2001. "Statewide Elective Executive Women 2001." Fact Sheet. New Brunswick, NJ: Center for American Women and Politics.

Clark, Janet. 1998. "Women at the National Level: An Update on Roll Call Voting Behavior." In *Women and Elective Office: Past, Present, and Future*, ed. Sue Thomas and Clyde Wilcox. New York: Oxford University Press.

Congressional Quarterly Weekly Report. 1997. February, 369.

Cook, Beverly Blair. 1980. "Women Judges and Public Policy on Sex Integration." In *Women in Local Politics*, ed. Debra W. Stewart. Metuchen, NJ: Scarecrow Press.

——1984. "Women on the State Bench: Correlates of Access." In *Political Women: Current Roles in State and Local Politics*, ed. Janet Flammang. Madison: University of Wisconsin Press.

Costantini, Edmond. 1990. "Political Women and Political Ambition: Closing the Gender Gap." *American Journal of Political Science* 34: 741–70.

Crowley, Patrick. 2001. "Connection Factor in Judgeships," *Cincinnati Enquirer*, 16 December.

Darling, Marsha J. 1998. "African American Women in State Elective Officeholding in the South." In *Women and Elective Office: Past, Present, and Future*, ed. Sue Thomas and Clyde Wilcox. New York: Oxford University Press.

Denmark, Florence L. 1977. "Styles of Leadership." *Psychology of Women Quarterly* 2: 99–113.

——1993. "Women, Leadership, and Empowerment." *Psychology of Women Quarterly* 17: 343–56.

Diamond, Irene. 1977. *Sex Roles in the State House.* New Haven: Yale University Press.

Dodson, Debra L., ed. 1991. *Gender and Policymaking: Studies of Women in Office.* New Brunswick, NJ: Center for the American Woman and Politics.

——and Susan J. Carroll. 1991. *Reshaping the Agenda: Women in State Legislatures.* New Brunswick, NJ: Center for the American Woman and Politics.

Dolan, Kathleen, and Lynne E. Ford. 1998. "Are All Women State Legislators Alike?" In *Women and Elective Office: Past, Present, and Future*, ed. Sue Thomas and Clyde Wilcox. New York: Oxford University Press.

Duerst-Lahti, Georgia, and Cathy Marie Johnson. 1990. "Gender and Style in Bureaucracy." *Women & Politics* 10: 67–120.

——and Rita Mae Kelly, eds. 1995. *Gender Power, Leadership, and Governance.* Ann Arbor: University of Michigan Press, 1995.

Eagly, Alice H., and Blair T. Johnson. 1990. "Gender and Leadership Style: A Meta-Analysis." *Psychological Bulletin* 108: 233–56.

Edwards, George C. III. 1989. *At the Margins: Presidential Leadership of Congress.* New Haven: Yale University Press, 1989.

Frankovic, Kathleen A. 1977. "Sex and Voting in the U.S. House of Representatives 1961–1975." *American Politics Quarterly* 5: 315–31.

Friedman, Sally. 1993. "Committee Advancement of Women and Blacks in Congress: A Test of the Responsible Legislator Thesis." *Women & Politics* 13: 27–52.

——and Robert T. Nakamura. 1991. "The Representation of Women on U.S. Senate Committee Staffs." *Legislative Studies Quarterly* 16: 407–27.

Gehlen, Freida. 1977. "Women Members of Congress: A Distinctive Role." In *A Portrait of Marginality: The Political Behavior of the American Woman*, ed. Marianne Githens and Jewell Prestage. New York: McKay.

Gertzog, Irwin N. 1995. *Congressional Women: Their Recruitment, Treatment, and Behavior.* 2nd ed. Westport, CT: Praeger.

Gierzynski, Anthony, and Paulette Burdreck. 1995. "Women's Legislative Caucus and Leadership Campaign Committees." *Women & Politics* 15: 37–54.

Githens, Marianne, and Jewell Prestage, eds. 1977. *A Portrait of Marginality: The Political Behavior of the American Woman.* New York: McKay, 1977.

Guy, Mary E., ed. 1992. *Women and Men of the States: Public Administrators at the State Level.* New York: M. E. Sharpe, Inc.

Hardy-Fanta, Carol. 1993. *Latina Politics, Latino Politics: Gender, Culture, and Political Participation in Boston.* Philadelphia: Temple University Press.

Havens, Catherine M., and Lynne M. Healy. 1991. "Cabinet-Level Appointees in Connecticut: Women Making a Difference." In *Gender and Policymaking: Studies of Women in Office*, ed. Debra L. Dodson. New Brunswick, NJ: Center for the American Woman and Politics.

Hill, David, B. 1984. "Female State Senators as Cue Givers: ERA Roll-Call Voting, 1972–1979." In *Political Women: Current Roles in State and Local Government*, ed. Janet A. Flammang. Beverly Hills: Sage.

Jennings, Jeanette. 1991. "Black Women Mayors: Reflections on Race and Gender." In *Gender and Policymaking: Studies of Women in Office*, ed. Debra L. Dodson. New Brunswick, NJ: Center for the American Woman and Politics.

Jennings, M. Kent. 1992. "Women in Party Politics." In *Women Politics and Change*, ed. Louise A. Tilly and Patricia Gurin. New York: Russell Sage Foundation.

Johannes, John R. 1984. "Women as Congressional Staffers: Does It Make a Difference?" *Women & Politics* 4: 69–81.

Johnson, Marilyn, and Kathy A. Stanwick. 1976. *Profiles of Women Holding Office.* New Brunswick, NJ: Center for the American Woman and Politics.

Johnson, Marilyn, and Susan Carroll. 1978. *Profile of Women Holding Office II.* New Brunswick, NJ: Center for the American Woman and Politics.

Kathlene, Lyn. 1989. "Uncovering the Political Impact of Gender: An Exploratory Study." *Western Political Quarterly* 42: 397–421.

——1992. "Studying the New Voice of Women in Politics." *The Chronicle of Higher Education.* November 18: B1–2.

——1994. "Power and Influence in State Legislative Policy Making: The Interaction of Gender and Position in Committee Hearing Debates." *American Political Science Review* 88: 560–76.

——Susan E. Clarke, and Barbara A. Fox. 1991. "Ways Women Politicians Are Making A Difference." In *Gender and Policymaking: Studies of Women in Office*, ed. Debra L. Dodson. New Brunswick, NJ: Center for the American Woman and Politics.

Kelly, Rita Mae, Michelle A. Saint-Germain, and Jody D. Horn. 1991. "Female Public Officials: A Different Voice?" *Annals of the American Academy of Political Science* 515: 77–87.

Kirkpatrick, Jeane J. 1974. *Political Woman.* New York: Basic Books.

Knoke, David. 1992. "The Mobilization of Members in Women's Associations." In *Women, Politics, and Change*, eds. Louise A. Tilly and Patricia Gurin. New York: Russell Sage Foundation.

Kunin, Madeleine. 1994. *Living a Political Life*. New York: Knopf.

Leader, Shelah G. 1977. "The Policy Impact of Elected Women Officials." In *The Impact of the Electoral Process*, ed. Joseph Cooper and Louis Maisels. Beverly Hills: Sage.

Margolies-Mezvinsky, Marjorie. 1994. *A Woman's Place . . . The Freshman Women Who Changed the Face of Congress*. New York: Crown.

Martin, Elaine. 1991. "Judicial Gender and Judicial Choices." In *Gender and Policymaking: Studies of Women in Office*, ed. Debra L. Dodson. New Brunswick, NJ: Center for the American Woman and Politics.

Martin, Janet M. 1997. "Women Who Govern: The President's Appointments." In *The Other Elites: Women, Politics, and Power in the Executive Branch*, ed. MaryAnne Borrelli and Janet M. Martin. Boulder, Colo.: Lynne Rienner Publishers.

McGlen, Nancy E., and Meredith Reid Sarkees. 1991. "The Unseen Influence of Women in the State and Defense Departments." In *Gender and Policymaking: Studies of Women in Office*, ed. Debra L. Dodson. New Brunswick, NJ: Center for the American Woman and Politics.

Meyer, Katherine. 1986. "The Influence of Gender on Work Activities and Attitudes of Senior Civil Servants in the United States, Canada, and Great Britain." In *Women and Politics: Activism, Attitudes and Officeholding*, ed. Gwen Moore and Glenna Spitze. Greenwich, Conn.: JAI Press.

Mezey, Susan Gluck. 1978a. "Support For Women's Rights Policy: An Analysis of Local Politicians." *American Politics Quarterly* 6: 485–97.

——1978b. "Women and Representation: The Case of Hawaii." *Journal of Politics* 40: 369–85.

——1978c. "Does Sex Make a Difference? A Case Study of Women in Politics." *Western Political Quarterly* 31: 492–501.

Mladenka, Kenneth R. 1989. "Blacks and Hispanics in Urban Politics." *American Political Science Review* 83: 165–92.

National Women's Political Caucus. 1994. "Why Don't More Women Run?" A Study Prepared by Mellman, Lazarus, Lake. Washington, DC.

Norris, Pippa. 1986. "Women in Congress: A Policy Difference." *Politics* 6: 34–40.

Norton, Noelle. 1995. "Women, It's Not Enough to Be Elected: Committee Position Makes a Difference." In *Gender Power, Leadership, and Governance*, ed. Georgia Duerst-Lahti and Rita Mae Kelly. Ann Arbor: University of Michigan Press.

Reingold, Beth. 1992. "Concepts of Representation among Female and Male State Legislators." *Legislative Studies Quarterly* 17: 509–37.

Rosener, Judy B. 1990. "Ways Women Lead." *Harvard Business Review*. November–December: 119–25.

Rosenthal, Cindy Simon. 1998. *When Women Lead: Integrative Leadership in State Legislatures*. New York: Oxford University Press.

Saint-Germain, Michelle A. 1989. "Does Their Difference Make A Difference? The Impact of Women on Public Policy in the Arizona Legislature." *Social Science Quarterly* 70: 956–68.

Schlozman, Kay Lehman. 1992. "Representing Women in Washington: Sisterhood and Pressure Politics." In *Women, Politics, and Change*. ed. Louise A. Tilly and Patricia Gurin. New York: Russell Sage Foundation.

——Nancy Burns, and Sidney Verba. 1994. "Gender and the Pathways to Participation: The Role of Resources." *Journal of Politics* 56: 963–90.

——Nancy Burns, and Sidney Verba. 1999. "What Happened at Work Today? A Multistage Model of Gender, Employment, and Political Participation." *Journal of Politics* 61: 29–53.

Stewart, Debra W., ed. 1980. *Women in Local Politics*. Metuchen, NJ: Scarecrow Press.

Stiehm, Judith Hicks. 1989. *Arms and the Enlisted Woman*. Philadelphia: Temple University Press.

Swers, Michelle L. 1998. "Are Congresswomen More Likely to Vote for Women's Issues Bills Than Their Male Colleagues?" *Legislative Studies Quarterly* 23: 435–48.

Takash, Paule Cruz. 1990. "A Crisis of Democracy: Community Responses to the Latinization of a California Town Dependent on Immigrant Labor." Unpublished dissertation, Department of Anthropology, University of California, Berkeley.

——1993. "Breaking Barriers to Representation: Chicana/Latina Elected Officials in California." *Urban Anthropology and Studies of Cultural Systems and World Economic Development* 22: 325–60.

Tamerius, Karen L. 1995. "Sex, Gender, and Leadership in the Representation of Women." In *Gender Power, Leadership, and Governance*, ed. Georgia Duerst-Lahti and Rita Mae Kelly. Ann Arbor: University of Michigan Press.

Thomas, Sue. 1991. "The Impact of Women on State Legislative Policies." *Journal of Politics* 53: 958–76.

——1992. "The Effects of Race and Gender on Constituency Service." *Western Political Quarterly* 45: 161–80.

——1994. *How Women Legislate*. New York: Oxford University Press.

——1997. "Why Gender Matters: The Perceptions of Women Officeholders." *Women & Politics* 17: 27–53.

——1998. "Legislative Careers: The Personal and the Political." Paper presented at the annual meeting of the Midwest Political Science Association, Chicago.

——and Susan Welch. 1991. "The Impact of Gender On Activities and Priorities of State Legislators." *Western Political Quarterly* 44: 445–56.

Tolleson-Rinehart, Sue. 1991. "Do Women Leaders Make a Difference? Substance, Style and Perceptions." In *Gender and Policymaking: Studies of Women in Office*, ed. Debra L. Dodson. New Brunswick, NJ: Center for the American Woman and Politics.

——and Jeanie R. Stanley. 1994. *Claytie and the Lady: Ann Richards, Gender, and Politics in Texas*. Austin: University of Texas Press.

Van Assendelft, Laura, and Karen O'Connor. 1994. "Backgrounds, Motivations and Interests: A Comparison of Male and Female Local Party Activists." *Women & Politics* 14: 77–92.

Vega, Arturo, and Juanita M. Firestone. 1995. "The Effects of Gender on Congressional Behavior and the Substantive Representation of Women." *Legislative Studies Quarterly* 20: 213–22.

Verba, Sidney, Nancy E. Burns, and Kay Lehman Schlozman. 1997. "Knowing and Caring about Politics: Gender and Political Engagement." *Journal of Politics* 59: 1051–72.

Welch, Susan. 1985. "Are Women More Liberal than Men in the U.S. Congress?" *Legislative Studies Quarterly* 10: 125–34.

Werner, Emmy E. 1968. "Women in the State Legislatures." *Western Political Quarterly* 21: 40–50.

—— 1966. "Women In Congress: 1917–1964." *Western Political Quarterly* 19: 16–30.

Whicker, Marcia, and Malcolm Jewell. 1998. "The Feminization of Leadership in State Legislatures." In *Women and Elective Office: Past, Present, and Future*, ed. Sue Thomas and Clyde Wilcox. New York: Oxford University Press.

Wurthnow, Robert, and William Lehrman. 1992. "Religion: Inhibitor or Facilitator of Political Involvement Among Women?" In *Women, Politics, and Change*, ed. Louise A. Tilly and Patricia Gurin. New York: Russell Sage Foundation.

5 ❖ Women, Women's Organizations, and Political Parties[1]

Denise L. Baer

Many, if not most, of the efforts through which women have sought power in American history have involved organized, collective action. Yet, political science research on women's organizations in both partisan and nonpartisan arenas has lagged behind recent real-world advances in women's status and roles. Consequently, we know less than we should about the role organized action has played in achieving these gains. To develop a twenty-first-century research agenda, there are three sets of interrelated gaps in our knowledge base that require cross-disciplinary collaboration and innovative research partnerships to answer old questions and provide new direction for research and practice:

- *theory gaps* between the subfields of women and politics versus interest groups and parties, which has led to
- *research gaps* on how the active and latent phases of the women's movement are linked, and how leadership, recruitment, and organizational culture impacts women's power, which in turn feeds into
- growing *research-practice gaps* which risk making research irrelevant and may undermine rights already gained.

The most serious set of gaps are theoretical, reflecting fundamental issues in epistemology, methodology, and paradigms that underlay our ability to define appropriate research questions.

❖ FUNDAMENTAL THEORY GAPS

Since the 1960s there have been two blind spots within behavioral political science that have discouraged much-needed research on women in groups. In fact, these two blind spots have operated as a "double-blind" where each has self-consciously ignored the other, when in fact, these two subfields in behavioral political science should have informed each other. The first overarching theoretical blind spot stems from the still dominant behavioral paradigm. Behavioralism directs our attention to individuals and views organizations primarily as the sum of individual behaviors. It is only in the 1990s that a new institutionalism (March and Olson 1989) reemerged and partially lifted these disciplinary blinders. Yet, women and politics researchers must be wary as the old institutionalism which preceded behavioralism also viewed women's interests as inherently nonpolitical.

There are two aspects to this theory/paradigm issue. First, old research may be inadequate to explain women's roles. Old questions previously studied using the behavioral paradigm (as well as the old institutionalism) may need fresh approaches to fully flesh out the historical record leading to the contemporary women's movement. These must include a closer attention to history and social change as well as numerical data.

For example, Jo Freeman's (2000) history of how women entered party politics "one room at a time" from the 1800s until 1970 fundamentally recasts that history by comparing the two key mechanisms of influence in electoral and party politics: individual sponsorship and organized blocs. Similarly, Kristi Andersen (1996) reexamines how the effects of women's suffrage reframed American culture through restructuring the practices of voting, pressure group politics, and the party machine. In doing so, Andersen's and Freeman's research questions the widely accepted notion of "forty years in the desert" (Sinclair Deckard 1983, 283) by providing new data about women in organizations and in parties, using contemporary theory to reevaluate these new data, and asking us to reconsider our views about women's accomplishments and the power of organization. We need more studies like these.

And second, research continues to be stymied because of disagreements over the best approach to use in studying women and politics. Early contemporary (i.e., 1960s–1970s) women and politics scholars maintained that participant observation and ethnography were essential to the study of women and politics and that survey research was limited as a technique for studying social and protest movements. However, the newer generations of women and politics scholars are trained in graduate schools often dominated by behavioral and quantitative approaches. As a result, the commitment to utilizing a range of techniques and methods remains at continual risk due to generational replacement.

As early ethnographic studies are replaced by newer quantitative/ behavioral studies, what will we lose in understanding the role of social movements in advances for women? The point is not that quantitative techniques do not shed critical light necessary for testing generalizable hypotheses (they do), but rather that quantitative techniques alone may not suffice to capture participation

(Verba, Schlozman, and Brady 1997) and the full range of influence of a social movement (Baer 1993*a*). For example, Christina Wollbrecht's (2000) analysis of the realignment of the Democratic and Republican parties in Congress uses measures of bill sponsorship to gauge whether the increasing number of women members (among other causes) best explains the issue evolution of women's rights issues. In this quantitative analysis the role of informal influence becomes invisible, and the qualitative impact of Sue Thomas' (1994) observation about the importance of proportionality for women's legislative effectiveness (the 30% threshold) disappears as an explanatory factor. This is relevant because the U.S. Congress still lacks gender parity, with women in 2001 comprising only 14% of representatives and 13% of senators (Center for American Women and Politics 2001).

To give another example, many qualitative studies of women activists suggest that women may become active through their role as mothers and specialize in grassroots, local politics (Collins 1990; Kaplan 1997; Naples 1998) while quantitative research finds little aggregate difference between men and women in the general public (Schlozman et al. 1995). Is it possible that both findings are true and that research using only one technique lacks context? Further, quantitative research considered alone may raise questions among casual readers about whether it makes a difference for women to be in office and may lead them to conclude that men may represent women just as well as women can, a perspective vigorously disputed by most social movement scholars, whose work stresses the role of leadership of women by women.

In addition to the problems created by behavioralism discussed above, a second theoretical blind spot stems from distinctive subfield paradigms that have inhibited useful cross-fertilization across similar areas of research. The contemporary subfield of women and politics has largely neglected organizational aspects of women's roles and influence in favor of political process explanations (Baer 1993*a*; Schlozman 1986). This has occurred for a variety of good reasons, probably the most important of which is the need for scholars in the subfield of women and politics to recover the study of women in politics from the intellectual dustbins reserved for nonpolitical entities and other curiosities. Now that women are entering into the political mainstream through group-based power, the "mainstream" interest group and political party subfields, with fewer good reasons, have likewise ignored the impact of the changing political roles of women. Many contemporary works still treat the political interests of women as tied to the presumably "nonpolitical," traditional roles of wife and mother.[2] For example, Byron Shafer's 1983 history of Democratic Party reform attributed women's role predominantly to the "immediate social access" of the wives of prominent reform leaders, rather than to their leadership of a genuine social movement with real grievances (1983, 471).

It is ironic that both women and politics scholars and party and interest group scholars have contributed to a scholarly gap in research at this juncture in history. The women and politics subfield has ignored parties and interest groups while the mainstream subfields have ignored women. Yet, political parties have become institutionalized, and parties and the groups with which they are allied are now the dominant actors in setting the public agenda. At a time when the grassroots movement phase of the contemporary women's movement is waning and women's leaders are turning to more mainstream mechanisms for access, this "double-blind" approach (the behavioral paradigm combined with subfield specialization) has stymied advances in our understanding of how women's organizations advocate their interests. The result is a growing intellectual and theoretical gap not only for scholars, but also for women's organizational leaders.

One goal of a new research agenda for women and politics scholarship must be to bridge this theoretical gap by borrowing those conceptual tools that are useful while challenging those theories that are wrong or inadequate. This chapter will consider first interest group scholarship, then political party research, and finally their growing intersection. Because of the research gap described above, some of the following discussion necessitates reviewing the basic history of women's organizations and party activism in order to identify what lines of future research might prove most fruitful.[3]

❖ RESEARCH–THEORY GAP, PART I: INTERESTS AND POLITICAL ORGANIZATION

The double-blind split between women and politics and mainstream scholarship is probably no more evident than in the study of the origins of the women's movement. Women and politics scholarship has accepted as its basic operating premise that the contemporary women's movement is a genuine, new social movement arising from a common *political* identity (Baer 1999; Baer and Bositis 1988, 1993; Freeman 1975, 1983; McGlen and O'Connor 1983). By contrast, mainstream interest group scholarship classifies the goals of movement-type organizations as an aberration due to the "free rider" problem (Olson 1965). Thus, any group based on concepts of group rationality and not organized around immediate *social* (i.e., familial, neighborhood) or *economic* (i.e., work and profession) needs is different. "While not denying that these [purposive] incentives do attract many activists, the logic indicates that such incentives, unreinforced by private benefits, have little staying power" (Schlesinger 1984, 387). From this perspective, all mass movements are similar in that they can only occur through outside sponsorship (McCarthy and Zald 1973) or the singlehanded actions of an entrepreneur (Salisbury 1969) who exchanges his or her assumption of the organizational costs for personal and professional gain.

❖ DENISE L. BAER

In ignoring the validity of their purposive goals, mainstream scholars view mass movements as irrational, extremist, and demagogic in nature (Gusfield 1962). This has meant that mainstream scholarship has ranged from treating the women's movement as illegitimate and potentially destructive of democracy (Polsby 1980, 133) to treating it merely as a trivial exception that proves the rule (e.g., Nagel 1987, 127). Outside the women and politics literature, it is common to see the women's movement treated as originating not in the widespread autonomous and spontaneous development of a variety of different organizations, but rather in the unscrupulous actions of irresponsible and self-interested elites. To go beyond this circumscribed approach to women's organizations and political interests requires starting at the beginning.

❖ Establishing the Women's Movement as a Cyclical Phenomenon

The women's movement, usually dated as originating in 1966 with the founding of the National Organization for Women, is no longer young. Commonly, active movements are thought to last only twenty years or so. While dates vary, many researchers view the women's movement as a cyclical phenomenon[4] occurring in three discrete movements, the Equal Rights Movement of the mid-1880s, the Suffrage Movement during the Progressive Era, and the contemporary Women's Rights Movement, each of which focused on different issues, created new organizations under new leadership, and utilized different repertoires of action (Baer 1999; Freeman 2000; McGlen and O'Connor 1983). By the early 1990s Anne Costain concluded that "the peak period has now passed . . . Political opportunities have narrowed, consciousness has diminished, and organizations . . . are now preoccupied with just maintaining themselves" (1992, 141). Yet, feminist consciousness, a key factor in the origins of the women's movement, increased in the 1990s among all generational cohorts, including the youngest cohort who came of age during the Clinton presidency and the 1992 "Year of the Woman" (Cook 1999). While it may be true that the organizing potential for women's groups in the 1990s was decidedly less than it was 30 years ago, the mixed presence of conditions necessary for the initiation of a fourth women's movement in the twenty-first century raises key questions about whether the next women's movement may be "jump-started" by existing women's leaders and women's organizations or whether it will arise from new organizations focusing on new issues.

Four competing theories are used to explain the origins of the contemporary women's movement:

- *Mass society theory*, derived from pluralist theory, emphasizes the irrational and dangerous participation of the rootless and the alienated urged by unscrupulous elites within a society undergoing social breakdown of values (Kornhauser 1959; Polsby 1983).

- *Resource mobilization theory* traces the origins of movements to resources provided from *outside* the group, particularly professional reformers, charitable trusts and foundations, and the growth of a large pool of activists willing to devote increasing discretionary time to causes (Conover and Gray 1983; McCarthy and Zald 1973).
- *Political process theory* de-emphasizes organizational factors, stressing instead the use of political leverage, public opinion, the structure of political opportunities, and the role of government (Costain 1992; McAdam 1982; Wollbrecht 2000).
- *Classic social movement theory* views social movements as a unique formation of the have-nots, distinguished by a group consciousness based in a social identity, which organizes for both social and political change and seeks to create new elites from within the group itself (Baer and Bositis 1993; Freeman 1975; McGlen and O'Connor 1983).

Of these four theories, only the first, mass society theory, has been applied to undermine the legitimacy of the women's movement. While mass society theory has not been used by women and politics scholars, it remains the dominant approach to the women's movement employed by mainstream scholars. As such, women and politics scholars need to be more aware of the key theoretical distinctions between mass society theory and the alternate theories utilized by women and politics scholars.

Resource mobilization, classic social movement, and political process theories differ in what they see as the primary factor driving women as a social movement—outside resources, government and the political process, or internal social mobilization. What they share in common is their emphasis upon a new mechanism by which nonelites can influence elites and their agreement that women do comprise a discriminated group with common interests. Unlike traditional forms of participation (e.g., voting, campaigning, volunteering for an existing group), *social movements are not constrained by alternatives already determined by existing elites.* Social movements create new elites, and they expand the public policy agenda in unique ways. But this is the old agenda.

Now that the contemporary women's rights movement has evidently peaked, women and politics scholars must seek new ways to explain the decline and changing circumstances of the women's movement. New directions for research would likely include empirical examination of the linkages among grassroots activism, group consciousness, political identity, and leadership. Reexaminations of woman suffrage have transformed our understanding of how leadership makes a difference in the directions, coalitions, and the long-term impact of movement goals (Andersen 1996; Banaszak 1996; Graham 1996; Marilley 1996). Freeman's new analysis of women in parties concluded that early women "laid the foundations" at a time when organized influence was not possible (2000, 235). These new directions for research, in turn, raise new questions about how women leaders can lead women.

❖ Understanding Women's Organizations and How They Link with the Women's Movement

What types of organizations are women's groups? First, while most interest groups represent economic interests, this is not true of most women's organizations. A 1980 survey of women's organizations found that seven of ten women's organizations were citizens' groups as opposed to nonprofit organizations or for-profit business groups (Walker 1991, 188). Second, most national women's organizations of all types seem to have been formed during one of two major "waves" (Truman 1971) of group organization: the 1890s–early 1900s and the 1960s–1970s (McGlen and O'Connor 1983). Prior to the Civil War there were two distinct phases of local organization: religiously based benevolent societies during the early-1800s and reform organizations springing from religious values during the early to mid-1800s. As Harriet Martineau noted in 1827, religion was the only "occupation" besides marriage open to women during this era. And historically it has been found that women's organizations and "clubs held a more significant place in women's lives than men's clubs and organizations did for men" (Blair 1989, x). While women's organizations may be different in type, they do seem to form during periods of economic and social change similar to those experienced by other segments of society, but in ways that are unique to women and not well understood by those who study predominantly "male" economic interest groups.

When we turn to a focus on "women's organizations," we must ask whether women's organizations are only those who seek to represent "women," or whether they also include groups whose membership is largely or wholly comprised of women, but organized around some other economic (e.g., the American Library Association, the Amalgamated Clothing and Textile Workers Union, National Education Association, Business and Professional Women (BPW)), associational (e.g., the American Association of University Women (AAUW)), religious (e.g., National Council of Catholic Women, B'NAI B'RITH Women), or public interest (e.g., the League of Women Voters) goal. The first definition would primarily limit us to the newer women's rights organizations (e.g., the National Women's Political Caucus (NWPC), the National Political Congress of Black Women (NPCBW)) while the second would lump together a disparate array of organizations, blurring distinctions usually considered critical by interest group scholars. For those who study interest groups, public and citizens' interest groups are qualitatively different from occupational and economic groups while both, in turn, are different from groups organized along neighborhood, ethnic, or racial lines. From this view, the interests of business (e.g., Women Business Owners) would be opposed to those of unions (e.g., the Amalgamated Clothing and Textile Workers Union), and a group like the NPCBW would be considered more like the National Association for the Advancement of Colored People (NAACP) or the National Urban League. Moreover, church organizations, still a predominant part of women's group participation (Schlozman 1986), would be considered nonpolitical.

The appropriate definition of "women's organizations" is an empirical and theoretical question. To the extent that women's organizations work together regardless of their origins or their group purpose, then it may be the case that all organizations that represent constituents of a social movement can be studied as social movement organizations. Current empirical evidence, while limited, does support this approach. One 1985 survey conducted by Kay Schlozman (1986) used the broader definition in a study of Washington representatives of women's organizations. Of the 89 organizations she surveyed in 1985, only four did not express support for "feminist goals" while another six offered only "passive" support. According to Schlozman, this indicates a high level of "sisterhood" and feminist activity. Further, Schlozman found that women's organizations, while sophisticated in working in coalition with any group which shared their goals, often made special efforts to work with other women's organizations, and that women's rights organizations were central in developing coalitions among women's organizations in the early 1980s. Even so, women's organizations were vastly under-represented in the nation's capital, comprising only about 1% to 2% of all organizations with representation in Washington.

From a theoretical perspective, the integration of women's interest groups poses several challenges to mainstream interest group theory. First, it undermines the traditional political science distinction between private and public spheres. The history of women's clubs finds them moving issues from the private to the public sphere. According to Anne Scott, women's volunteerism serves as an "early warning system" in "identifying emergent social needs and trying to deal with them, first on their own and then by persuading some government body to undertake responsibility" (1990, 46).

Second, adopting a broad definition of women's organizations delimits the Durkheimian view that a division of labor characterizes organizations. Women's clubs, as forums for social and political expression, became political instruments for women through separate institution building (Freedman 1979). While the newly federated organizations in the early twentieth century did become increasingly specialized (Breckinridge 1972), they continued to cooperate to a degree unparalleled by other groups.

Third, a broad definition of women's organizations challenges the assumption that economic interests are paramount. Women's organizations have increasingly crossed class barriers (Kaminer 1984). This has been particularly

true for Black women's organizations which began forming in large numbers
during the late 1800s and later for white women's organizations (Watts 1993).

Traditional versus women's rights organizations. If women's rights organizations
occupy a central position among women's groups generally, is this based on distinctive characteristics of the women's movement, or is it true of all movements?
Jo Freeman (1983) concluded that the women's movement differed from the
civil rights movement because women, unlike Blacks, had no preexisting group
like the NAACP to lay the groundwork for a grassroots movement or to work for
constitutional change. Despite growing ferment among activists in the 1960s,
existing women's organizations, like BPW, AAUW, and women's colleges, were
uninterested in leading the movement. This meant that new organizations
had to be formed to lead the movement–the National Organization for Women
(NOW) in 1966, the Women's Equity Action League (WEAL) in 1968, the
Women's Lobby in 1970, and the NWPC in 1971. Despite their failure to lead the
women's movement, mainstream women's organizations, according to recent
work by Anne Costain (1992, 52), devoted significant resources to ratification of
the Equal Rights Amendment throughout the 1970s, thereby adopting more of
a follower role.

Do older, traditional women's organizations continue to take follower roles
among women's organizations? Or is this conceptual distinction increasingly a
blurred one? This is an important empirical research question with both theoretical and practical implications. The older generation of women's organizations themselves arose at a time when the creation of a women's sphere was
a radical innovation mobilizing women previously confined to the home to
engage in the public sphere (Freedman 1979). As Mildred Wells stated in her
history of the General Federation of Women's Clubs (GFWC), "the early history of every women's club shows it to be the group in each community which
sponsored the progressive movements which were later taken over by the
municipal government or by specialized welfare organizations" (1975, 461).

The reform basis of today's traditional organizations could not help but be
reactivated by the growth spurt in women's coalitional activity, particularly
with the change in focus after the Equal Rights Amendment failed to be
ratified in 1983, which allowed attention to turn from legal equality to broader
and substantive policy issues. One key transition point occurred with the
adoption of the Women's Agenda in Des Moines, Iowa, in January, 1988. A
broad array of 42 women's organizations (including occupational, labor union,
civic, ethnic, and church groups as well as the new women's rights organizations) adopted the Women's Agenda. The Agenda encompassed family
policies, economic opportunity for women, comprehensive health care,
women's rights, and a federal budget which balanced global human and
economic development with defense. The conference represented a new level

of formal coalition-building because all declared presidential candidates were invited to speak, and traditional groups embraced an increased activism between 1988 and 1992.

BPW, previously a predominantly Republican leaning group with little political involvement, now has a political action committee which endorsed Bill Clinton in 1996 and has embraced comparable worth and pay equity. AAUW supports reproductive rights and the Equal Rights Amendment (ERA) and has made child care, family leave, pay equity, and education funding priority issues. Similarly, occupational groups like the American Nurses Association (ANA), the National Association of Social Workers (NASW), and the National Educational Association (NEA) have adopted formal positions advocating pay equity, family leave, civil rights, and affirmative action.

The convergence of "traditional" and "feminist" organizations deserves recognition and analysis among women and politics scholars, who continue to focus almost exclusively on the latter. As Disney and Gelb point out, the dichotomy of social service versus social change is a false one (2000, 68). Suffrage organizations defeated the anti-suffrage organizations; they did not join forces with them. What this seems to demonstrate—in the absence of research—is that while there was a time lag, the traditional women's organizations were responding to the same dynamics as the feminist organizations.

Women's activity in organized groups seems to be structured around the changing fabric of family and work. Even the exclusive Junior League, probably the most prototypical middle- and upper-class leisure service organization, has become more feminist. The Junior League did not stagnate in the 1970s in response to the women's movement and the increasing labor force participation of women. Instead, Kaminer (1984) points out that about one–third of Junior League members worked, and that half either worked or attended graduate school. If research can establish this as fact, then the distinction made by many mainstream scholars between "legitimate" traditional women's organizations and "extremist" non-grassroots feminist organizations loses credibility.

While the trend is for women's groups to cooperate, there is a recent and growing split between organizations for women of color and women's rights organizations. While women of color have experienced sexism from men of color (Reid-Merrit 1996; Scruggs 1996), African American, Latina, and Asian American women have increasingly formed their own political organizations. Why is this? Is it because they have separate issues from "white" women's organizations, or is it because they feel discriminated against by these groups (Giddings 1984, 1988; Graham 1996; hooks 1981; Marilly 1996)? Interestingly, some of these organizations formed after the peak of the women's movement (e.g., NPCBW organized in 1984), while others, like MANA, reorganized as a pan-Latina organization in 1994, after initially organizing in 1974 as the Mexican American Women's Association. As the movement overall is declining,

❖ DENISE L. BAER

does this mean that increasingly leadership will come from women of color? One notable group is the National Council of Negro Women (NCNW), a federation of 34 national voluntary associations, originally organized in 1935. NCNW, the African American counterpart to the National Council of Women's Organizations (NCWO), is a mature organization of substance and leadership among African American women (Noble 1996). Yet, we know little about the genesis of these groups of women of color or their activities—an unacceptable research gap.

Issue networks. In recent years the growth of what interest group scholars call "issue networks" (Berry 1989; Heclo 1978) has been evident among women's groups, and these issue networks merit more attention from researchers. While some maintain that the women's movement has become professionalized and institutionalized (Minkoff 1997), we do not know enough about the way that women's organizations operate to represent women or work through other, related issue networks. Women's organizations have now developed a formal organization called the National Council of Women's Organizations (NCWO) through which the presidents of over 100 women's organizations meet on a monthly basis in Washington, D.C. to discuss shared interests and develop consensus positions and organized actions. Lead influential groups within the NCWO include such traditional first wave groups as the General Federation of Women's Clubs (GFWC) and the Young Women's Christian Association (YWCA) as well as the AAUW and BPW. Organized labor is increasingly an allied group which now actively supports women's issues and is influential through weekly meetings at the AFL–CIO headquarters.

Another aspect of this issue network that should be studied is the mainline churches, particularly since the Christian Coalition, which opposes the women's movement, is in turn opposed by mainstream faith organizations such as the newly formed Interfaith Alliance. Few of the conservative Christian organizations appear to be headed by women,[5] but this is a speculation that requires investigation. If women in the aggregate are more active in church organizations (as Schlozman, Burns, and Verba 1994 have found), is this as true within the Christian Coalition as it is for mainline churches? What role does the politicization of faith have in mobilizing both evangelical and mainline church-women women to political activity?

A research agenda on women and politics must include a mapping of the overlapping and intersecting issue networks among women's organizations, particularly as these have developed since the 1980s. What are the dynamics of women's issue networks? While several research efforts have focused on the divide between pro- and anti-ERA groups (e.g., Mansbridge 1986), few have looked at the broader women's policy agenda. Walker (1991) finds that women's organizations seem to confront a more conflictual policy environment than is true for the "average" group. Has increased conflict for women's organizations, particularly during the Reagan years, in turn increased awareness of shared interests among women's organizations? E. E. Schattschneider (1975) and Jeffrey Berry (1989) find that conflict qualitatively changes the policy agenda. Has the policy agenda of women's organizations changed because of conflict? Also, to what extent has the growth of issue networks altered the older pattern of overlapping and cross-cutting group memberships? Are feminist women increasingly only members of groups supporting women's rights? Unfortunately, we know little about this aspect of women's organizational involvement because mainstream political science has excluded newer women's organizations from national election studies and limited their analysis to categories of group membership rather than a mapping of group activity (Walker and Baumgartner 1988, 1990).

❖ What is the Impact of Group Formation and Membership on Women's Organizations?

The ability of groups to attract and retain members is critical. Many of the women's groups which began in the 1960s and early 1970s started as leadership or cadre groups and only later gained a mass base (Gelb and Palley 1982, 25). While any group may form around a crisis, it is sustained membership that provides resources for long-term influence and success in the policy arena. Most feminist organizations have had collective origins, yet traditional interest group theory stresses that no group can survive for long on collective goals alone. For interest group theorists, only those groups which can develop a local, communal base tied by friendship networks (solidary incentives) and financial gain (economic incentives) can maintain themselves.

Some interest groups have been formed by entrepreneurs—John Gardiner of Common Cause, for example. A major indicator of this type of organization is a single leader who, lacking or having lost other "portfolio" in national policymaking, maintains control permanently or semi-permanently in order to have a platform in national politics. Other cadre-style interest groups may rotate leaders but never meet face-to-face and lack members in the usual sense of the term. Such organizations are called "letterhead" groups (referring to the letterhead listing an advisory board which never meets) or "checkbook" organizations (referring to donors sending checks as the only "members"). Still other "groups" might exist only over the airwaves, like the "electronic" church. A major question is to what extent do these structures occur among women's organizations? Prominent examples of membership-style entrepreneurs would be Phyllis Schafly of the Eagle Forum or Beverly LaHaye of Concerned Women of America, both organizations of the new or Christian right. Another model might be those women entrepreneurs who have formed small, "boutique" think-tanks, rather than membership organizations. Examples would include Linda Tarr-Whelan (Center for Policy Alternatives), Betty Dooley (Women's Research and Education Institute), Heidi Hartman (Institute for Women's Policy Research) and Leslie Wolfe (Center for Women Policy Studies). New research is required to learn how common this is and whether there is a trend that separates anti-women's rights groups from feminist groups.

For the most part women's groups are membership-based organizations which have emphasized internal democracy. As Chris Bosso (1995) observes for environmental organizations, in difficult times membership maintenance can prove problematic. Yet, women's organizations to differing degrees have proclaimed a commitment to democratic procedures—what Carole Pateman (1970) would call partial to full or participatory democracy. This has been true, for example, of the League of Women Voters, which takes no national position until a majority of local groups has engaged in a year of self-study and has endorsed the position. Yet, the precise degree of commitment of women's organizations to internal democracy, especially compared to other "male" organizations, has never been gauged. This type of research would require an organizational or institutional analysis (e.g., Disney and Gelb 2000), rather than a survey of members.

Membership size is an important resource in and of itself. It permits development of a professional staff and the use of greater resources for specialized operations. For example, compare the NEA with a professional staff of over 400 to the NWPC, which declined to a staff of seven by 1996. Yet there are more important issues to consider: have women's organizations of all types declined or gained? This is clearly an area which requires research. An informal survey of women's organizations by this author finds that many major organizations have experienced declines in membership, and some groups, like WEAL, have ceased to exist. Does this mean, however, that women are now less likely to belong to organizations, including women's organizations? It may be the case that proportionally just as many (or more) women belong to organizations but that the number of members in individual groups has declined simply because the numbers are spread across a larger number of groups. Disney and Gelb contend that movement of activists and leaders from one organization to another can be a sign of organizational success even if the organization disappears (2000, 48).

There is an active debate among interest group scholars over the question of whether women's organizations have declined to which women and politics scholars can usefully contribute.[6] Responding to this question would require defining what a group is, and paying particular attention to historical factors intrinsic to women's political activity that may not be apparent to "male" scholars.

❖ *What is the Role of Organized Leadership in Maintaining the Women's Movement?*

Leaders are central to organizations. Yet organized leadership has not been systematically studied in large part because the women's movement sought to work without hierarchy. This does not mean that there have been no leaders, but it does mean that these leaders have been working at times inconsistently and at cross purposes. Costain argues that "the movement's own conscious decision to forego hierarchical leadership, which thereby prevented the movement from speaking in one voice . . . doomed its efforts to pursue a diverse agenda" (1992, 138). Leadership is discussed elsewhere in this volume (see Chapter Four). The focus here is on three elements specifically related to organizations.

First, some attention needs to be paid to how organizations act to mobilize and recruit women to politics. Schlozman, Burns, and Verba found that women's organizations (1994) and the workplace (1999) still provide fewer opportunities for women to gain important political skills. In terms of women's organizations, while it is true that the gender segregation increases the opportunities for gaining skills in making presentations, fewer women than men have had these opportunities (1994).

Second, some research attention needs to be paid to the difference in the gender gap among women leaders and activists compared to the gender gap among voters. Some research has argued the gender gap among leaders divides along feminist lines (over issues such as equal rights, abortion, affirmative action) while among voters the gender gap divides over issues of the economy, environment, and war and peace (Baer and Bositis 1988). If this finding is confirmed more generally, then some research attention must be devoted to learning why this is so and how the dynamic changes as women become more involved in politics. This is important because research now suggests that activists are not a single, core group who always participate because of their internalized attitudes, but rather a highly variable, larger pool of volunteers who are mobilized by groups and candidates in some elections but not others (Carmines and Stimson 1989; Rosenstone and Hansen 1993). Thus, women and politics scholars must ask how women's groups act to maximize the increasingly feminist gender gap among the politically active.

Third, anecdotal evidence seems to credit women's organizations with recruiting women to elite political positions. For example, Congresswoman Rosa DeLauro (D-CT) was Executive Director of EMILY's List in 1989; Clinton White House Political Director Ann Lewis started in politics as the NWPC Political Director; and former Maryland State Senate President Mary Boergers began working in politics for NOW. How common is this path from feminist organizational leader to more general political leader for the first generation of 1960s–1970s women's rights organizational leaders? If validated, does this remain true for the second and third generation of women's organizational leaders who are increasingly recruited from within their organizations? (It is difficult to imagine women members of Congress resigning a safe seat to head women's organizations as did former Congressmen Bill Gray and Kweise Mfume for Black organizations.) If the women's movement is entering a more latent phase and declining in activism, it may be that women's groups may be less fruitful in producing or recruiting new leaders. If so, then political recruitment of women activists generally may decline as well unless new avenues of recruitment are found. This is an area of immense practical importance to which women and politics scholars may usefully contribute.

❖ RESEARCH–THEORY GAP PART II: WOMEN AND INTEREST GROUP CLOUT

Interest groups engage in a wide variety of tactics to influence the political process. And women can work either within women's organizations or as representatives within other interest groups. Both aspects of women's political role must be considered.

❖ *How Effective is Lobbying by Women and Women's Organizations Who Lobby?*

Women lobbyists have greatly increased in number but still remain underrepresented. In the late 1950s, women were only 7% of a sample of all Washington lobbyists (Milbrath 1961). By 1985, women comprised as many as 22% of all Washington lobbyists (Schlozman 1986). Nevertheless, in a more selective sample of four economic policy domains (agriculture, energy, health, labor), women comprised only 12% of lobbyists in 1982–83 (Heinz et al. 1993).

Women lobbyists have been less associated with business interests than male lobbyists. According to Schlozman, in 1985, 49% of women lobbyists compared to 61% of male lobbyists represented business organizations (1986). The Heinz et al. (1993) economic policy domain study found that women lobbyists were much more common in government affairs offices (a staff position) than as higher status executives of Washington organizations, and only 7% of women were executives in business organizations while 17% were business government affairs representatives. While citizen and good government associations were a small portion of the economic policy domain study, women lobbyists were most prevalent as citizen group executives (29%) and government affairs representatives (19%).

Does it make a difference whether women or men lobby for an organization? Schlozman (1986) suggests that it might, at least in terms of organizations she categorizes as "women's" organizations. In terms of ideology, policy agenda, and willingness to work in coalition with other women's organizations, organizations of women represented by men were less feminist. Alan Rosenthal, in his analysis of lobbyists and lobbying in the states, believes that the 1980s increase in women lobbyists is tied directly to the increase in women state legislators and the changed legislative culture:

> Take Colorado, where one–third of the legislators are women. The "good ol'" boy atmosphere is practically gone in Colorado and is no longer as pervasive even in Florida and Texas, which now has a female governor. (1993, 85)

How effective are women's organizations in lobbying? One of the few studies of lobbying by women's organizations has found that many if not most of the advances in federal law occurred in advance of significant lobbying by women's organizations (Costain 1992). Women's organizations have become more active in lobbying, but we know little about how they lobby now or what women's organizations did in earlier eras. For example, Pendleton Herring found that women's lobby groups were second in number to trade associations in the 1920s and that the women's suffrage associations introduced new techniques of lobbying in their systematic campaign to gain suffrage (1941, 34–46, 186). But there has been little subsequent research in this area. Further, groups like NOW and NWPC, which formerly had in-house lobbyists, no longer lobby in Washington, D.C. Have traditional women's organizations like AAUW, the LWV, and BPW expanded their lobbying on women's issues? Or has elite-level lobbying also declined with the peaking of the women's movement among the grassroots? These are critical and unanswered questions.

❖ How Do Women's Organizations Act as Agents for Change?

The role of women's groups in acting as agents and leaders for change has received little research attention. While there are many anecdotal stories, there has been no systematic research on how effective different initiatives have been. For example, the AAUW in 1992–94 embarked upon a study of girls and self-esteem, a high profile project which produced a research report and prompted congressional hearings as well as a 1995 attack by Christina Hoff Sommers in *Who Stole Feminism* (1994). Was the AAUW study effective in bringing about change? According to what measures?

Another example is the 1996 Women's Vote Project, chaired by Irene Natividad, which involved a large coordinated effort by 110 women's organizations to increase voter turnout among women. This effort was more sophisticated than earlier efforts launched in 1988 and 1992 which relied on media efforts. The 1996 Project utilized grassroots efforts to identify and register previously inactive women and targeted ten states where women's voting had been historically low. These states included Arkansas, Colorado, Georgia, Massachusetts, Minnesota, Missouri, North Carolina, Pennsylvania, Tennessee, and Texas.

Was this effort effective? While preliminary data suggest a drop-off in women's voting in 1996 (Baer 1998), systematic research is needed to weigh the impact of this mobilization effort as well as others initiated by women's organizations.

❖ RESEARCH–THEORY GAP, PART III: POLITICAL PARTIES

The women's movement has largely concentrated its efforts to influence mainstream politics within the two major political parties. The Democratic Party, founded in 1796, and the Republican Party formed in 1860, both predate the three identified women's movements. While there have been many third party efforts in American history and within the African American community, "suffrage activism normally institutionalized itself in interest group activism" rather than choosing the party path (Gillespie 1993, 143). There have been a few rare exceptions of women organizing separate women's parties. These efforts include: the Equal Rights Party which ran Belva Lockwood for President in 1884 and 1888; Alice Paul's National Women's Party (organized in 1916) which did not formally nominate candidates, and the Twenty-First-Century Party, launched by NOW in August, 1992, which has yet to run candidates under its own label.

Within the two major political parties, women have had significant successes in obtaining parity, but have made few inroads in opening the remaining nearly "closed doors" among leadership ranks. In part, this pattern has resulted from a continuing focus on absolute numbers of group representatives—an issue of procedural fairness—rather than on clout as an organized group. The origins of this focus date from the early days of the suffrage movement, with the emphasis on the "50/50 Rule" used to guarantee parity by state statute and internal party rules.

❖ *What is the Impact of Quotas on Influence? The 50/50 Rule and Women's Clout*

The 50/50 Rule has a long and varied history in party politics. First adopted in Colorado in 1910 by state statute, the 50/50 Rule gained momentum after adoption of the Nineteenth Amendment on August 20, 1920, guaranteeing women the right to vote, when the Democratic and Republican parties adopted the 50/50 Rule for their national committees. But the two parties have differed in their implementation in ways which must be understood to be able to define appropriate party-focused research agendas (See Freeman 2000).

The Democratic Party moved first, adopting a new rule at its 1920 Convention declaring that the DNC was to be composed of one man and one woman from each state and territory. The Democratic Party Charter adopted in 1974, while enlarging the DNC to encompass a broader cross-section of party activists, maintained the 50/50 gender split. In 1980, the Charter was amended to provide equal division for all party groups—namely "the Democratic National Committee, the Executive Committee, Democratic state central committees, commissions, and like bodies" (Article Eleven, Section 16). Interestingly, the DNC has not tried to demand compliance with this rule since an early and incomplete effort in 1981–82.

The Republican Party did not adopt equal division until 1924. Since the Republican convention had already met by the time the Nineteenth Amendment was adopted, the RNC, following party tradition, refused to institute the 50/50 Rule without authorization of the national convention. Instead, in 1921, a prominent suffrage leader was appointed vice-chairman of the National Republican Executive Committee, with seven other women appointed to serve on the Executive Committee, and the states were directed in 1923 to appoint women as associate members (meaning without a vote) to the RNC.

The 1924 Republican Convention reconstituted the RNC, providing that it be composed of one man and one woman from each state. In 1940, the Republican Convention passed Rule 29, providing for equal representation of women on all committees of the RNC. The 50/50 balance on the RNC (but not RNC committees) ended in 1952 with the addition of Republican state chairs, an overwhelmingly male group, to the RNC. Today, the RNC has a minimum of one-third female representation by specification (or quota). State parties are not regulated by the RNC (again, following party tradition). However, some state parties (e.g., New York) have voluntarily chosen to require 50/50 representation for their state central committees.

In essence, the 50/50 rule constitutes a quota. One set of new research questions should focus on whether a quota can ever result in genuine influence in institutions like parties in whom influence is based upon organizational interdependence, an integrative community life, formal factions, and informal networks (Baer 1993b). As Freeman concludes in her review of the 50/50 Rule, "Over time women became disenchanted with its actual results," agreeing with Eleanor Roosevelt's observation that where a slot is to be filled by existing leaders, the men "naturally pick women who will go along with them, and not give them any trouble" (2000, 120).

❖ How Did Women Contribute to Party Reform and Women's Representation in the Parties?

This is a key question whose history has been inadequately incorporated into women and politics and party research. Following adoption of suffrage, the Republican Party more easily adjusted itself to the inclusion of women. When Alice Paul sought a partisan strategy to get suffrage adopted, she targeted the Democratic Party as the opposition party. And it was the Republican Party which first added the Equal Rights Amendment to its party platform in 1940, followed by the Democrats in 1944. Though women were not an organized political group, the Republican Party was relatively more open to including Republican women based on their contributions to the party than was the more traditional Democratic Party. Cotter and Hennessy (1964) found as many as half of Democratic national committeewomen, but only one-third of Republican committeewomen, were rated quite unimportant by their peers in the early 1960s.

The watershed event was the demand for parity at party conventions; the Democrats reformed and the Republicans refused. Women were central, not peripheral, to reform of the Democratic Party (Baer and Bositis 1988), contrary to the views expressed by Byron Shafer in his early history (1983). But the implications and consequences of these changes have been recognized little among women and politics scholars while political party scholars have attacked the idea of a quota for women (Baer 1993*a*). It is helpful to briefly recount this history to consider how future research might be redirected.

Contrary to the pervasiveness of the 50/50 Rule in formal party organizations, there were no efforts to demand parity in convention delegate selection prior to 1972. The nominating conventions, where control of the party by a dominant faction and the selection of party leaders as well as recruitment and vetting of cabinet and subcabinet appointees were determined, remained within the informal, but closed, "old boy" network.

The NWPC, founded in 1971, chose as its inaugural reform initiative the reform of the Democratic and Republican parties. While both parties underwent a reform period in the 1970s, they chose different routes for inclusion structured largely by their differing political cultures (Freeman 1986).

This was an important political battle. After suffrage was granted, women found the inner circles of party power closed to them (Cotter and Hennessy 1964). The first woman delegate was seated in 1900 in both the Democratic and Republican conventions. The numbers did not increase until after suffrage was granted in 1920. From 1924 to 1968, the proportion of women at both two major party conventions was similarly and consistently low—an informal "glass ceiling" ranging from a low of 6% to a relative high of 18% in 1964 (see Figure 5.1). It was not until party reform took effect for the 1972 conventions that the proportion of women delegates increased markedly. In 1960, Republican women gained a significant advance when the convention adopted a rule providing for 50/50 representation of women delegates with men on all convention committees. Ironically, this meant that Republican convention committees over represented female convention delegates. During this early period, the Republican Party was relatively more open to women than the Democratic Party so long as Republican women sought upward mobility through traditional channels of elite sponsorship.

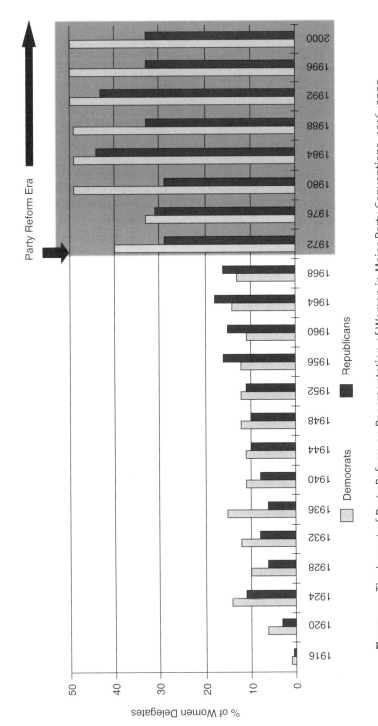

Figure 5.1 The Impact of Party Reform on Representation of Women in Major Party Conventions, 1916–2000

Source: Data for 1988–2000 calculated by the author from official lists of delegates provided by the national parties. Data for earlier years from CAWP.

For Democrats in 1972, a revolution was wrought via party reform—change which fundamentally and permanently altered women's roles within the party. The dominance of the Democratic Party by the southern wing (traditionally least supportive of women's rights) and by organized labor (then quite hostile to the women's movement) meant no change would come easily. An important precedent was set in 1964 when the Mississippi Freedom Democratic Party (MFDP) led by an African American women, Fannie Lou Hamer, led a challenge to the all-white official Mississippi delegation at the convention in Atlantic City. The MFDP demonstrated the impact of discriminatory delegate selection procedures in the Democratic Party, and the party responded informally by promulgating a set of six basic principles opposing discrimination. The 1968 convention, the precursor to reform, occurring at the height of anti-war protest and racial tensions, was a public debacle that produced the appointment of the McGovern–Fraser Commission on delegate selection and other issues. The McGovern–Fraser report detailed extensive evidence of active discrimination in the party, as well as a lack of written rules and procedural biases within state parties which had no parallel within the Republican Party.

It was the McGovern–Fraser Commission, under pressure from NWPC (and other groups), which *mandated* proportional representation for women, Blacks, and youth (those under 30) for the 1972 Democratic convention. As a result, the proportion of women tripled from 13% in 1968 to 40% in 1972.

Following McGovern's defeat, party reform came under attack by dominant party forces. In response, the Mikulski Commission rewrote delegate selection rules, banning "quotas" in favor of affirmative action efforts. Since states which filed an affirmative action plan were granted immunity from credentials challenges, efforts to include women were dependent upon local party culture and traditions. Without external intervention by party leaders, the proportion of women dropped sharply to 34%, a proportion higher than the pre-reform era, and quite similar to the Republican share in 1976.

In 1974 Democratic women gained a significant advance by using the historical precedent of the 50/50 Rule. First, the 1974 Democratic Party Charter established the supremacy of national party law, a move which permanently reduced the power of sectional and local interests to oppose inclusion of women. And second, while the McGovern–Fraser quotas were "banned," the Charter expressly exempted equal division of men and women from the ban (Article Ten, Section 11). This was done at the behest of women delegates to the 1974 Mid-Term Convention following a contentious session in which both Black and women delegates walked out, protesting efforts to undermine party reform. In 1980, the Democratic National Committee, acting under the Charter exemption, adopted the 50/50 Rule for delegates. In 1988, at the behest of presidential candidate Jesse Jackson, the 1988 Convention amended the Charter to extend the 50/50 Rule from the final statewide delegation to each candidate's delegation within each state.

The two parties have different traditions, and there are party-specific factors which affect the proportion of delegates who are women. The Republican Party has traditionally regarded the selection of delegates as a state matter. While there were two reform commissions appointed (DO—Delegates and Organization—and Rule 29 committees), party traditions prevailed. The Republican Party, adamantly refusing to mandate parity, remains unreformed. However, following the dramatic upsurge of Democratic women delegates in 1972, the proportion of Republican women delegates also rose in the years 1972–80 to about one-third of the delegates. After discovery that the new gender gap in voting threatened the prospects of Republican presidential candidates, Republican leaders have grown more concerned about how the low proportion of women at Republican conventions makes the party look unresponsive. In the absence of official rules, however, efforts to include women rests with the traditional mechanism of personal intervention by influential leaders,[7] which is affected by whether an incumbent is running for re-election. In 1984 the proportion of Republican women increased to a record 44% largely through the intervention of President Reagan's campaign manager, Ed Rollins, who personally called each state party. In 1988, however, when the race involved a contested primary and no incumbent, the proportion of women delegates returned to one-third. With an incumbent president, Republican women delegates increased to 41% in 1992, only to drop in both 1996 and 2000 to 33% following contested primary campaigns. In the post-reform era, without extraordinary efforts (on the Republican side) and without the DNC mandate (on the Democratic side), there seems to be an informal "glass ceiling" for women of about one-third of the delegates (see Figure 5.2).

Party differences appear to be structured by partisan culture. Despite the lack of parity, Republican women have achieved considerable influence at the leadership levels that is unparalleled in the Democratic Party. In 1985 the DNC under Chair Paul Kirk disestablished the DNC Women's Caucus. In sharp contrast, in 1988, the National Federation of Republican Women (NFRW) was granted a voting seat on the 28-member Council which governs the RNC between its quadrennial meetings. A key research question is whether Democratic Party culture has advanced to the point that women have equal influence, not just parity, so that mandated rules are no longer necessary to break the "glass ceiling."

In 1996 EMILY's List developed a structural relationship with the DNC to conduct research on the gender gap, to coordinate get-out-the-vote efforts, to recruit women volunteers for the coordinated state campaigns, and to raise money. Because EMILY's List is an organization with no real members in local groups, one must wonder if this collaboration represented greater party power

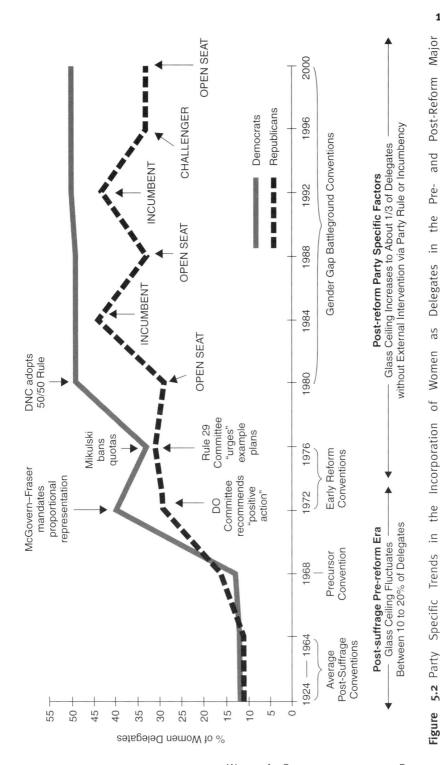

Figure 5.2 Party Specific Trends in the Incorporation of Women as Delegates in the Pre- and Post-Reform Major Party Conventions, 1924–2000

Source: Data for 1988–2000 calculated by the author from official lists of delegates provided by the national parties. Data for earlier years from CAWP.

WOMEN'S ORGANIZATIONS AND PARTIES ❖

for Democratic women or merely the exploitation of the women's funding community by (male) Democratic party leaders for their own purposes. It may be that women's influence has actually dropped within the Democratic Party even as parity has increased the number of delegates. As Cotter and Hennessy concluded of the pre-reform party system, "In most states, at most levels of the party organization, women have *equal representation* with men; there is no evidence that they have ever had *equal influence*" (1964, 58). In 1984 and 1988, the power of the women's caucus at the convention was such that key platform debates were brokered during its daily meetings. In contrast, in 1996, while the pro-choice plank had become an unquestioned part of the Democratic Party platform, President Clinton's signing of the welfare reform bill immediately before the convention provided no cause for complaint despite the fact that most major women's organizations opposed the bill.

Parity has different meanings for Republican women than it does for Democratic women. Within the Republican Party the feminist and anti-feminist forces have been opposed since 1980 when anti-feminist forces were able to remove the pro-choice plank from the Republican Party platform. The key question for Republicans, beyond mere numbers of women, is *what kind of woman* (Baer 1993*a*)? The two parties have provided entirely different and culturally distinct arenas for women's participation (Freeman 1986, 2000). Participation of Republican women occurs through the large network of local Republican women's clubs, the state federations, and the National Federation of Republican Women (NFRW). Apart from the Ripon Society, which represents only a small part of the Republican Party, the NFRW monopolizes the organized factional participation of Republican women. While NFRW members are more likely than non-members to be active in traditional as well as newer feminist groups, the proportions who are active remain quite low (Baer and Dolan 1994).

Women and politics scholars must advance beyond examining mere numerical parity to investigating more sophisticated measures of political influence. Leadership is one such measure.

❖ Why is Party Leadership for Women Still Rare in Party Organizations?

While there is parity in party organizational membership, party leadership for women remains rare. The tradition in both parties has been that the permanent chair of the national convention is the party's leader in the House of Representatives, a post never held by a woman. Since 1972, Democratic rules requiring that the permanent convention chair rotate between a man and a woman have produced three female Democratic convention chairs.[8] The Democratic and

Republican parties have each had only one woman elected[9] as national party chair, Jean Westwood and Mary Louise Smith, respectively. In 2001 women served as state chairs in seventeen Democratic state parties[10] (34% of the total) and nine Republican state parties[11] (12% of the total). Since 1996 the rate of increase in women state chairs in Democratic parties (70%) has been more than double that in Republican parties (33%).

Jean Westwood, a Utah native, stands as the first woman chair of a major party in the U.S. Westwood, while not nationally active, was a supporter of the women's movement. A veteran of many senatorial, gubernatorial, and presidential campaigns, Westwood was elected Democratic National Committee (DNC) Chair as the personal choice of nominee George McGovern at the conclusion of the convention where she managed the rules and credentials challenges for McGovern.[12] A national co-chair of the McGovern campaign and regional campaign director in 1971–72, Westwood rose the old-fashioned way to the DNC Chair post.

Mary Louise Smith of Iowa was chosen by Gerald Ford to follow George Bush as Republican National Committee (RNC) Chairman[13] in September, 1974. Serving until 1977, Smith became the first woman to organize and call to order the national convention of a major party in the U.S. A founding member of the Iowa Women's Political Caucus and a member of the advisory board of the National Women's Political Caucus (NWPC), Smith expanded opportunities for women in the Republican Party by appointing women to senior positions in the RNC. Long associated with reform forces (the Ripon Society and the Mainstream Coalition), Smith was known for her work in rebuilding the Republican Party after the Watergate scandal.

There are key similarities to Westwood's and Smith's tenures. Neither Westwood nor Smith served as the elected chair of a party out of power during the critical party-building years (i.e., outside of the immediate election year). *This means that women have not yet gained power as a dominant faction within either major party with enough clout to take control without endorsement or support from an established male leader.* Party power is factional power[14] (Baer and Dolan 1994). Further, since both Westwood and Smith served during the early years of the women's movement and were associated with ascendant reform forces, their selection occurred during unique circumstances not likely to be recreated in today's conservative environment.

The rarity of political party leadership for women makes those women who have served in leadership a set of case studies.[15] Too often prior research has focused on elucidating the "case studies" by focusing upon the unique characteristics of individual women which allowed them to assume unusual leadership roles. Other studies have stressed discrimination as the major barrier and viewed parity in numbers as the major criterion of success. But focusing solely upon the numbers of women who have obtained a position may ignore more important questions. Obtaining the post may not be the real test of women's acceptance and influence within political circles.

To what extent are women leaders able to capitalize on their leadership posts as progressive stepping stones to higher office or greater political influence? Neither Westwood or Smith gained the usual perks of office granted to former national party leaders. After the McGovern defeat Westwood was challenged and ultimately replaced by Robert Strauss as DNC Chair in 1973. Westwood later retired to Arizona. Smith, while appointed to the U.S. Civil Rights Commission by Ronald Reagan in 1981, was ousted two years later after controversy developed over her views on civil rights.

In the post-reform party system, the post of state party chair now serves as a stepping stone to elective office.[16] This is important because a major avenue of political recruitment—business—remains relatively closed to women. While there have been few women state party chairs, this avenue of political recruitment now seems more open to women. Current House members Nancy Pelosi (D-CA) (elected in 1987) and Jennifer Dunn (R-WA) (elected in 1992) served as chairs of their state parties prior to gaining elective office.

❖ Understanding the Partisan Cleavage Over Women's Issues

We now know that the parties are realigned on women's rights issues (Melich 1996; Wollbrecht 2000). Based on her path-breaking research at successive Democratic and Republican conventions since 1976, Jo Freeman has concluded that the parties are in the early stages of a realignment over gender and culture. These realigning issues include "gender roles, sexual behavior, reproduction, care of children, family structure, intersection of work and family obligations, military service" while traditional issues like race, welfare, and education have been transformed by this cleavage. Quoting Pat Buchanan's fears of a "cultural war" in his speech before the 1992 Republican convention, Freeman speculates that "the realignment of the next 20 years will transform the nature of party competition from a mere fight for office to a surrogate civil war" (1993, 27). If Freeman is correct, then one area where we need more research is how women's organizations work within parties.

Women's organizations have by and large employed a bipartisan strategy. A central question that must be considered is whether this strategy remains a viable one during an era in which groups are increasingly tied to one party.

Writing in 1974 at the beginning of the revolution in political parties, sociologist Ann Oakley wrote that as the "term 'housewife' can and is, applied to the majority of female population . . . a mass revolt of women must involve housewives as the largest single group" (1974, 193). While it is true that the majority of women now work, it is precisely over these kinds of issues that the parties are split.

This split is obvious among the party coalitions, their platforms, and their activists (Freeman 1993). Baer and Dolan found that Republican Party elites are much more likely to be married and living in traditional families (Baer and Dolan 1994). Over four-fifths of Republican elites are married, and of these, 28% of the women identify themselves as housewives and 44% of the Republican men say their wives are housewives. By contrast, only 7% of Democratic women are housewives, and only 28% of Democratic men so identify their wives. To the extent that more Republican women are housewives, this becomes an identity that structures their participation and affects male/female status differentials. The more traditional roles among Republican activist women are reinforced by their lesser achieved status. Less than half of Republican women (42%) are employed full-time, compared to two-thirds (66%) of Democratic women. By contrast, a similar proportion of Republican men (82%) and Democratic men (85%) are employed full-time. Only 37% of Republican women are employed in professional or technical occupations, compared to at least three-fifths of Republican men (60%), Democratic women (62%), and Democratic men (70%) (Baer and Dolan 1994).

Groups are important within the parties not only because they comprise a communications network, but also because they provide scarce potential campaign resources. The activities of campaigns and parties center around existing groups and networks. As Rosenstone and Hansen have explained, "Anxious to involve the greatest number of the right people with the least amount of expense, [campaigns] mobilize people who are known to them, who are well placed in social networks, whose activities are effective, and who are most likely to act" (1993, 162).

While women have traditionally comprised the ranks of the party volunteers, the party as a vehicle for leadership and office-holding provides fewer opportunities for women. In the pre-reform party system, women used to be recruited to political activism and office-holding primarily outside of the party system via women's organizations. The advent of true factions within the institutionalized party system enhances the impact of informal associations, apprenticeships, and recruitment among party activists within the parties. Therefore, the more active women are within the party, the more opportunity they have to be recruited via party-linked factions and groups—a fundamentally decentralized and "privatized" process. *This means that women are increasingly dependent on the extent to which they have organized clout within the party. Recruitment previously controlled by party bosses is now in the hands of party factions and informal networks of associations.*

This fundamental fact explains why Republican women have achieved such power within the national party despite the lack of formal parity. Those studies which find that the parties treat announced men and women candidates about the same (Biersak and Herrnson 1994; Darcy, Welch, and Clark 1987) do not address the actual recruitment process whereby party activists garner the appropriate apprenticeship for waging competitive campaigns, but rather only how parties treat those who have *already* gained that experience. As Browning, Marshall, and Tabb (1997) make clear, those outgroups seeking incorporation of group members within leadership circles usually obtain greater government responsiveness than do those who merely protest or seek symbolic appointment of a few leaders. A research focus limited to the party organization (i.e., the headquarters) cannot investigate how informal associations may differentially structure or retard women's advancement.

Assisting declared women candidates and encouraging potential women candidates to be both more ambitious and to actually run for office, the contemporary foci of women's political groups, only helps at the later stages after the recruitment pool has been reduced within the party crucible. It is important for women's organizations to concentrate their efforts on increasing the critical mass of women candidates and elected officials because women candidates do more than provide role models for other potential leaders. They also help to educate voters on a broader and more inclusive policy agenda because "campaigns are a time of relatively intense political learning [and] candidates are the teachers" (Carmines and Stimson 1989, 136). Further, the issue is incorporation rather than mere representation (Browning, Marshall, and Tabb 1997). A central research issue is not so much the obvious fact that the glass ceiling bars the advancement of women, but rather the question of whether women and women's organizations are able to choose their own leaders within male-dominated organizations and male-dominated parties.

This is also relevant to assessing the extent to which women's organizations are able to lead on gender-gap issues. While most women's organizations are in agreement on issues that are usually found within the Democratic Party platform, and increasingly, most national women's organizations (whether organized as a nonpartisan or as a Democratic partisan group) do work with the Democratic Party, women leaders are just as prominent in both party caucuses and conventions. While the Democratic Party provides more compatible policies, its policies have not been defined by women's leaders. This lessens the degree to which "gender bloc" voting could develop, leaving the gender gap an ill-understood secular phenomenon.

❖ BRIDGING THE RESEARCH–PRACTICE GAP: OF GLASS CEILINGS AND SYMBOLIC POWER

If contemporary politics is increasingly a zero-sum game that is now "no place for amateurs" (Johnson 2001), we need to close the research-practice gap to enable women to gain power as a group. There have been several themes to this chapter: the need for more theory-relevant research, the need to include greater historical context, and the need for a more in-depth focus on topics of leadership, recruitment, and organizational culture. Future research must be collaborative and interdisciplinary in the broadest sense. We can no longer rely solely on individual researchers pursuing separate research projects, and we can no longer ignore the active organization of women of color, who in some cases have attained higher leadership roles than white women (e.g., in the Congressional Black Caucus). This effort will require the use of techniques such as participant and nonparticipant observation to supplement survey research as well as greater attention to history and historical cycles. Women and politics scholars must begin to engage more seriously basic theories within political science and sociology. If women continue to be considered deviant by mainstream scholarship, then women and politics scholarship must challenge and redefine basic theories undergirding social science disciplines to include women as legitimate political actors.

The cost of this research gap has been threefold. First, mainstream political science as a discipline has been retarded by its ignorance of the changes wrought by the women's movement, changes that challenge the very foundations of many political science theories. As a result, discussions of women's role in politics by many mainstream political scientists have been dominated by cultural archetypes of a bygone era. Second, women and politics scholarship, while focused on increasing knowledge of women as political actors, has left the field of general political science theory to those most ignorant of women's roles, thus permitting political science scholarship to present women's roles negatively. And third, women and politics scholars have failed to engage basic tools of political science analysis in the service of advancing women and politics research, leaving us largely ignorant of the effectiveness of women's influence within mainstream politics and less able to advise women political leaders about effective, practical techniques of influence and organization. After all, scholars are leaders as well.

❖ NOTES

1 The author wishes to thank Marie Page Gatti for her assistance with graphics.

2 Robert Lane's *Political Life* (1959) provides a classic example of traditional political science conceptions of women when he dismisses trying to get women more involved in politics because of their political opinions as expressed through their voluntary groups.

3 Much of the history included here is based on unpublished, original research conducted by the author while serving as a staffer of the House Democratic Caucus in the 103rd Congress and conducting observational research at the 1988–2000 Democratic

and Republican conventions, as well as work done as a consultant for various women's organizations.

4 While dates vary, most scholars (e.g., Baer and Bositis 1993; McGlen and O'Connor 1983) divide women's rights efforts into three discrete movements: 1848–1875; 1980–1920; 1966-present era.

5 In 1994 I unsuccessfully tried to get a woman from the Christian Coalition to speak to my women and politics class at American University. After several telephone calls in which I sought to reassure the Christian Coalition that we wished to consider all views, I was finally told that their *only* female spokesperson was leaving the group to go abroad and that there was no other woman in the national office who could speak about women in the Christian Coalition.

6 Compare, for example, the discussion in Gant and Luttbeg (1990, 106–8) to Baumgartner and Walker (1989, 1990) and Rosenstone and Hansen (1993).

7 At the state level, some state parties have voluntarily chosen to employ equal division (e.g., the California Republican delegation in 1988).

8 These include Rep. Corrine "Lindy" Boggs (D-LA), Gov. Martha Layne Collins (D-KY), and Gov. Ann Richards (D-TX). For the Republicans, Sen. Nancy Kassebaum (R-KS) served as the temporary Chair in 1980.

9 Debra DeLee did serve as interim (appointed) chair of the DNC for two months after David Wilhelm resigned in November, 1994, following the loss of the Democratic majority in the House of Representatives to the Republicans. Don Fowler was elected as DNC Chair in January, and DeLee was appointed CEO of the Democratic Convention as had been announced prior to her interim appointment.

10 These include the states of Hawaii, Idaho, Iowa, Kentucky, Maine, Nebraska, New Hampshire, New Mexico, New York, North Carolina, Pennsylvania, South Dakota, Texas, Utah, Vermont, Wisconsin, and Wyoming. If the position of General Chair in Virginia were to be counted, then the number would rise to 18. In 1996, the states were Florida, Maine, Nebraska, Nevada, New York, North Carolina, Oklahoma, Oregon, Virginia, and Wyoming.

11 The states are Hawaii, Kentucky, Louisiana, Maine, Maryland, Missouri, Tennessee, Texas, and Wyoming. If D.C. is included, the number of Republican Chairs rises to 10. In 1996, this included the states of Arizona, Hawaii, Maryland, Michigan, Montana, and Oklahoma.

12 Since 1992, DNC Chairs are only elected once, after the November election, rather than twice during the presidential election year (at the convention and after the election).

13 Republican Party tradition dictates use of this term even for female chairs.

14 While Freeman correctly stresses that groups are different in the two parties, factions are associated with influential leaders in the GOP while they are more freestanding within the Democratic Party.

15 Party leadership is also rare in the U.S. Congress for women members. Until 2002, with the election of Nancy Pelosi as House Democratic Caucus Whip, no woman in either party had ever served in the upper ranks of elected formal party

leadership (e.g., as Speaker of the House, Majority Leader, Whip, or Caucus or Conference Chair).

16 This has been true, for example, for Representatives Bart Gordon (D-TN) (elected in 1984); David Price (D-NC) (elected in 1986–1994; reelected in 1996); and Senator Spencer Abraham (R-MI) (elected in 1994).

❖ REFERENCES

Andersen, Kristi. 1996. *After Suffrage: Women in Partisan and Electoral Politics Before the New Deal.* Chicago: University of Chicago Press.

Baer, Denise L. 1993*a*. "Political Parties: The Missing Variable in Women and Politics Research." *Political Research Quarterly* 46: 547–76.

——1993*b*. "Who Has the Body? Party Institutionalization and Theories of Party Organization." *American Review of Politics* 14: 1–32.

——1998. "The Gender Gap in Turnout and Preference in 1996: Strategic Implications for the Political Empowerment of Women." In *Women's Progress*. Washington, DC: Institute for Women's Policy Research.

——1999. "The Political Interests of Women: Movement Politics, Political Reform and Women's Organizations." In *Women in Politics: Outsiders or Insiders?* 3rd ed., ed. Lois Duke Whitaker. Upper Saddle River, NJ: Prentice Hall.

——and David A. Bositis. 1988. *Elite Cadres and Party Coalitions: Representing the Public in Party Politics*. Westport, Conn.: Greenwood Press.

——and David A. Bositis. 1993. *Politics and Linkage in a Democratic Society*. Westport, Conn.: Prentice Hall.

——and Julie A. Dolan. 1994. "Intimate Connections: Political Interests and Group Activity in State and Local Parties." In *Comparative State Parties: Their Electoral, Organizational and Governing Roles*, ed. Sarah P. Morehouse and Malcolm E. Jewell. A special issue of the *American Review of Politics* 15: 257–89.

Banaszak, Lee Ann. 1996. *Why Movements Succeed or Fail: Opportunity, Culture and the Struggle for Woman Suffrage*. Princeton: Princeton University Press.

Baumgartner, Frank R., and Walker, Jack L. 1988. "Survey Research and Membership in Voluntary Associations." *American Journal of Political Science* 32: 902–28.

—— ——1990. "Response." *American Journal of Political Science* 34: 662–70.

Berry, Jeffrey M. 1989. "Subgovernments, Issue Networks and Political Conflict." In *Remaking American Politics*, ed. Richard A. Harris and Sidney M. Milkis. Boulder, Colo.: Westview Press.

Biersak, Robert, and Paul S. Herrnson. 1994. "Political Parties and the Year of the Woman." In *The Year of the Woman: Myths and Realities*, ed. Elizabeth Adell Cook, Sue Thomas, and Clyde Wilcox. Boulder, Colo.: Westview Press.

Blair, Karen J. 1989. *History of American Women's Voluntary Organizations, 1810–1960: A Guide to Sources*. Boston: G. K. Hall.

Bosso, Christopher. 1995. "The Color of Money: Environmental Groups and the Pathologies of Fund Raising." In *Interest Group Politics*, 4th ed., ed. Allan J. Cigler and Burdett A. Loomis. Washington, DC: CQ Press.

Breckinridge, Sophonisba P. [1933]1972. *Women in the Twentieth Century.* New York: ARNO Press.

Browning, Rufus P., Dale Rogers Marshall, and David H. Tabb. [1990]1997. "Has Political Incorporation Been Achieved? Is It Enough?" In *Racial Politics in American Cities*, ed. Rufus P. Browning, Dale Rogers Marshall, and David H. Tabb. New York: Longman.

Carmines, Edward G., and James A. Stimson. 1989. *Issue Evolution: Race and the Transformation of American Politics.* Princeton: Princeton University Press.

Center for American Women and Politics. 2002. "Women in the U.S. Congress 2001." Fact Sheet. New Brunswick, NJ: Center for American Women and Politics.

Collins, Patricia Hill. 1990. *Black Feminist Thought: Knowledge, Consciousness, and the Politics of Empowerment.* Boston: Unwin, Hyman.

Conover, Pamela J., and Virginia Gray. 1983. *Feminism and the New Right: Conflict Over the American Family.* New York: Praeger.

Cook, Elizabeth Adell. 1999. "The Generations of Feminism." In *Women in Politics: Outsiders or Insiders?*, 3rd ed., ed. Lois Duke Whitaker. Upper Saddle River, NJ: Prentice Hall.

Costain, Anne N. 1992. *Inviting Women's Rebellion: A Political Process Interpretation of the Women's Movement.* Baltimore: Johns Hopkins University Press.

Cotter, Cornelius P., and Bernard Hennessy. 1964. *Politics Without Power.* New York: Atherton Press.

Democratic National Committee. *Democratic Party Charter.* 1974. Washington, DC: Democratic National Committee.

Darcy, Robert M., Susan Welch, and Janet Clark. 1987. *Women, Elections and Representation.* New York: Longman.

Disney, Jennifer Leight, and Joyce Gelb. 2000. "Feminist Organizational 'Success': The State of U.S. Women's Movement Organizations in the 1990s." *Women & Politics* 21: 39–76.

Freedman, Estelle B. 1979. "Separatism as Strategy: Female Institution Building and American Feminism, 1870–1930." *Feminist Studies* 5: 512–29.

Freeman, Jo. 1975. *The Politics of Women's Liberation.* New York: Longman.

—— 1983. "On the Origins of Social Movements." In *Social Movements of the Sixties and Seventies*, ed. Jo Freeman. New York: Longman.

—— 1986. "The Political Culture of the Democratic and Republican Parties." *Political Science Quarterly* 101: 327–56.

—— 1993. "Women at the 1992 Democratic and Republican Conventions." *PS: Politics and Political Science* 26: 21–28.

—— 2000. *A Room at a Time: How Women Entered Party Politics.* New York: Rowman and Littlefield.

Gant, Michael M., and Norman R. Luttbeg. 1990. *American Electoral Behavior, 1952–1988.* Itasca, Ill.: F. E. Peacock.

Gelb, Joyce, and Marian Palley. 1982. *Women and Public Policies.* Princeton: Princeton University Press.

Giddings, Paula. 1984. *When and Where I Enter: The Impact of Black Women on Race and Sex in America.* New York: William Morrow.

——1988. *In Search of Sisterhood: Delta Sigma Theta and the Challenge of the Black Sorority Movement.* New York: William Morrow.

Gillespie, J. David. 1993. *Politics at the Periphery: Third Parties in Two-Party America.* Columbia: University of South Carolina Press.

Graham, Sara Hunter. 1996. *Woman Suffrage and the New Democracy.* New Haven: Yale University Press.

Gusfield, Joseph R. 1962. "Mass Society and Extremist Politics." *American Sociological Review* 27: 19–30.

Heclo, Hugh. 1978. "Issue Networks and the Executive Establishment." In *The New American Political System*, ed. Anthony King. Washington, DC: American Enterprise Institute.

Heinz, John P., Edward O. Laumann, Robert L. Nelson, and Robert H. Salisbury. 1993. *The Hollow Core: Private Interests in National Policy Making.* Cambridge: Harvard University Press.

Herring, E. Pendleton. [1929]1941. *Group Representation Before Congress.* Baltimore: The Johns Hopkins Press.

hooks, bell. 1981. *Ain't I a Woman? Black Women and Feminism.* Boston: South End Press.

Johnson, Dennis. 2001. *No Place for Amateurs.* New York: Routledge.

Kaminer, Wendy. 1984. *Women Volunteering: The Pleasure, Pain and Politics of Unpaid Work from 1830 to the Present.* Garden City, NY: Anchor.

Kaplan, Temma. 1997. *Crazy for Democracy: Women in Grassroots Movements.* New York: Routledge.

Kornhauser, William. 1959. *The Politics of Mass Society.* Glencoe, Ill.: The Free Press.

Lane, Robert E. 1959. *Political Life: Why People Get Involved in Politics.* Glencoe, Ill.: The Free Press.

Mansbridge, Jane. 1986. *Why We Lost the ERA.* Chicago: University of Chicago Press.

March, James G., and Johan P. Olson. 1989. *Rediscovering Institutions: The Organizational Basis of Politics.* New York: Free Press.

Marilley, Suzanne M. 1996. *Woman Suffrage and the Origins of Liberal Feminism in the United States, 1820–1920.* Cambridge: Cambridge University Press.

McAdam, Doug. 1982. *Political Process and the Development of Black Insurgency, 1930–1970.* Chicago: University of Chicago Press.

McCarthy, John D., and Mayer N. Zald. 1973. *The Trends of Social Movements in America: Professionalization and Resource Mobilization.* Morristown, NJ: General Learning Press.

McGlen, Nancy E., and Karen O'Connor. 1983. *Women's Rights: The Struggle for Equality in the 19th and 20th Century.* New York: Praeger.

Melich, Tanya. 1996. *The Republican War Against Women.* New York: Bantam Doubleday.

Milbrath, Lester. 1961. *The Washington Lobbyists.* 2nd ed. Chicago: Rand McNally.

Minkoff, Debra. 1997. "Organizational Mobilizations, Institutional Access, and Institutional Change." In *Women Transforming Politics: An Alternative Reader*, ed. Cathy J. Cohen, Kathleen B. Jones, and Joan C. Tronto. New York: New York University Press.

Nagel, Jack H. 1987. *Participation.* Englewood Cliffs, NJ: Prentice Hall.

Naples, Nancy A. 1998. *Community Activism and Feminist Politics: Organizing Across Race, Class and Gender.* New York: Routledge.

Noble, Joanne. 1996. "Paradigm Shifts Facing Leaders of Black Women's Organizations." In *Voices of Vision,* ed. Julianne Malveaux. Washington, DC: National Council of Negro Women.

Oakley, Ann. 1974. *The Sociology of Housework.* London: Martin Robinson.

Olson, Mancur. 1965. *The Logic of Collective Action.* Cambridge, Mass.: Harvard University Press.

Pateman, Carole. 1970. *Political Participation and Workplace Democracy.* Cambridge: Cambridge University Press.

Polsby, Nelson. 1980. "The News Media as an Alternative to Party in the Presidential Selection Process." In *Political Parties of the Eighties,* ed. Robert M. Goldwin. Washington, DC: American Enterprise Institute.

——1983. *Consequences of Party Reform.* New York: Oxford University Press.

Reid-Merritt, Patricia. 1996. "Black Female Leadership: Standing on the Verge of a New Movement for Social Change." In *Voices of Vision,* ed. Julianne Malveaux. Washington, DC: National Council of Negro Women.

Rosenstone, Steven J., and John Mark Hansen. 1993. *Mobilization, Participation and Democracy in America.* New York: Macmillan.

Rosenthal, Alan. 1993. *The Third House: Lobbyists and Lobbying in the States.* Washington, DC: CQ Press.

Salisbury, Robert H. 1969. "An Exchange Theory of Interest Groups." *Midwest Journal of Political Science* 13: 1–32.

Schattschneider, E. E. 1975. *The Semisovereign People.* Hinsdale, Ill.: The Dryden Press.

Schlesinger, Joseph. 1984. "On the Theory of Party Organization." *Journal of Politics* 46: 369–400.

Schlozman, Kay Lehman. 1986. "Representing Women in Washington: Sisterhood and Pressure Politics." Paper presented at the 1986 Annual Meeting of the American Political Science Association, Washington Hilton, Washington, DC, 28–31 August.

——Nancy Burns, and Sidney Verba. 1994. "Gender and the Pathways to Participation: The Role of Resources" *Journal of Politics* 56: 963–90.

——Nancy Burns, and Sidney Verba. 1999. " 'What Happened at Work Today?' A Multistage Model of Gender, Employment, and Political Participation." *Journal of Politics* 61: 29–53.

——Nancy Burns, Sidney Verba, and Jesse Donahue. 1995. "Gender and Civic Participation: Is There a Different Voice?" *American Journal of Political Science* 39: 267–93.

Scott, Anne Firor. 1990. "Women's Voluntary Associations: From Charity to Reform." In *Lady Bountiful Revisited: Women's Philanthropy and Power,* ed. Kathleen D. McCarthy. New Brunswick, NJ: Rutgers University Press.

Scruggs, Yvonne. 1996. "American Women and Political Empowerment." In *Voices of Vision,* ed. Julianne Malveaux. Washington, DC: National Council of Negro Women.

Shafer, Byron. 1983. *Quiet Revolution: The Struggle for the Democratic Party and the Shaping of Post-Reform Politics.* New York: Russell Sage.

❖ Denise L. Baer

Sinclair Deckard, Barbara. 1983. *The Women's Movement: Political, Socioeconomic, and Psychological Issues.* New York: Harper and Row.

Sommers, Christina Hoff. 1994. *Who Stole Feminism?: How Women Have Betrayed Women.* New York: Simon and Schuster.

Thomas, Sue. 1994. "Women in State Legislatures: One Step at a Time." In *The Year of the Woman,* ed. Elizabeth Adell Cook, Sue Thomas, and Clyde Wilcox. Boulder, Colo.: Westview Press.

Truman, David. [1951]1971. *Governmental Process: Political Interests and Public Opinion.* New York: Alfred Knopf.

Verba, Sidney, Kay L. Schlozman, and Henry E. Brady. 1997. "Reply to Reviews." *American Political Science Review* 91: 427–30.

Walker, Jack L., Jr. 1991. *Mobilizing Interest Groups in America: Patrons, Professions and Social Movements.* Ann Arbor: University of Michigan Press.

——and Frank R. Baumgartner. 1988. "Survey Research and Membership in Voluntary Associations." *American Journal of Political Science* 32: 908–28.

——and Frank R. Baumgartner. 1990. Measurement Validity and the Continuity of Results in Survey Research. *American Journal of Political Science* 34: 662–70.

Watts, Margit Misangyi. 1993. *High Tea at Halekulani: Feminist Theory and American Clubwomen.* Brooklyn, NY: Carlson.

Wells, Mildred White. 1975. *Unity in Diversity: The History of the General Federation of Women's Clubs.* Washington, DC: General Federation of Women's Clubs.

Wollbrecht, Christina. 2000. *The Politics of Women's Rights: Parties, Positions, and Change.* Princeton: Princeton University Press.

6 ❖ The Gender Gap: Old Challenges, New Approaches

Pippa Norris

The 1980 election signified a critical realignment in American gender politics. It revealed a seismic shift in voting choice and party identification, which has subsequently been consolidated over successive elections. This development has had important consequences for party competition, for the recruitment of women candidates for elected office, and for the salience of gendered issues on the American policy agenda.

References to the "gender gap" have become commonplace in the popular press and the scholarly literature in the United States. Yet despite considerable research, the precise reasons for the realignment in American politics, and its implications, remain under debate. The key issues explored by this chapter are threefold: What are the trends in the gender realignment that need to be explained? What are the central theoretical issues about the causes and consequences of this phenomenon that continue to prove puzzling? And what are the research designs and methodological approaches that might help to tackle these questions? The review of the literature suggests that many American studies are limited to the analysis of voting behavior in specific presidential or congressional elections, rather than developing broader generalizations. The scattering of studies in other countries remains inconclusive. To learn more about this phenomenon, the chapter argues that we need systematic analysis that is sensitive to comparisons over time and place, as well as to differences between different groups of women. Most importantly, with a "new institutionalism" perspective we need to understand the complex interaction between electoral behavior and party strategies, using multi-level and multi-method analysis, so that we start to reintegrate our understanding of how women and men respond to the context in which they make their political decisions.

In developing this argument, this chapter does not attempt to provide a comprehensive review of the extensive literature on the relationship between gender, voting behavior, and public opinion. We cannot therefore discuss the issues raised by the growing body of research on gender consciousness, feminist attitudes, and support for the women's movement (for a review, see Rinehart 1992; Wilcox 1991); the general literature on public attitudes towards women in politics (cf. Bennett and Bennett 1992; Simon and Landis 1989); research on gender differences in political efficacy, interest, and participation (see Bennett and Bennett 1989; Inglehart 1981; Hayes and Bean 1993; Conway, Steuernagel, and Ahern 1997); and studies of the gender gap among politicians at elite level (for example, Thomas and Welch 1991; Dodson and Carroll 1991; Dodson 1991; Thomas 1991, 1996; Berkman and O'Conner 1993; Mezey 1994; Rosenthal 1998). Although all of these are important topics, this chapter focuses specifically on what we know, and do not know, about the nature of the gender gap in voting and partisanship and identifies new research designs and methodological approaches that would help us to expand this understanding.

❖ GENDER REALIGNMENT IN AMERICAN POLITICS

First, we need to clarify the key trends in the phenomenon under question, confirming some conventional perceptions but rejecting others. The first use of the term "gender gap" is credited to the then-President of the National Organization of Women, Eleanor Smeal, in 1981 (Bonk 1988). The phrase rapidly popularized as convenient shorthand for American journalists, scholars, and pollsters, referring to gender differences in support for the Democrat and Republican parties. The concept has subsequently been employed loosely to cover a diverse range of political phenomenon, such as gender differences in levels of electoral participation, political attitudes, issue priorities, and so on, at mass and elite levels, not to speak of the extension of the term even more broadly within the social sciences to describe other differences between women and men, such as in educational achievement and labor force participation.

Political analysis of the "gender gap" in the United States and elsewhere has focused mainly, as we shall, on explaining differences between men and women in their party identification and voting choice. The American gender gap in votes can be measured as the percentage difference between the two-party lead among women and men, as follows:

$$\frac{(\% \text{ Women Dem vote} - \% \text{ Women GOP vote}) - (\% \text{ Men Dem vote} - \% \text{ Men GOP vote})}{2}$$

E.g., 1996:

$$\frac{\text{Women } (60\% \text{ Clinton} - 34\% \text{ Bush} = 26\%) - \text{Men } (46.5\% \text{ Clinton} - 44.6\% \text{ Bush} = 1.9\%)}{2}$$

$$= \frac{26\% - 1.9\%}{2}$$

$$= 12.0\%$$

Key developments in the early 1980s fueled interest in the gender gap in American elections: for the first time, proportionately more women than men voted, a significant gender cleavage emerged in Democratic and Republican party support, and the women's movement seized on these developments to advance their agenda. During the 1980 and 1984 elections the gender gap could be dismissed as a short-term reaction to President Reagan's leadership and the mobilization of the New Right around issues like abortion rights and welfare cutbacks. But an enduring electoral cleavage since the early 1980s, with American women consistently leaning more Democratic while men favored the Republicans, convinced even the most skeptical observer that this was not merely a temporary blip.

❖ THE REVERSAL OF THE PARTICIPATION GAP

The first significant factor fueling interest in this phenomenon has been the mobilization of women voters, who have become the majority of the electorate. For successive decades since 1920, when the franchise was first granted, women had slightly lower levels of turnout than men (for a discussion of the reasons, see Andersen 1996, 49–75). According to U.S. census data, gender differences in voting participation gradually diminished in the 1980s in the United States (see Figure 6.1), as in many other countries (Christy 1987). The 1980 election was the first where there was parity in turnout. In successive elections since then, women have voted at slightly higher rates than men, although it should be noted

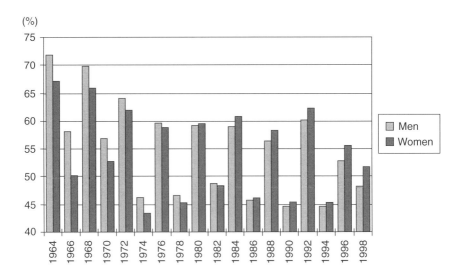

Figure 6.1 U.S. Voting Turnout, 1964–98

Source: www.census.gov.

that women still tend to engage in fewer campaign activities and other types of conventional activities than men (for a discussion, see Conway et al. 1997, 77–94; Verba, Schlozman, and Brady 1995, 228–66). The participation gap in voting turnout remains modest in size but it does mean that American women cast more votes at the ballot box; in the 1996 presidential election, for example, 101 million women voted compared with 92.6 million men, producing a participation gap of 8.4 million votes. Nor is this pattern simply a product of women's greater longevity, since turnout was also higher for women in the younger (18–44 year old) age group (www.census.gov/population).

❖ THE REVERSAL OF THE GENDER GAP IN VOTING CHOICE AND PARTY IDENTIFICATION

The second significant development was the male and female *reversal* in voting choice and party identification. The central puzzle is why women, who were more right-wing than men in the 1950s, became more left-wing in the 1980s. Just as some naive accounts suggest that sex was invented by the younger generation in 1964, so some popular accounts suggested the gender gap in voting started in 1980. Even recent scholarship reflects these assumptions: "The gender gap (typically understood as the partisan difference in voting behavior between men and women) was not a feature of political commentary prior to Ronald Reagan's election in 1980" (Kaufman and Petrocik 1999). "In fact, not until the 1980 presidential election, when 8% fewer women than men voted for Ronald Reagan, did anyone take much notice of the male/female split" (Sigel 1999). Not so. This foreshortened understanding of the literature leads to a serious misunderstanding of trends, typically encouraging studies to focus on developments since 1980 (see, for example, Chaney, Alvarez, and Nagler 1998). As always, any interpretation of trends depends critically upon the choice of starting and closing dates, and wherever possible the longest time-series is desirable for the most comprehensive picture.

In fact, the analysis of sex differences in voting behavior was established in the earliest pioneering works of empirical political sociology. The gender gap was studied in 1937 by Herbert Tingsten, in 1949 by Henry Durant, in 1955 by James Ross, and above all by Maurice Duverger in his classic work, *The Political Role of Women,* published for UNESCO in 1955. Duverger established the conventional wisdom that prevailed in political behavior textbooks for many decades, namely early polls revealed that women voters were slightly more *right wing* than men in many countries, including in Norway, France, and Germany (see, for example, the literature review in Randall 1987). This pattern can be termed the *traditional* gender gap. Although the early studies were essentially descriptive, based on simple cross-tabulations of face-sheet variables, theories commonly explained women's conservatism by their greater longevity, greater religiosity (linked to their support for Christian Democrat parties), and lower trade union membership, rather than by gender *per se* (Lipset 1960; Blondel 1970; Baxter and Lansing 1983; see, however, the critique of the literature by Goot and Reid 1984). Moreover, this phenomenon was not confined to Western Europe since similar trends were established in the earliest surveys in the United States. *The American Voter* (Campbell et al. 1960) found that in presidential elections from 1952 to 1960 women were slightly more Republican than men, with a gender gap in the region of 3–5 percent. In the 1956 mid-term elections, for example, men voted decisively (58%) in favor of the Democrats while women gave the edge to the Republicans (52%). The pattern in NES data was confirmed by Gallup polls, which registered stronger female support for the Republican presidential candidate, Dwight D. Eisenhower, in both elections during the 1950s (for a discussion see Stoper 1989).

During the 1960s and 1970s, the traditional gap closed and became insignificant in successive American presidential and congressional elections (see Figures 6.2 and 6.3). The *modern* gender gap in voting first became evident in the Reagan *v.* Carter contest in 1980, and since then American women have consistently given stronger support to Democratic candidates in successive presidential and congressional elections. As a result, in the 1996 presidential race women favored Clinton over Bush by a margin of 60% to 34% while men split by a far narrower margin of 46% to 45% respectively, with the remainder supporting Perot, producing the substantial gender gap already noted of 12 percentage points. As Carroll noted, for the first time in history, feminist activists could claim that the votes of women determined the president of the United States (Carroll 1999; see also Mattei and Mattei 1998). The size of the gender gap has fluctuated substantially, however, which may provide important clues to the causes of this phenomenon; for example, in the 1998 Congressional mid-term elections the gender gap shrank to only 4 percentage points. The gender gap is usually evident at many other levels of elected office although in statewide races women have occasionally given stronger support to Republican candidates (for details, see Center for American Women and Politics 2000).

Evidence for gender realignment in the United States, signifying a long-term shift in the loyalties of male and female voters, displays a slightly different pattern in terms of partisan identification. As demonstrated in Figure 6.4, from 1952 to 1970 there were only modest differences in the party loyalties of women and men, and the pattern is one of trendless fluctuations over time. In contrast, male support for the Democrats started to erode after 1972, producing a gender gap that expanded in the 1980s. In 1998, according to NES data, men split 54% self-identified Republicans to 46% Democrats, whereas women were evenly divided between the parties. As Kaufmann and Petrocik emphasize (1999), the primary change in partisanship has been the growing Republicanism of men, not a substantial change in female party loyalties. Yet this observation in itself

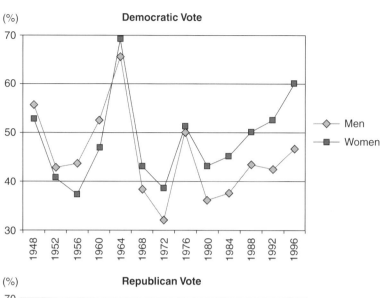

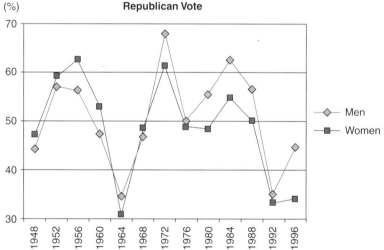

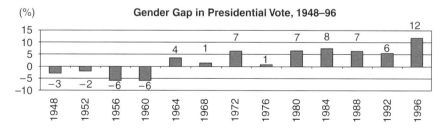

Figure 6.2 Presidential Vote, 1948–96

Source: National Election Studies, 1948–98.

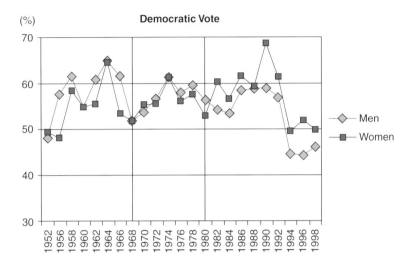

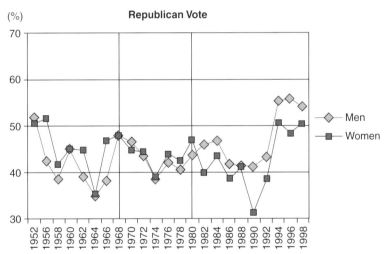

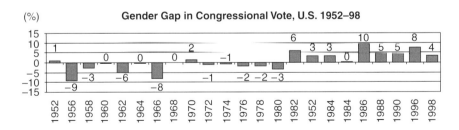

Figure 6.3 Congressional Vote by Gender, 1952–98

Source: National Election Studies, 1952–98.

❖ PIPPA NORRIS

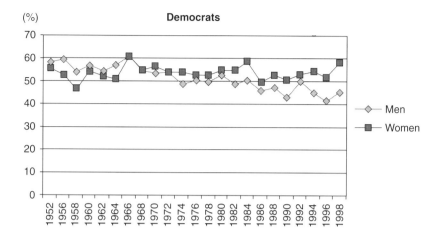

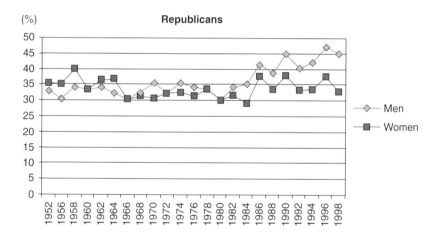

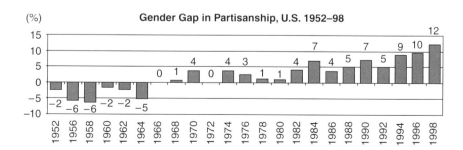

Figure 6.4 U.S. Partisan Identification, 1952–98

Source: National Election Studies, 1952–98.

does not provide many novel insights since the gender gap is, after all, a relative phenomenon. The puzzle is *why* there is a difference between women and men, and why the gender-related electoral cleavage should have *reversed* over time, more than whether one or the other sex "caused" this development.

❖ GENDER REALIGNMENT AND PARTY COMPETITION

The third related development was the way that the organized feminist movement and women political activists seized the emergence of the gender gap to advance their agenda, and the news media rapidly adopted this frame (see Bonk 1988; Smeal 1984; Abzug and Kelber 1983). As a result, press coverage of the gender gap expanded dramatically as a popular framing device or "peg" for a wide variety of electoral stories in the mainstream media from the early 1980s onwards (see Figure 6.5). The story first broke with Judy Mann in an article entitled "Women are Emerging as Political Force" in *The Washington Post* (October 16, 1981). The theme was picked up by Adam Clymer in a lengthy, front-page article in *The New York Times* in June 1982, which throughout focused on the change among women rather than men. Content analysis reveals that this frame is apparent in every election; it dominates coverage in 1988 and is the most common gender-related theme in 1982, and 1984, before surging in 1996. The "angry white male" story in 1994 and the "soccer mom" story in 1996 are perhaps most appropriately considered as variations of the gender gap frame employed by journalists to fit the peculiarities of each election—why the GOP surged in 1994 and why Clinton rebounded in 1996 (Carroll and Norris 1997; Carroll 1999).

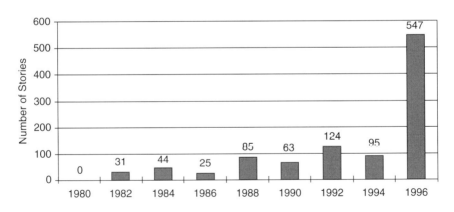

Figure 6.5 Press Coverage of the Gender Gap

Note: Nexis-Lexis keyword search of "Major Papers" database using term "gender gap and election" for September 1 through November 30 per election year. Table entries reflect number of stories using these terms.
Source: Carroll and Norris 1997.

Therefore, in the United States the gender gap in most presidential and statewide elections has not been great—in the region of 4 to 10 percentage points—but it has been politically significant. The women's movement mobilized around this development, it affects millions of votes, these votes are dispersed across every electoral district, press coverage has been extensive, the gender gap cannot be explained (and therefore modified) by a single issue, and it is a relatively recent phenomenon. As a result, party strategists have sought to compete for women's and men's ballot box power, with only an incomplete understanding of what steps are necessary to obtain maximum advantage of this development.

❖ EXPLAINING THE CAUSES OF GENDER REALIGNMENT

How do we explain the gender realignment in American elections? Studies have generally worked within alternative explanatory frameworks in electoral studies based on theories of issue voting, structural change, political mobilization, and generational value-change. "Issue-based" explanations commonly point to gender differences in policy priorities and attitudes. Structural explanations are based on the classic "Michigan" model of group voting, which suggests that objective socio-economic differences in the lifestyle of women and men determine their voting behavior. Political mobilization theories suggest the gender gap emerged largely among self-identified feminists as a result of the second-wave women's movement. Lastly, generational accounts emphasize the glacial process of value-evolution, in the United States and elsewhere, associated with societal modernization. How persuasive are these alternative accounts?

❖ *Issue Voting*

One of the most common ways of explaining the gender gap is by theories of issue voting. In the classic account by Campbell et al. (1960), the necessary conditions of issue voting are threefold:

(1) The public needs to be divided on the issue.
(2) The issue needs to be salient to voters.
(3) Candidates or parties need to take a distinct stance on the issue.

Unless all these conditions are met, issues are unlikely to affect voting choice. The public may disagree about whether American and allied troops should intervene in Bosnia, for example, but this will not influence electoral behavior if the issue is overshadowed by others such as health care reform or the state of the economy. Or the public may be sharply polarized on the question of abortion services, important as a "hot-button" issue, but candidates may seek to minimize damage by taking a bipartisan stance on the policy. To influence gender realignment, issues need to divide women and men, to be salient, and to distinguish candidates or parties.

Studies within this theoretical framework usually restrict themselves to the first condition, commonly focusing on differences in the political attitudes of women and men on one or two issue dimensions. Most have compared the sexes in their attitudes towards issues of war and peace, such as defense spending or the deployment of troops (Frankovic 1982; Smith 1984; Shapiro and Mahajan 1986; Gilens 1988). "Compassion issues" have also been seen as important, notably attitudes towards social welfare and racial equality (Piven 1990; Erie and Rein 1988; Shapiro and Mahajan 1986; Seltzer, Newman, and Leighton 1997). Lastly support for feminist issues of abortion and women's rights have commonly been studied, such as Reagan's opposition to ERA (Smeal 1984; Abzug and Kelber 1983), although research has challenged the idea that feminist issues *per se* were responsible for the gap (Klein 1984; Mansbridge 1986; Seltzer, Newman, and Leighton 1997). The most plausible pattern to emerge from this body of work indicates that women and men differ most consistently on issues related to the use of force and violence. These attitudes may influence support for foreign and domestic policy issues, including levels of defense spending and weapons build-ups, military intervention, and nuclear weapons, as well as approval of gun control and capital punishment (Smith 1984; Poole and Zeigler 1985; Clark and Clark 1993). Moreover women have also been found to be more strongly in favor of environmental protection and recycling initiatives and more opposed to nuclear power stations (Wirls 1986). On "compassion issues", women are generally more supportive of welfare programs for the elderly, sick, and poor, as well as government spending on education, health, and urban development (Deitch 1988; Page and Shapiro 1992). In contrast, on attitudes towards specifically feminist issues like abortion and the Equal Rights Amendment, gender differences have usually been found to be small or nonexistent (Shapiro and Mahajan 1986).

But if we accept this evidence, do attitudinal differences between women and men—whether on foreign policy, the role of government, or social issues—provide plausible explanations for gender realignment? For a convincing case, studies need to demonstrate not just that women and men have different attitudes today, but also that these attitudes relate systematically to voting choices. In particular, it is not enough to show that in any particular election these attitudes are associated with Democratic or Republican support, which is the common approach. The central challenge is to account for the partisan realignment that occurred in the early 1980s by demonstrating that either (1) the attitudes of women and men, *or* (2) the policies of parties, *reversed* on these issues around this period.

Did attitudes change? Unfortunately the available evidence of long-term trends in public opinion towards these issues remains patchy, at best, due to the limitations of time-series survey data. An analysis of gender differences in public opinion polls from the 1960s to the 1980s by Shapiro and Mahajan (1986) established only modest changes in women's and men's political attitudes on most issues at the aggregate level. Nevertheless this pattern could disguise countervailing trends among different groups of women, and the study found some evidence of greater polarization over time between liberal and conservative women. Another study by Page and Shapiro (1992) compared trends over fifty years in aggregate differences between men's and women's policy preferences. They concluded that out of hundreds of comparisons, in all but a handful of cases the attitude gap remained largely constant over time. That is, on issues like gun control, support for capital punishment, or welfare spending, the study confirmed the existence of some consistent differences between women and men, but the attitude gap has not expanded in recent decades. As always, a dynamic process fails to be explained by a constant.

Therefore, the core puzzle remaining for the issue-voting model is to explain why attitudinal differences between men and women on certain issue dimensions should have generated gender realignment in the American electorate in the 1980s. What does this suggest for the research agenda on issue voting? If the gender gap in attitudes has remained stable, answers within this framework must be sought by analyzing possible changes in the salience of these issues on the public policy agenda, or alternatively, possible strategic changes in the position of parties and/or candidates. Although systematic evidence is lacking, there are plausible grounds to believe that both these factors may have altered in the early 1980s. Thorson and Stambough (1994) measured trends in the salient issues facing the electorate from 1960 to 1992, and the results suggest that women and men became increasingly polarized over the most important issue facing the country. During the 1960–1972 period women and men expressed similar concerns about issues like the economy, the environment, and economics. The main gender difference during the 1968 and 1972 elections revolved around foreign policy, with far more women than men prioritizing the bloody conflict in Vietnam. Most strikingly, however, from 1976 to 1992 a pattern of increased polarization developed, with women far more likely than men to stress welfare as an important problem, while conversely men gave greater priority to the economy. This reflects gender differences in issue priorities similar to those found in some other countries like Sweden (Wangnerud 1994). Kaufmann and Petrocik (1999) found that the salience of issues, not just attitudinal differences, contributed towards the gender gap in the 1992 and 1996 presidential elections.

Moreover, many have observed how congressional parties in Washington have become increasingly polarized over social and economic policy issues, starting in the late 1970s and early 1980s (Aldrich 1995). President Reagan's alliance with the Christian Coalition and the New Right, coupled with the long-term decline of the southern Democratic "Boll Weevils", led to greater divisions between congressional parties. Support for reproductive rights, affirmative action, and child care, which had previously been bipartisan, became more strongly linked with the Democrats. Moreover President Reagan's commitment to cutting back government services, the welfare state, and particularly AFDC, greatly increased the salience of these issues on the policy agenda. The 1994 Republican sweep of Congress, under Newt Gingrich's leadership, reinforced party divisions over welfare reform while the impeachment proceedings further polarized Washington politics. The challenge for the research agenda within this framework is to use systematic evidence such as content analysis of party manifestoes or analysis of roll call voting to document these trends, and then to demonstrate how these developments have altered the issue agenda facing women and men voters since the 1980s. This research therefore needs to link survey analysis of electoral behavior with an awareness of the choices facing voters, reintegrating our understanding of voters and parties (for an illustration of this approach, see Evans and Norris 1999).

❖ Structural Explanations

Structural theories are commonly used to explain the link between social groups and party identification. In the United States the "Michigan" theory by Campbell et al. (1960) established the conventional wisdom throughout the 1960s. Democratic and Republican support was seen as rooted in long-standing and complex historical alignments based on successive waves of external and internal immigration, regional polarization over the Civil War, racial divisions over civil rights, the urban–rural split, and to a lesser extent the cleavage between unionized workers and employers. Once established, party loyalties maintained group support for decades.

The analysis of group voting support during the last forty years shows the Democratic base today remains a faded print of the classic New Deal coalition—Jewish liberals, low income whites, African Americans, Hispanics, union households, older voters. The old Democratic coalition has lost some support among certain groups—whites (especially southern whites) who deserted in the mid-1960s, men, the young, union households, and Catholics who gradually lost their Democratic faith. Some of these groups have themselves been transformed; in the 1950s "Catholics" usually meant Italian-Americans, Polish-Americans, and other ethnic groups from southern, central, and eastern Europe. Today this group has become more socially and politically diverse with the entrance of new Hispanic émigrés from central and southern America. In counterbalance the Democrats have made gains among African Americans, older voters, and women. There have been temporary shifts over time relating to a particular candidate, for example the rise in Catholic votes for John

Kennedy in 1960, the overwhelming support among blacks for Johnson in 1964, and the increased southern support for Carter in 1976, but overall the general pattern is one of trendless fluctuations and broad continuity. The structural shrinkage in the size of the Democratic base has proved more significant than behavioral shifts among voting groups.

In the classic theory of Lipset and Rokkan (1967), social class, region, and religion were regarded as the most important political cleavages in many European countries because they reflect broadly based and longstanding social and economic divisions within society at the time when Western democracies were emerging. Contemporary party systems resulted from complex historical processes, notably the national and industrial revolutions experienced by societies from the seventeenth century onwards. In Europe the division between church and state produced religious support for Christian Democrat parties, the division between landowners and industrialists helped create agrarian parties, and the division between employers and workers generated left-wing parties.

Therefore, groups in different countries—whether based on social class, religion, language, ethnicity, or region—became the primary building blocks for the political system. Parties mobilized coalitions of social groups and appealed to their interests. In contrast to these blocks, gender was usually regarded as secondary since women's interests were seen as divided by crosscutting cleavages such as class, ethnicity, and generation. The varying pattern of social cleavages across Europe in the nineteenth and early twentieth century established the essential framework for contemporary party systems. After the systems were established, Lipset and Rokkan (1967) suggest they "froze" as parties strengthened links with their supporters and integrated new social cleavages. In most countries women won the franchise after the modern party system was established, and they were therefore absorbed into the existing framework.

The gender gap can be explained by this theory if, like race, ethnicity, class, and religion, gender can be seen as a basic social cleavage reflecting distinctive political interests. Women's life styles, based on their roles within families, the labor market, the welfare state, and the community, may be expected to lead to different patterns of political participation, partisan loyalties, and political priorities on a wide range of issues: child care, family support, public transport, environment and technology, reproductive rights, welfare, education, and defense.

Why should the American gender gap have emerged in the last two decades? A number of interpretations within this theoretical framework are possible. For dealignment theorists, this development can be seen as part of a broader loosening of the traditional ties between social groups and parties, particularly the weakening of class alignments (Franklin et al. 1992; Dalton et al. 1984). In recent decades party fragmentation has grown in many established democracies, symbolized by the sudden rise of new regional, racist, or Green parties in countries like Italy, Canada, France, and Germany. For Inglehart new cleavages in society, produced by the "post-material" revolution, have changed priorities on the policy agenda, with a decline in the old left–right politics of redistribution and a rise in concern about issues of the environment, women's rights, and the quality of life (Inglehart 1977, 1990, 1997; Inglehart and Norris 2000). If the old cleavages of class and religion have declined in importance, this opens the way for the politics of gender, region, and ethnicity to become increasingly salient.

In a related explanation, it can be argued that in America structural change has produced a divergence in the socio-economic position of women and men. If this has affected the gender gap in voting behavior, we would expect considerable differences in the size of the gap depending on levels of education, income, age, occupational status, and marital status. The results of previous studies are divided. Miller (1988, 264) concluded that the socio-economic experiences of women and men are not sufficient to explain gender differences in the vote. The gender gap persisted even after controlling for demographic and social characteristics. On the other hand, Susan Carroll (1988) noted that the gender gap was strongest for two groups of women in the early 1980s: on the one hand, professional, college-educated, and fairly affluent women and on the other hand the less well-off and unmarried groups. The common factor linking these two groups, Carroll suggests, is economic and psychological independence from men. A continuing pattern of gender differences by high and low-income groups has been confirmed by more recent studies (Clark and Clark 1993). Plissner (1983) suggested the gender gap is essentially a "marital" gap, with polarization around marital status. Research among European voters suggests that rather than a simple gender gap, we can identify a "gender-generation gap". Younger women in many European countries prove more left-wing than younger men, while the pattern reverses among the middle-aged and older generations, where women remain more right-wing than men in their voting choice and ideological self-placement (Norris 1993, 1996b, 1999; Inglehart and Norris 2000).

One way to analyze this is to merge the NES surveys and then break down the analysis into two periods: the era of the traditional gender gap where American women leaned towards the Republicans (1952 to 1960) and the era of the modern gender gap (1980 to 1998) where women leaned Democrat. The social basis of the gender gap can then be examined to see where sex differences are greatest and also what has changed over time. The results in Table 6.1 and Figure 6.6 show that the size of the gender gap varies substantially by major social sector. In the traditional era, women leaned towards the right in most of the categories, especially the oldest age cohort and the unmarried. The exceptions where women proved more Democratic than men were among the youngest group, college graduates, and women in working-class jobs. In contrast, by the

Table 6.1 Profile of the Gender Gap, U.S. 1952–98

	1952–60 Gender Gap	1980–98 Gender Gap
ALL	−4.5	7.9
AGE GROUP		
17–34	0.7	9.5
35–44	−6.8	7.4
45–54	−5.3	11.8
55–64	−4.1	4.7
65+	−10.1	4.5
BIRTH COHORT		
1959–1974 Gen X		6.0
1943–1958 Boomers		9.2
1927–1942 New Dealers	0.6	10.7
1911–1926 Inter-War	−4.0	4.1
1895–1910 Pre-War	−5.1	2.4
Pre-1895 Victorians	−7.6	
MARITAL STATUS		
Married	−3.4	7.5
Not Married	−9.0	3.5
EDUCATION		
Grade school or less	−3.0	−2.6
High school	−6.8	6.6
Some college	−4.6	6.4
College or Advanced Degree	5.7	12.6
RACE/ETHNICITY		
White	−4.5	6.3
African American	0.9	3.5
OCCUPATION		
Professional or Manager	2.5	12.2
Clerical and Sales	0.7	−0.9
Manual	6.7	0.5
HOUSEHOLD INCOME		
Lowest	−7.8	−2.6
Low	−3.5	−1.5
High	−11.0	27.2
Highest	−0.4	7.2
RELIGION		
Protestant	−5.5	10.0
Catholic	−1.9	4.8
Jewish	−2.4	4.2

Note: The gender gap if defined as the difference between the Democrat–Republican voting lead among women and men. A positive figure means stronger female than male support for Democrats. A negative figure means stronger female than male support for Republicans.

Source: 1952–98 American National Election Studies.

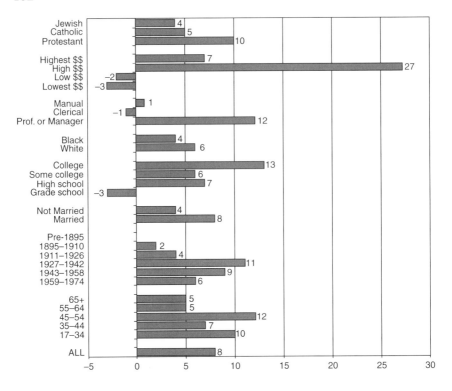

Figure 6.6 The Gender Gap in Vote, U.S. 1980–98

Source: NES 1980–98. See Table 1 for the definition and measures of the gender gap.

modern era women were more left-leaning across almost all the categories, with the gap strongest among middle-aged women, middle- to high-income, college graduates, those in professional and managerial occupations, whites, and Protestants. The pattern suggests that the gender gap is a crosscutting cleavage, strongest among many of the groups of women who would traditionally have been expected to vote Republican. Further studies of gender realignment among different categories of women are needed using multivariate analysis before we can claim to understand the reasons for these variations. One problem with analyzing this phenomenon is that the gender gap is often relatively small, with few cases within each sub-group in standard social surveys. If existing surveys are consolidated, this can help overcome the common problems of sample size, as well as allow generalizations about longer- term patterns evident over successive elections. Moreover, where robust and significant gender gaps among sub-groups of the population are identified, like those of marital status or socioeconomic class, then we need much further theoretical development to provide plausible explanations of these differences.

❖ PIPPA NORRIS

❖ *Feminist Mobilization*

Another school of thought emphasizes theories of political mobilization relating to the development of the women's movement and the growth of feminist consciousness. Early studies by Friedan and Dector (1982) first suggested a link between the gender gap and the strength of the women's movement. This explanation has been developed most fully by Pamela Conover (1988), who suggested that American women as a whole do not differ much from men in their political values on issues such as egalitarianism, individualism, and liberal self-identification. Nevertheless, the study found that a feminist identity was significantly related to a range of domestic and foreign policy preferences and political values. Conover concludes that becoming a feminist may act as a catalyst that helps women recognize their underlying "female" values. This interpretation is interesting, but it has attracted criticism. Cook and Wilcox (1991) argued that the relationship between feminism and policy preferences is reciprocal; developing a feminist consciousness may lead to more egalitarian values, but at the same time more liberal and egalitarian people become feminists. Without time-series panel data, it is difficult to disentangle the direction of causality in these claims, which have to remain theoretical.

❖ *Modernization Theory and Value Change*

Lastly, the process of societal modernization provides an alternative explanatory framework. The process of gender realignment in the United States raises the question of whether similar developments are emerging elsewhere. There are two perspectives on this issue. If the gender gap in American politics is caused by common structural and/or cultural trends affecting modern societies, such as increased female participation in the paid workforce, the break-up of traditional family units, or the transformation of gender roles, then we would expect to find similar gender gaps in other nations. But if the American gender gap is caused by factors that are distinctive to American politics, such as the traditional lack of a strong class cleavage in the electorate, the centrist pattern of two-party competition, or the salience of issues like abortion and affirmative action, then the modern gender gap in the United States may be *sui generis*, or at least contingent upon particular conditions found in particular countries, such as the predominant issue agenda, patterns of party competition, or cultural values. Exploring this issue is important both to compare, understand, and map the pattern worldwide and to provide further theoretical insights into the reasons for the emergence of the modern gender gap in the United States.

Unfortunately the previous comparative literature has been unable to resolve this issue, with different studies producing somewhat contradictory and ambiguous findings in different countries (see DeVaus and McAllister 1989; Everitt 1998*a*, 1998*b*; Haavio-Mannila 1985; Hayes and MacAllister 1997; Hayes

1997; Jelen, Thomas, and Wilcox 1994; Listhaug, Miller, and Valen 1985; Lovenduski and Norris 1993; Mayer and Smith 1995; Norris 1985, 1988; Oskarson 1995; Renfrow 1994).

Evidence from the World Values Surveys from 1981 to the mid-1990s indicates that gender differences in voting behavior have been realigning in post-industrial societies. Inglehart and Norris (2000) found that by the 1990s, women voters in most postindustrial societies had become significantly more left-wing than men, even after introducing a range of social controls. The modern gender gap is not confined only to the United States, as particularistic accounts suggest, but is also evident by the 1990s in some West European states. Nevertheless this pattern was not yet established in post-communist societies or developing societies, where the traditional gender gap persists into the mid-1990s with women voters continuing to be more right-wing than men. The main reason for the emergence of the modern gender gap in post-industrial societies, Inglehart and Norris argue, is that structural and cultural trends have transformed the values of women, particularly among the younger generation. We need further comparative studies examining the reasons for this pattern and exploring other cross-national differences in political attitudes and behavior.

❖ Conclusions: A New Research Agenda

Despite the extensive body of research, many aspects of gender realignment remain an unresolved puzzle. Certain issues emerge from this discussion, which help define the principles guiding any new research agenda. New approaches have to consider methodological innovations and the theoretical importance of contextual factors. Studies of the gender gap have usually followed the traditional methodology of public opinion research. Work has been based on individual-level analysis using existing cross-sectional survey data, usually items from the American National Election Studies or NORC. This has provided only limited answers to the key questions.

To expand the research agenda we need to move towards multi-method approaches. The re-analysis of aggregate trend data from opinion polls provides a rich source of data to consider the dynamics of changes in gender politics and the decisive realignment in the early 1980s. The use of qualitative interviews and focus groups allows us to explore whether women and men structure their thoughts and beliefs about political issues, candidates, and government in a similar or different fashion. It may be that women and men come to the same voting choices, but for different reasons, or that women and men take account of different considerations when evaluating candidates or prioritizing issues. Given what we know about gender differences in speech patterns, it seems wholly plausible that women and men talk about politics in distinctive ways. More qualitative approaches could explore these avenues of research.

Moreover, for those skeptical of qualitative approaches, experimental designs allow us to analyze how women and men respond to campaign messages and news within a controlled setting and to investigate their responses to different types of issues, candidates, and formats (see Iyengar et al. 1996). Multi-method research designs, however, are insufficient by themselves without theoretical developments. In particular, it can be argued that we need to take account of contextual factors, including temporal, social, and national contexts.

First, the gender gap varies over time, in size, and in direction. A comprehensive theory needs to account for these variations. Many of the early studies were limited to static, cross-sectional survey data, focusing on one, or perhaps two successive, elections. Explanations of gender realignment need comparisons over time to explain why this voting shift occurred in the early 1980s, rather than before or after. Research replicating Page and Shapiro's (1992) analysis of fifty years of trends in public opinion, focusing on aggregate changes among women and men, could help illuminate these issues. Moreover, the analysis of cross-sectional data needs to be sensitive to the context of the particular campaign—with its particular mix of issues, candidates, and events—rather than assuming that the gender gap is constant and invariable. Studies need to consider how the gender gap in presidential support may vary according to the configuration of women's races at U.S. House, U.S. Senate, and gubernatorial levels.

Second, studies need to be sensitive to social context and therefore to significant diversity among groups of women—by race, generation, and class, as well as between self-identified feminists and others—rather than treating women as a single, homogeneous group. Research needs to build on the foundation of previous studies by Susan Carroll (1988) analyzing women's autonomy and Pamela Conover (1988) focusing on feminist women, which have provided some of the richest theoretical work in this field. Initial comparison of the social profile of the gender gap since the 1980s (Table 6.1) suggests some interesting patterns that deserve far closer examination and multivariate analysis. Cohort analysis shows that the gender-generation gap, found elsewhere, is also evident in the United States. Education, income, and education are all important factors in distinguishing among groups of women, with a large gender gap among college graduates as well as among those with professional or managerial occupations. Far more work using multivariate analysis needs to be done to explore differences within and between groups of women, as well as between women and men.

Lastly, convincing theories of trends in American public opinion need to be evaluated within a cross-national context. This is particularly true of accounts that suggest "essentialist" explanations based on the changing role of women as child-rearers and homemakers. The tendency for women to favor right-wing parties during the 1950s was regarded as a cross-cultural pattern. In contrast, during the 1980s the gender realignment in American politics has seen parallel developments in some post-industrial democracies, but not everywhere (Inglehart and Norris 2000; Rusciano 1992; Haavio-Mannila 1985; Listhaug et al. 1985). More comparative research is needed to map out and explain the reasons for this pattern more fully. In particular, cross-cultural differences point to the need to be aware of a broader range of systemic factors influencing the relationship between social cleavages and party loyalties, including the role of party systems and party competition, electoral systems, political culture, and the agenda and strength of the organized women's movement. A cross-cultural perspective also highlights the need to be aware of "top-down" explanations of gender realignment, based on changes in party/candidate strategies, policies, and images, as well as "bottom-up" explanations based on changes in men's and women's attitudes, values, and policy priorities.

Gender realignment has now become an established part of American elections, taken for granted by commentators, journalists, and politicians. It provides a useful frame or "peg" on which to hang different stories about the election. Nevertheless, we should not be seduced by the conventional wisdom as many assumptions surrounding this phenomenon remain underexplained, and the challenge is to provide fresh ways of understanding the complex relationship between gender, voting behavior, and public opinion.

❖ REFERENCES

Abzug, Bella, and M. Kelber. 1983. *Gender Gap*. Boston: Houghton Mifflin.

Aldrich, John H. 1995. *Why Parties?* Chicago: University of Chicago Press.

Andersen, Kristi. 1996. *After Suffrage*. Chicago: University of Chicago Press.

Baxter, Sandra, and Marjorie Lansing. 1983. *Women and Politics*. Ann Arbor: University of Michigan Press.

Bennett, Linda, and Stephen Bennett. 1989. "Enduring Gender Differences in Political Interest." *American Politics Quarterly* 17: 105–22.

Bennett, Stephen Earl, and Linda Bennett. 1992. "From Traditional to Modern Conceptions of Gender Equality in Politics." *Western Political Quarterly* 45: 93–111.

Berkman, Michael, and Robert O' Conner. 1993. "Do Women Legislators Matter? Female Legislators and State Abortion Policy." *American Politics Quarterly* 21: 102–24.

Blondel, Jean. 1970. *Votes, Parties and Leaders*. London: Penguin.

Bonk, Kathy. 1988. "The Selling of the 'Gender Gap': The Role of Organized Feminism." In *The Politics of the Gender Gap*, ed. Carol M. Mueller. Beverly Hills, Calif.: Sage.

Campbell, Angus, Philip Converse, Warren E. Miller, and Donald E. Stokes. 1960. *The American Voter*. New York: Wiley.

Carroll, Susan J. 1988. "Women's Autonomy and the Gender Gap: 1980 and 1982." In *The Politics of the Gender Gap*, ed. Carol M. Mueller. Beverly Hills, Calif.: Sage.

——1999. "The Dis-Empowerment of the Gender Gap: Soccer Moms and the 1996 Elections." *PS: Political Science & Politics* 32 (March 1999): 7–11.

——and Pippa Norris. 1997. "The Dynamics of the News Framing Process: From

Reagan's Gender Gap to Clinton's Soccer Moms." Presented at the annual meeting of the Southern Political Science Association, Norfolk, VA.

Center for American Women and Politics. 2000. "The Gender Gap." Fact Sheet. *http://www.rci.rutgers.edu/~cawp/ggap.html*

Chaney, Carol K., Michael Alvarez, and Jonathan Nagler. 1998. "Explaining the Gender Gap in US Presidential Elections, 1980–1992." *Political Research Quarterly* 51(2): 311–40.

Christy, Carol. 1987. *Sex Differences in Political Participation: Processes of Change in Fourteen Nations.* New York: Praeger.

Clark, Cal, and Janet Clark. 1993. "The Gender Gap 1988: Compassion, Pacifism and Indirect Feminism." In *Women in Politics: Outsiders or Insiders?* ed. Lois Lovelace Duke. Englewood Cliffs, NJ: Prentice Hall.

Clymer, Adam. 1982. *The New York Times.*

Conover, Pamela Johnston. 1988. "Feminists and the Gender Gap." *Journal of Politics* 50: 985–1010.

Conway, Margaret, Gertrude A. Steuernagel, and David Ahern. 1997. *Women and Political Participation.* Washington, DC: CQ Press.

Cook, Elizabeth A., and Clyde Wilcox. 1991. "Feminism and the Gender Gap: A Second Look." *Journal of Politics* 53: 1111–22.

Cook, Elizabeth Adell, Sue Thomas, and Clyde Wilcox, eds. 1998. *The Year of the Woman: Myths and Realities.* Boulder, Colo.: Westview Press.

Costain, Anne N., and Heidi Berggren. 1998. "The Gendered Electorate." Paper presented at the annual meeting of the American Political Science Association, Boston, September.

Dalton, Russell J., Scott C. Flanagan, Paul A. Beck, and James E. Alt. 1984. *Electoral Change in Advanced Industrial Democracies: Realignment or Dealignment?* Princeton: Princeton University Press.

Deitch, Cynthia. 1988. "Sex Differences in Support for Government Spending." In *The Politics of the Gender Gap,* ed. Carol M. Mueller. Beverly Hills, Calif.: Sage.

DeVaus, David, and Ian McAllister. 1989. "The Changing Politics of Women: Gender and Political Alignments in 11 Nations." *European Journal of Political Research* 17: 241–62.

Dodson, Debra L., ed. 1991. *Gender and Policymaking: Studies of Women in Office.* New Brunswick, NJ: Center for the American Woman and Politics, Rutgers University.

——and Susan J. Carroll. 1991. *Reshaping the Agenda: Women in State Legislatures.* New Brunswick, NJ: Center for the American Woman and Politics, Rutgers University.

Durant, Henry W. 1949. *Political Opinion.* London.

——1969. "Voting Behavior in Britain 1945–1966." In *Studies in British Politics,* ed. Richard Rose. London: Macmillan.

Duverger, Maurice. 1955. *The Political Role of Women.* Paris: UNESCO.

Erie, Stephen P., and Rein Martin. 1988. "Women and the Welfare State." In *The Politics of the Gender Gap,* ed. Carol M. Mueller. Beverly Hills, Calif.: Sage.

Everitt, J. 1998a. "Public Opinion and Social Movements: The Women's Movement and the Gender Gap in Canada." *Canadian Journal of Political Science* 31(4): 743–65.

——1998b. "The Gender Gap in Canada: Now you See It, Now You Don't." *Canadian Review of Sociology and Anthropology* 35(2): 191–219.

Evans, Geoffrey, and Pippa Norris, eds. 1999. *Critical Elections: British Parties and Voters in Long-term Perspective.* London: Sage.

Franklin, Mark, Thomas T. Mackie, Henry Valen, and Clive Bean. 1992. *Electoral Change: Responses to Evolving Social and Attitudinal Structures in Western Countries.* Cambridge: Cambridge University Press.

Frankovic, Kathleen. 1982. "Sex and Politics–New Alignments, Old Issues." *PS* 15: 439–48.

Friedan, Betty, and Midge Dector. 1982. "Are Women Different Today?" *Public Opinion* 5: 20.

Gilens, Martin. 1988. "Gender and Support for Reagan: A Comprehensive Model of Presidential Approval." *American Political Science Review* 32: 19–49.

Goot, Murray and Elizabeth Reid. 1984. "Women: If Not Apolitical, Then Conservative." In *Women and the Public Sphere,* ed. Janet Siltanen and Michelle Stanworth. London: Hutchinson.

Haavio-Mannila, Elina et al., eds. 1985. *Unfinished Democracy: Women in Nordic Politics.* Oxford: Pergamon Press.

Hayes, Bernadette. 1997. "Gender, Feminism and Electoral Behavior in Britain." *Electoral Studies* 162: 203–16.

—— and Clive S. Bean. 1993. "Gender and Local Political Interest: Some International Comparisons." *Political Studies* 41: 672–82.

—— and Ian McAllister. 1997. "Gender, Party Leaders and Election Outcomes in Australia, Britain and the United States." *Comparative Political Studies* 30: 3–26.

Inglehart, Margaret L. 1981. "Political Interest in West European Women: An Historical and Empirical Comparative Analysis." *Comparative Political Studies.* 14: 299–326.

Inglehart, Ronald. 1977. *The Silent Revolution: Changing Values and Political Styles Among Western Publics.* Princeton: Princeton University Press.

—— 1990. *Culture Shift in Advanced Industrial Society.* Princeton: Princeton University Press.

—— 1997. *Modernization and Postmodernization: Cultural, Economic and Political Change in 43 Societies.* Princeton: Princeton University Press.

—— and Pippa Norris. 2000. "The Developmental Theory of the Gender Gap: Women's and Men's Voting Behavior in Global Perspective." *International Political Science Review* 21(4): 441–63.

Iyengar, Shanto, Nicholas Valentino, Stephen Ansolabehere, and Adam Simon. 1996. "To Be or Not To Be: Campaigning as a Woman." In *Women, the Media, and Politics*, ed. Pippa Norris. New York: Oxford University Press.

Jelen, Ted G., Sue Thomas, and Clyde Wilcox. 1994. "The Gender Gap in Comparative Perspective." *European Journal of Political Research* 25: 171–86.

Kaufmann, Karen M., and John R. Petrocik. 1999. "The Changing Politics of American Men: Understanding the Sources of the Gender Gap." *American Journal of Political Science* 43(3): 864–87.

Kiernan, Kathleen. 1992. "Men and Women at Work and at Home." In *British Social Attitudes the 9th Report,* ed. Roger Jowell et al. Aldershot: Dartmouth.

Klein, Ethel. 1984. *Gender Politics.* Cambridge, Mass.: Harvard University Press.

Lipset, Seymour M. 1960. *Political Man: The Social Bases of Politics.* Garden City, NY: Doubleday.

—— and Stein Rokkan. 1967. *Party Systems and Voter Alignments.* New York: Free Press.

Listhaug, Ola, Arthur H. Miller, and Henry Vallen. 1985. "The Gender Gap in Norwegian Voting Behavior." *Scandinavian Political Studies* 83: 187–206.

Lovenduski, Joni, and Pippa Norris, eds. 1993. *Gender and Party Politics*. London: Sage Publications.

——1996. *Women in Politics*. Oxford: Oxford University Press.

Mann, Judy. 1981. "Women Are Emerging as Political Force." *The Washington Post*, 16 October.

Mansbridge, Jane. 1986. *Why We Lost the ERA*. Chicago: University of Chicago Press.

Mayer, Lawrence, and Roland E. Smith. 1995. "Feminism and Religiosity: Female Electoral Behavior in Western Europe." In *Women and Politics in Western Europe*, ed. Sylvia Bashevkin. London: Frank Cass.

Mattei, Laura R. Winsky, and Franco Mattei. 1998. "If Men Stayed Home . . . The Gender Gap in Recent Congressional Elections." *Political Research Quarterly* 51: 411–36.

Mezey, Susan Gluck. 1994. "Increasing the Number of Women in Office: Does it Matter?" In *The Year of the Woman*, ed. Elizabeth Adell Cook et al. Boulder, Colo.: Westview Press.

Miller, Arthur. 1988. "Gender and the Vote: 1984." In *The Politics of the Gender Gap*, ed. Carol M. Mueller. Beverly Hills, Calif.: Sage.

Norris, Pippa. 1985. "The Gender Gap in America and Britain." *Parliamentary Affairs* 38: 192–201.

——1986. "Conservative Attitudes in Recent British Elections: an Emerging Gender Gap?" *Political Studies* 34: 120–28.

——1988. "The Gender Gap: A Cross National Trend?" In *The Politics of the Gender Gap*, ed. Carol M. Mueller. Beverly Hills, Calif.: Sage.

——1993. "The Gender-Generation Gap in British Elections." In *British Elections and Parties Yearbook 1993*, ed. David Denver, Pippa Norris, David Broughton, and Colin Rallings. London: Harvester Wheatsheaf.

——1996a. "Gender Realignment in Comparative Perspective." In *The Paradox of Parties*, ed. Marian Simms. Australia: Allen & Unwin.

——1996b. "Mobilising the Women's Vote: The Gender-Generation Gap in Voting Behaviour." *Parliamentary Affairs* 491: 333–42.

——1997. *Electoral Change Since 1945*. Oxford: Blackwell Publishers.

——1999. "A Gender-Generation Gap?" In *Critical Elections: British Parties and Voters in Long-term Perspective*, ed. Geoffrey Evans and Pippa Norris. London: Sage.

——and Geoffrey Evans. 1999. "Introduction: Understanding Electoral Change." In *Critical Elections: British Parties and Voters in Long-term Perspective*, ed. Geoffrey Evans and Pippa Norris. London: Sage.

Oskarson, Maria. 1995. "Gender Gaps in Nordic Voting Behavior." In *Women in Nordic Politics*, ed. Lauri Karvonen and Per Selle. Aldershot: Dartmouth.

Page, Benjamin I., and Robert Y. Shapiro. 1992. *The Rational Public: Fifty Years of Trends in Americans' Policy Preferences*. Chicago: University of Chicago Press.

Piven, Frances Fox. 1990. "Ideology and the State: Women, Power, and the Welfare State." In *Women, the State, and Welfare*, ed. Linda Gordon. Madison: University of Wisconsin Press.

Plissner, Martin. 1983. "The Marriage Gap." *Public Opinion* 53.

Poole, Keith T., and L. Harmon Zeigler. 1985. *Women, Public Opinion and Politics: The Changing Political Attitudes of American Women.* New York: Longman.

Randall, Vicky. 1987. *Women and Politics.* London: Macmillan.

Renfrow, Patty. 1994. "The Gender Gap in the 1993 Election." *Australian Journal of Political Science* 29: 118–33.

Rinehart, Sue Tolleson. 1992. *Gender Consciousness and Politics.* New York: Routledge.

Rokkan, Stein. 1970. *Citizens, Elections, Parties. Approaches to the Comparative Study of the Processes of Development.* Oslo: Universitetsforlaget.

Ross, James F. S. 1955. *Elections and Electors: Studies in Democratic Representation.* London: Eyre & Spottiswoode.

Rosenthal, Cindy Simon. 1998. *When Women Lead.* Oxford: Oxford University Press.

Rusciano, Frank L. 1992. "Rethinking the Gender Gap: The Case of West German Elections, 1949–87." *Comparative Politics* 243: 335–57.

Seltzer, Richard A., Jody Newman, and Melissa V. Leighton. 1997. *Sex as a Political Variable.* Boulder, Colo.: Lynne Reinner.

Shapiro, Robert Y., and Harprett Mahajan. 1986. "Gender Differences in Policy Preferences: A Summary of Trends from the 1960s to the 1980s." *Public Opinion Quarterly* 50: 42–61.

Sigel, Roberta. 1999. "Gender and Voting Behavior in the 1996 Presidential Election: An Introduction." *PS: Political Science & Politics* 32 (March 1999): 5–6.

Simon, Rita J., and Jean M. Landis. 1989. "Women's and Men's Attitudes about a Woman's Place and Role." *Public Opinion Quarterly* 53: 265–76.

Smeal, Eleanor. 1984. *Why and How Women Will Elect the Next President.* New York: Harper & Row.

Smith, Tom. 1984. "The Polls: Gender and Attitudes Towards Violence." *Public Opinion Quarterly* 48: 384–96.

Stoper, Emily. 1989. "The Gender Gap Concealed and Revealed: 1936–1984." *Journal of Political Science* 17: 50–62.

Thomas, Sue. 1991. "The Impact of Women on State Legislative Policies." *Journal of Politics* 532: 958–76.

—— 1996. *How Women Legislate.* Oxford: Oxford University Press.

—— and Susan Welch. 1991. "The Impact of Gender on Activities and Priorities of State Legislators." *Western Political Quarterly* 44: 445–56.

Thorson, Gregory, and Stephen J. Stambough. 1994. "Understanding the Gender Gap through the Paradigm of a Revised Michigan Model." Paper presented at the annual meeting of the American Political Science Association, New York.

Tingsten, Herbert L. G. 1937. *Political Behavior: Studies in Election Statistics.* London: P. S. King.

Verba, Sidney, Kay Schlozman, and Henry E. Brady. 1995. *Voice and Equality.* Cambridge, Mass.: Harvard University Press.

Wangnerud, Lena. 1994. "Male and Female Party Images in Sweden." *Scandinavian Political Studies* 172: 143–70.

Wilcox, Clyde. 1991. "The Causes and Consequences of Feminist Consciousness among Western European Women." *Comparative Politics* 23: 519–45.

Wirls, Donald. 1986. "Reinterpreting the Gender Gap." *Public Opinion Quarterly* 50: 316–30.

❖ **Part III**

New Directions in Women and Politics Research

7 ❖ Assessing the Media's Impact on the Political Fortunes of Women

Kim Fridkin Kahn

How does the media influence women's role in politics? Given the pervasiveness of the media in our political system, this is an important question which remains greatly understudied. In this chapter, I begin by describing what we know about the media's treatment of women in politics. Next, I identify five potential areas of future research: (1)an analysis of the news treatment of women officeholders; (2)the effectiveness of women candidates' media strategies; (3) an investigation of how men and women politicians deal with the press when running for office and when governing; (4)an examination of how the gender of journalists influences the content and consequences of political information; and (5)an examination of how the media socialize children about the role of women in politics. In discussing future research questions, I offer some preliminary ideas regarding potential research designs.

❖ REVIEW OF LITERATURE

Women are largely under-represented in the media's presentation of news. In the first place, women are rarely used as sources in news stories, and when they are quoted, women are more likely to represent private citizens than experts or authorities. For example, Rakow and Kranich (1991), in their study of the three network news programs, found that women were used as on-camera sources only 15% of the time while men were sources 85% of the time. Budge (1996), in her study of national newspapers, reported a strikingly similar trend. Men were referred to or solicited for comment 85% of the time in stories reported on the front page while women were referred to only 15% of the time. Furthermore, men were four times as likely as women to be pictured on the front page.

Johnson and Christ (1988) examined how newsmakers have been covered in *Time* magazine and found that only 14% of the covers of *Time* have shown

images of women and many of these images (37%) were of artists and en-
tertainers. Only 12 of the women who were shown on the cover of *Time* were
political leaders, government officials, or activists. Relatedly, between 1928 and
1985, only two women were sole recipients of *Time*'s annual choice for "Man
of the Year."

This research suggests that the news media do not regard women as authoritative or newsworthy sources of political information. When women do receive
attention, it is primarily reserved for celebrities or sources representing the
"woman on the street." Women in government and politics are rarely relied
upon for their professional expertise. This underrepresentation of women
may signal to the public that women are not legitimate sources of political
news.

Some scholars have argued that the scarcity of coverage of women in the
news is driven by the dominance of men in the news room (e.g., Braden 1996).
According to a 1992 survey by the *Columbia Journalism Review*, 84% of
reporters and editors in local newspapers were male, and the proportion of
females working for national newspapers and in broadcast journalism was only
marginally better (Smith 1997). Budge (1996), in her content analysis of 20
newspapers, documented the underrepresentation of women reporters. In
particular, she found men wrote 65% of all front page stories and 74% of the
opinion pieces examined in her study.

Weaver and Wilhoit (1996), in their landmark study of journalists, found
that women reporters may be more open to women as sources and as subjects.
For instance, in an examination of news stories written by men and women
reporters, Weaver and Wilhoit found that women journalists are more likely
than their male colleagues to use female sources. Furthermore, Mills (1997)
explained that women reporters, because they have different life experiences
than men, will cover news stories differently, relying on different sources and
emphasizing alternative perspectives.

Women's underrepresentation in the media is not restricted to news;
women also receive less attention than men in entertainment programming
(e.g., Alger 1989; Paletz 1999). For example, between 1950 and 1980 male characters outnumbered female characters on prime-time television by a margin of
three to one. In recent years, these numbers have improved, but only marginally. Vande Berg and Streckuss (1992) found that twice as many male characters as
female characters appeared in prime-time programs during the mid-1980s. In
addition, they discovered that women are consistently portrayed in a much
narrower range of roles than men–primarily as wives and parents–while men
are more often portrayed as being employed and holding higher status occupations. Similarly, while census figures indicate that women constitute more than
half of the U.S. work force, women appear as employed outside of the home
only about one-third of the time in entertainment programs. Finally, women

are more likely than men to be portrayed as sensitive, in need of emotional support, and nurturing. Men, in contrast, are shown as decision-makers, assertive, and economically productive (Vande Berg and Streckuss 1992).

Gender differences in the representation of women in entertainment programs is likely to influence socialization patterns among younger viewers. Since children between the ages of 2 and 17 watch more than 20 hours of television each week (Graber 1997), they are likely to be exposed to television's portrayal of men as authority figures and women as supportive and subordinate to men. These stereotypical views of men and women may influence boys' and girls' expectations regarding their future position in the world (Bennett and Bennett 1989). Owen and Dennis (1992) argued, for example, that unflattering portraits of women's position in society may explain why girls have lower levels of political knowledge and political interest than boys.

The coverage of women's issues has also been scant and stereotypical. For example, during the late 1960s and early 1970s, coverage of the women's movement tended to appear on the women's pages and not in the news section of daily newspapers (Bonk 1988). As the movement developed, coverage increased but serious coverage was still hard to come by. Stories concentrated on the sensational, not the substantive issues of the movement. Like other protest activities and social movements seeking media attention, what became newsworthy about the women's movement focused on style rather than substance and on features that discouraged expanded membership (Paletz 1999).

In a recent study Terkildsen and Schnell (1997) examined how the framing of the women's movement in major national news magazines shaped the public's views of the movement. Relying on both content analysis and an experimental design, Terkildsen and Schnell showed how the dominant frame for the women's movement (i.e., "feminism") encouraged negative views of the women's movement. However, an alternative frame (i.e., "political rights"), while rarely used by news media, encouraged people to develop more favorable attitudes towards the women's movement.

Huddy (1997), in a similar study, examined the framing of the terms "feminist" and "feminism" in the *New York Times* and in major news magazines from 1965 to 1992. Huddy showed that reporters discussed feminism narrowly, touching on women's private roles but rarely discussing feminism in terms of women's public roles at work or their rights within the legal system. Furthermore, feminists were identified as a small set of flamboyant women involved in the women's movement (e.g., Bella Abzug, Betty Friedan).[1]

Just as poor news coverage probably limited and slowed the growth of the women's movement, coverage of a gender gap in vote choice in the 1980s created a favorable atmosphere for female candidates and fostered more serious discussion of women's issues. Feminist leaders encouraged news coverage of the gender gap because they believed that a gender gap would force mainstream politicians to take the women's vote seriously (Bonk 1988). By making themselves and their polling information easily accessible to "friendly" reporters, activists helped generate and sustain coverage of the gender gap in the press (Barker-Plummer 1995).

The coverage of the gender gap varies quite dramatically across election years, depending upon the size and breadth of the gap in any given election. For example, Frankovic (1999) found a dramatic increase in coverage of the gender gap in 1996 compared to 1992. Coverage of the gender gap tripled in the *Washington Post* and quadrupled in the *Wall Street Journal* from 1992 to 1996. Frankovic believes the increase in coverage of the gender gap is partly explained by prominent Democratic women talking about issues associated with the gender gap. Furthermore, the gender gap in support for different issues was evident in polls through out the campaign season and clearly visible to reporters.

In addition to examining how the media has portrayed women's issues, recent research has examined how the news media treat men and women candidates for electoral office and whether gender differences in press treatment influence people's views of the candidates (e.g., Braden 1996; Fox 1997; Kahn 1996; Smith 1997; Williams 1998).

In a content analysis of newspaper coverage in 47 statewide campaigns between 1982 and 1988, Kahn (1996) found that the press differentiate between male and female candidates in their campaign coverage. Women consistently received less campaign coverage than their male colleagues, and when women did receive press attention, the coverage was disproportionately negative–emphasizing their unlikely chances of victory. Furthermore, the news media differed in their representation of the messages of men and women candidates. The news media's agenda almost mirrored the messages disseminated by male candidates, as represented by the male candidates' political advertisements. For women candidates, there was considerable distortion between the themes articulated by women candidates in their ads and coverage of those themes in the news. In a series of experiments seeking to examine the impact of gender differences in news coverage, Kahn found that gender differences in news coverage lead citizens to develop less favorable impressions of women candidates compared to their male colleagues.

Smith (1997) examined news coverage of women candidates in 1994, seeking to establish if the gender differences in news coverage found by Kahn (1996) have persisted. Smith examined newspaper coverage for 11 of the 19 women running for U.S. Senator and governor in 1994 and found few gender differences in press treatment. However, Smith's study may be limited because his sample of women candidates overrepresented competitive women candidates. In particular, in Smith's sample, 36% of the women running for election were victorious. However, for the population of women candidates running in 1994, only 16% were successful. Since Smith examined the most competitive women candidates, Smith may have underestimated the amount of gender bias in news coverage.

Fox (1997), in his book, *Gender Dynamics in Congressional Elections*, examined differences in perceptions of gender bias in news coverage among candidates running for the U.S. House of Representatives in 1992 and 1994. Relying on a survey of campaign managers, Fox found that managers for women candidates were much more likely than their male counterparts to feel a "media bias" against their candidate. Furthermore, 36% of the managers for female candidates thought there was "a gender bias in media coverage" during the campaign (Fox 1997, 132). Poole (1993), in a study of state legislative campaigns in Illinois, also found evidence for a gender bias in reporting. As one women candidate interviewed by Poole explained, the media covering the race concentrated "on stupid, little things such as clothes, hair, etc, which never comes up with men. They also use loaded adjectives to describe us such as feisty, perky, small, and lively" (Poole 1993, 6–7).

❖ AREAS FOR FUTURE RESEARCH

❖ *News Media Treatment of Women Officeholders*

While research in the last twenty years has shown us ways in which the media can influence women's role in the political system, many important questions have yet to be explored. First, we have some evidence that the news media treat men and women candidates differently. However, we know little about whether these gender differences in press patterns persist when candidates take office. In other words, do men and women officeholders receive the same treatment by the press? A pioneering study by Carroll and Schreiber (1997) offers a first look at media coverage of women officeholders. Carroll and Schreiber looked at media treatment of women in the 103rd Congress from 1993 to 1995. They found that women in Congress are portrayed as "agents of change" and the bulk of their coverage emphasizes their concern for health, abortion, and, to a lesser extent, sexual harrassment. Carroll and Schreiber also showed that news coverage downplays women's involvement in other issues, such as foreign affairs, international trade, the appropriations process, and regulatory reform.

The implementation of additional studies examining news treatment of women officeholders is important for a number of reasons. First, gender bias in news coverage of women incumbents could hinder women's chances of re-election. We know that local news coverage is a significant resource for House incumbents; local news is largely uncritical and provides members with an unobstructed line of communication with their constituents (Cook 1989). However, we do not know whether women members of the House enjoy the same incumbency advantage in press coverage as their male counterparts.

In addition to concerns about re-election, nonelectoral coverage is important because of the politician's legislative or executive goals. For example, if the media offer women governors more critical coverage and misrepresent their messages when reporting, then female governors may be less successful in implementing their agendas. Similarly, if women members of Congress are less likely to receive national coverage, their ability to champion major legislative initiatives may be inhibited. Pat Schroeder described her frustration with the *Washington Post* for inadequate coverage of her legislative priorities:

> When we talk about women's health, women's economic status, violence against women, it gets put on the style section by this city's major paper, and they talk about what we wear. It is time we move those issues to the front page. It is time they are taken seriously. And it is time that women lawmakers are given the same play in the paper with their issues [as men are given] by that newspaper. (Carroll and Schreiber 1997, 132)

Finally, attention in the national media spotlight is an important resource for officeholders as they aspire to higher political office (Cook 1989, 1998; Graber 1997). If women officeholders are less likely to receive fair treatment in the national media, then their national ambitions may be thwarted.

In examining news coverage of women officeholders, several related hypotheses need to be examined. First, if women officials are treated differently than their male colleagues (controlling for relevant political characteristics like tenure in office and campaign resources), are these differences found consistently across different offices (e.g., appointive *v.* elective, executive *v.* legislative)? Research on campaign coverage (Kahn 1996) suggests that settings which reinforce people's beliefs about women's stereotypical strengths (i.e., office of governor) may generate more favorable coverage of women officeholders.

Similarly, if women officials are covered differently than similarly situated men, these differences may be more evident in certain mediums and among certain reporters. It may be the case, for example, that the greater flexibility inherent in newspaper coverage as compared to television news (Graber 1997; Paletz 1999) creates more significant gender differences in newspaper treatment of women officeholders. Other structural differences between mediums may affect coverage patterns. Television news, in contrast to newspapers and radio, is a visual medium which places a premium on novelty (Epstein 1973). The demand for interesting visuals on television may lead to more coverage of women officials who are unusual and may be viewed as more "visually exciting."

In addition, the type of coverage given to women in office may be dependent upon characteristics of the reporter. Research in the campaign setting shows that women reporters are more likely than male reporters to focus on issues that correspond to a woman candidate's stereotypical strengths (Brader 1996; Mills 1997). In addition, women reporters do a better job than male reporters in representing the issue agendas of women senate candidates (Kahn 1996). If these differences hold in nonelectoral settings, then women reporters may be an important resource for women officeholders.

Finally, press treatment may also differ for women of color compared to other women officeholders, and researchers should try to sort out how race and gender influence coverage in the news. In examining the impact of race, scholars need to compare the press coverage given to various types of officeholders: women of color, white women, men of color, and white men. In making comparisons, one needs to make sure that race and gender are the only potentially politically relevant characteristics that differ across these different types of officeholders (i.e., control for characteristics like length of tenure, type of office held).

An examination of content differences in coverage of men and women officeholders is a worthwhile endeavor likely to improve our understanding of potential obstacles to women's chances for re-election and their ability to govern and legislate. Although content analysis of news coverage can be tedious, recent technical improvements (e.g., optical scanning of written documents, availability of news documents on the internet) has made content analysis less time-consuming. In addition, problems with the examination of television news is reduced in studies of national news because of the availability of tapes from the Vanderbilt Television Archive as well as Vanderbilt's published abstracts of stories from the three network news programs.

❖ Effectiveness of Men's and Women's Campaign Strategies

Research on the content of campaign messages suggests that men and women often articulate different themes when campaigning for electoral office (e.g., Benze and Declerq 1985; Fox 1997). Women, for example, are more likely than their male colleagues to emphasize their competence and credentials in their political advertisements. Similarly, men and women focus on different policy areas. In races for the U.S. House and U.S. Senate, women are more likely to focus on education, health, and environmental issues while men spend more time discussing taxes, the deficit, and trade. While we know that men and women stress different campaign themes, the effectiveness of these alternative strategies has not been explored. For example, do women gain electoral support when they focus on certain issues (e.g., education, healthcare) and avoid others (e.g., the economy, foreign affairs)?

Similarly, men and women candidates differ in their reliance on negative advertisements. Researchers examining congressional campaigns, for example, find that women are more likely than men to rely on negative appeals in their campaigns (Fox 1997; Williams 1998). Does this gender difference in reliance on negative advertisements reap electoral benefits for women candidates, or does such a strategy produce less favorable views of women candidates? Few scholars have examined the electoral consequences of negative campaigning by men and women candidates.[2]

The experimental method may be the best way to examine the impact that different campaign strategies have on people's perceptions of men and women candidates. The experimental method is ideally suited to study this question because of the greater degree of control available as compared to alternative designs, such as surveys or field studies. In the experiment, the investigator intrudes upon nature to provide authoritative answers to causal questions (Kinder and Palfrey 1993).

Two distinct elements of control enable experiments to provide important insights into causality. First, by creating the experimental conditions, the investigator holds all extraneous factors constant and makes sure that participants encounter stimuli that differ only in theoretically important ways. Second, by assigning participants randomly to treatment conditions, the experimenter can be confident that observed differences between the participants are caused by differences in the treatment conditions. Since proper randomization ensures that participants in the various conditions begin the experiment as approximately equivalent, group differences in the attitudes and behavior of respondents at the end of the experiment must be due to the experimental stimulus.

In designing an experiment to test the effectiveness of certain campaign strategies, the researcher needs to develop advertisements that look realistic and differ only in prescribed ways. With such a design, one can address a number of questions about the impact of different types of advertisements:

(1) Are people more persuaded by negative advertisements presented by female candidates, compared to male candidates?
(2) Do people develop more favorable views of women candidates when they focus on "female" issues (e.g., education, health care) as opposed to "male" issues (e.g., economic issues)?
(3) Are women as successful as men in creating positive images of their candidacies when the they emphasize "male" personality traits, such as competence, in their commercials?

❖ Gender Differences in Political–Press Relationships

Given the centrality of the news media in today's political system, an examination of how politicians deal with the press is crucial for understanding the media's role in campaigns and in government. While the symbiotic relationship between the press and elected officials has been examined at the presidential and congressional levels (e.g., Clarke and Evans 1983; Cook 1989, 1998; Kernell 1993), no systematic study of how men and women politicians differ in their relationship with the press has been conducted. This is a potentially important question because if women differ from men in how they design their press operations and interact with reporters, these differences can affect how men and women are treated by the news media and how successful they are as officeholders and in seeking re-election.

Beginning with the campaign setting, men and women candidates may have alternative views about the usefulness of various press strategies. For instance, male candidates may feel more comfortable pursuing free coverage in newspapers and television since they are more likely to receive favorable treatment as compared to their female counterparts. Women, in contrast, may allocate more of their campaign budget to controlled media communications like televised political advertising. Relatedly, since men may be more confident that their messages will be reported accurately by reporters, they may spend more time submitting press releases to local newspapers and local television news stations. Women, on the other hand, may feel that such an effort will not pay significant electoral dividends.

In setting up press operations in their campaigns, men and women may adopt different organizational styles. Women and men have different experiences and these differences are likely to influence how they conduct their business (Boxer 1994; Braden 1996). For example, some feminist theorists contend that women's experience as mothers makes women more empathetic, more open, and more cooperative (see Okin 1990 for a review). These qualities may lead women to organize their office–and their press operations–in a more open and democratic fashion. Men, in contrast, may adopt a more hierarchical system and closed structure for dealing with the press. These different organizational designs may influence how reporters relate to the candidates.

Finally, it is important to understand why men and women adopt different campaign strategies when running for office. Are men and women purposely adopting alternative strategies in their electoral bids? If so, why do they think their respective strategies will be more effective? By examining the candidate's campaign organization and by interviewing members of the candidate's staff, we can learn the answers to these questions.

Once a candidate successfully wins political office, he or she needs to organize his or her office and decide how to deal with the press (Foerstel and Foerstel 1996). Officeholders have several goals which they pursue during their period of tenure and these goals will affect how they decide to deal with the press. First, and foremost, elected officials want to ensure re-election, since without re-election they cannot achieve their other goals. In trying to gain re-election, members of Congress tend to rely on local news coverage which is easy to obtain and easy to control (Cook 1989).

In addition to the goal of re-election, politicians often want to accomplish specific policy outcomes while in office. Similarly, some elected officials want to gain power and prestige within their governing body, while others use their elected office as a stepping stone to higher office. For these three goals, national coverage is seen as more worthwhile than local coverage (Cook 1989).

By looking at the press organizations of men and women officeholders, we can compare their preference for local and national media attention and see whether these preferences correspond to their perceived goals. In addition, we can look at potential differences in the use of different types of mediums like local cable programming, C-SPAN, direct mail, and the internet. Women and men have different experiences and different constraints, which are likely to influence how they choose to deal with the media.

Several complementary designs can be used to examine gender differences in how men and women candidates and officeholders deal with the press. On the campaign side, a field study where a researcher follows various candidates on the campaign trail can yield valuable insights into how men and women candidates view the press and how their campaign seeks to encourage favorable coverage of their candidacies (see Fenno 1978, 1996 for classic examples of campaign field research).

To examine gender differences in how men and women officeholders deal with the press, researchers may want to use a panel survey where press secretaries are interviewed several times during a politician's tenure in office. For example, press secretaries for newly elected senators can be interviewed just after senators set up their office, after a few years in office, and when the senators are getting ready to run for re-election.

In addition, a survey of news reporters would provide useful insights into reporters' impressions of the politicians' choice of press strategies and the perceived effectiveness of these strategies. As with the survey of press secretaries, researchers could survey the reporters just after the election, during the middle of the senator's term, and before the re-election campaign. Interviewing both national and local reporters may provide interesting and alternative impressions of the officeholders' "press savvy."

Finally, to examine if men and women officeholders differ in their ability to generate coverage of their preferred messages, a researcher can conduct a content analysis comparing the officeholders' press releases with the press coverage they receive in their local newspapers. The researcher can also examine the amount of national news attention devoted to the politicians' messages. In studying U.S. Senators, for example, the researcher can collect a sample of press releases for all women serving in the U.S. Senate, as well as a sample of male senators, stratifying by party, ideology, and seniority. In selecting the press releases, it may make sense to look at a specific period and examine all press releases from each senator's office.[3]

To see whether senators receive news coverage for their preferred messages, the researcher can examine press coverage in the senator's home state newspaper for two weeks following each press release. Following Cook's (1989) lead, the *New York Times* can also be examined for the same time period to see whether the senators' messages receive national press attention.

❖ How the Gender of Journalists Influences the News

Do people react differently to news presented by men and women reporters, especially with regard to news about politics? While the appearance of women anchors, women political correspondents, and women talk-show pundits has increased, we know little about whether there are differences in how men and women journalists influence people's understanding of politics.

First, do women reporters talk about politics differently than their male counterparts? Prior research has documented some differences (Braden 1996; Kahn 1996; Mills 1997). For example, women journalists are more likely than their male colleagues to talk about personality characteristics like honesty and compassion when covering women running for statewide office. Future scholars may want to explore differences in coverage by men and women reporters and explore whether such differences persist across mediums (i.e., radio, newspaper, television), formats (e.g., talk shows, news programs), and topics (e.g., election news, foreign news, business news).

In addition to documenting differences in how men and women report the news, it is important to explore the impact that men and women journalists have on people's attitudes toward politics. While several different methods are available, I suggest using an experimental design to investigate the effect that men and women reporters have on people's understanding of politics. As a preliminary step, a content analysis of news reports (e.g., political reporting on network newscasts) should be conducted. This content analysis may show that men and women correspondents report news differently. For example, men may rely more heavily on sports metaphors to report the outcomes of political debates (e.g., "The incumbent senator scored a knockout punch during the second debate") compared to female reporters.

After assessing differences in reporting styles by men and women journalists, the investigator can develop stereotypical news stories simulating these differences (if there are differences). For example, one broadcast story may report a story in the style of a male reporter while a second story would report the same story in the style of a female reporter. In the experiment, one could vary both the gender of the reporter *and* the style of the story (i.e., style of male reporter, style of female reporter) to create four experimental conditions: (1) *male* journalist reporting story in style of *male* journalist, (2) *female* journalist reporting story in style of *male* journalist, (3) *male* journalist reporting story in style of *female* journalist, and (4) *female* journalist reporting story in style of *female* journalist.

This research design could answer a number of questions regarding the impact that male and female journalists have on people's understanding about politics. First, the content analysis segment of the design will help assess whether male and female reporters differ in how they report political news. Second, the experimental segment can tell us: (1) if people react differently to the "male" style of reporting as compared to the "female" style of reporting, (2) whether the gender of the reporter, independent of the style of reporting, influences people's interpretation of news, and (3) if the gender of the journalist and style of reporter cumulatively affect people's understanding of political reports.

❖ How the Media Affect the Political Socialization of Children

The impact that the mass media have on the political socialization of children has received surprisingly little attention by political scientists. In fact, many of the classic studies of political socialization conducted between the 1950s and 1970s (e.g., Greenstein 1965; Hess and Torney 1967; Jennings and Niemi 1974) have not been replicated or revised. This is an important oversight since television is much more important now than when these original studies were undertaken. Today, children between 5 and 11 years old spend more time watching television (an average of 30 hours a week) than they do in school (Graber 1997). Furthermore, the reliance on cable and internet sources has skyrocketed in recent years (Paletz 1999).

By examining the media's impact on children's views on politics, we gain insights into the attitudes and behaviors of adults (Greenstein 1965; Hyman 1959). For instance, researchers have demonstrated that women are less interested, informed, and efficacious than men (Corbett 1991). In addition, women are less likely to engage in political proselytizing than men (Hansen 1997). Are these gender differences in the political attitudes of adults the consequence of the media's impact of childhood socialization? This is an important question that has received little scholarly attention.[4]

Gender differences in the representation of women in entertainment programs, the absence of women as authoritative sources on news programs, and the negative portrayal of many women candidates, may lead children to see women as playing a less influential role than men in the U.S. political system.

First, since children watching prime-time television see men as authority figures while women are presented as supportive and subordinate to men, these stereotypical views may influence children's expectations regarding their perceived role in the system. Boys may develop optimistic views regarding their future opportunities while girls may sense that only certain careers paths are available to them.

❖ KIM FRIDKIN KAHN

Similarly, since women are rarely relied upon as expert sources for news stories on television, radio, and in the press, boys and girls may come to view women as less competent and knowledgeable than men in arenas such as politics and economics. These media-driven assessments of women may influence children's evaluations of men and women politicians as well as their own self-image.

Finally, children who pay attention to the mass media will see some women candidates portrayed in a stereotypical fashion (e.g., news coverage emphasizing "female" personality characteristics) and this may lead children to develop stereotypical views of women. In addition, since some women candidates are portrayed as less electable than men, children may learn that women candidates are likely to be long-shot candidates, with little chance of victory. Relatedly, children who follow the news will see that women hold very few positions of power in the country. Therefore, girls may learn that the political system is not very open to them and they may be discouraged from participating in politics. If the perception that the U.S. electoral system is closed to women promotes alienation among girls, then young women may forsake careers in public service and choose a career in the private sector instead. These young women, who might make excellent leaders, may stay away from government because their likelihood of success looks extremely limited.

To examine the role of the mass media on the political socialization of children, a panel design is desirable. For the proposed study, children should be interviewed, along with their primary agents of socialization (i.e., parents, peers, teachers), several times during childhood and as young adults. For instance, it may be worthwhile to start studying children early in grade school (e.g., first or second grade) when they are first developing attitudes towards the political system (Dawson, Prewitt, and Dawson 1977). Since children's attitudes and understanding toward politics change a great deal during these early years, the same children should be re-interviewed late in grade school (e.g., fifth grade). Interviewing of the children and their primary socialization agents should continue at prescribed intervals through young adulthood (e.g., eighth grade, senior year of high school, senior year of college or equivalent).

Given the ambitious nature of such a study, it would probably be more economical to target a specific metropolitan area than to try to draw a national representative sample. By targeting a smaller area, it would be easier to obtain the final data source: the content of the mass media that children rely upon. Since many potential news sources may be local, a more targeted study would make content analysis of these local media sources more manageable. Of course, national media sources of news would also need to be analyzed when children indicate their reliance on these sources.

By assembling these complimentary data sources, we could look at the correspondence between the children's political beliefs and the beliefs of their parents, friends, and teachers. More importantly, with information describing children's patterns of media use as well as the content of these media sources, we could see whether different patterns of media usage influence the children's views of politics and their view of women's role in politics. A panel design also would allow us to see how the impact of these agents changes over time. While we are primarily interested in examining the media's role in political socialization, it is necessary to examine the influence of alternative agents so that we can properly assess the media's effect, controlling for these other sources of influence.

❖ CONCLUSION

The mass media is a powerful force in today's political system. Given the media's pivotal role, systematic research examining how the media influence the political fortunes of women is surprisingly scarce. While research in this area is expanding, many questions remain unanswered. In this paper, I have identified five areas for future research. These areas do not represent an exhaustive list of unanswered questions. Instead, they illustrate questions that may improve our understanding of how the media affect the status of women in the United States.

In general, scholars need to spend more time looking creatively at gender differences in media coverage, how these differences affect the views of children and adults, and how men and women politicians and journalists influence patterns of media coverage. To explore these questions, researchers will need to adopt innovative and complimentary research designs. Multi-methodological approaches, relying on experiments, content analysis, field research, and traditional surveys, should be employed.

Examining the interplay between the media and women in politics is a fertile area for future research. Since research in this area is so sparse, future studies will significantly increase our understanding of how the media affect the political careers of women. While this type of information will be useful to scholars, these findings will also help activists and politicians as they make decisions regarding their media strategies.

❖ NOTES

1 For additional studies examining media coverage of the women's movement, see Costain, Braunstein, and Berggren 1997; Barker-Plummer 1995; Ashley and Olson 1998.

2 For two recent exceptions, see Hitchon and Chang 1995 and Iyengar, Valentino, Ansolabehere, and Simon 1997.

3 Press releases are routinely posted on each senator's web page.

4 For a recent exception, see Owen and Dennis 1992.

❖ REFERENCES

Alger, Dean E. 1989. *The Media and Politics.* Englewood Cliffs, NJ: Prentice-Hall.

Ashley, Laura, and Beth Olson. 1998. "Constructing Reality: Print Media's Framing of the Women's Movement, 1966 to 1986." *Journalism and Mass Communication Quarterly* 75: 263–77.

Barker-Plummer, Bernadette. 1995. "News as a Political Resource: Media Strategies and Political Identity in the U.S. Women's Movement, 1966–1976." *Critical Studies in Mass Communication* 12: 306–24.

Bennett, Linda, and Stephen Bennett. 1989. "Enduring Gender Differences in Political Interest: The Impact of Socialization and Political Dispositions." *American Politics Quarterly* 17: 105–22.

Benze, J. G., and E. R. Declerq. 1985. "Content of Television Political Ads for Female Candidates." *Journalism Quarterly* 62: 278–83,288.

Bonk, Kathy. 1988. "The Selling of the 'Gender Gap': The Role of Organized Feminism." In *The Politics of the Gender Gap: The Social Construction of Political Influence*, ed. Carol M. Mueller. Beverly Hills, Calif.: Sage.

Boxer, Barbara. 1994. *Strangers in the Senate: Politics and the New Revolution of Women in America.* Washington, DC: National Press Books.

Braden, Maria. 1996. *Women Politicians and the Media.* Lexington, Ky.: University Press of Kentucky.

Budge, M. Junior. 1996. "Teaching Women in the News: Exposing the 'Invisible Majority.'" *PS: Political Science and Politics* 29: 513–18.

Carroll, Susan J., and Ronnee Schreiber. 1997. "Media Coverage of Women in the 103rd Congress." In *Women, Media, and Politics*, ed. Pippa Norris. New York: Oxford University Press.

Clarke, Peter, and Susan H. Evans. 1983. *Covering Campaigns.* Stanford: Stanford University Press.

Cook, Timothy E. 1989. *Making Laws and Making News: Media Strategies in the U.S. House of Representatives.* Washington, DC: Brookings.

——1998. *Governing with the News: The News Media as a Political Institution.* Chicago: University of Chicago Press.

Corbett, Michael. 1991. *American Public Opinion: Trends, Processes and Patterns.* New York: Longman Publishing.

Costain, Anne N., Richard Baunstein, and Heidi Berggren. 1997. "Framing the Women's Movement." In *Women, Media, and Politics*, ed. Pippa Norris. New York: Oxford University Press.

Dawson, Richard E., Kenneth Prewitt, and Karen S. Dawson. 1977. *Political Socialization.* Boston: Little Brown.

Epstein, Edward Jay. 1973. *News From Nowhere.* New York: Vintage Books.

Fenno, Richard. 1978. *Homestyle: House Members in Their Districts.* New York: HarperCollins.

——1996. *Senators on the Campaign Trail: The Politics of Representation.* Norman: University of Oklahoma Press.

Foerstel, Karen, and Herbert N. Foerstel. 1996. *Climbing the Hill: Gender Conflict in Congress.* Westport, Conn.: Praeger Publishing.

Fox, Richard Logan. 1997. *Gender Dynamics in Congressional Elections.* Thousand Oaks, Calif.: Sage Publications, Inc.

Frankovic, Kathleen. 1999. "Why the Gender Gap Became News in 1996." *PS: Political Science and Politics* 32: 20–23.

Graber, Doris. 1997. *Mass Media and American Politics.* Washington, DC: Congressional Quarterly Press.

Greenstein, Fred I. 1965. *Children and Politics.* New Haven: Yale University Press.

Hansen, Susan B. 1997. "Talking about Politics: Gender and Contextual Effects on Political Proselytizing." *Journal of Politics* 59: 73–103.

Hess, Robert D., and Judith V. Torney. 1967. *The Development of Political Attitudes in Children.* Chicago: Aldine.

Hitchon, Jacqueline C., and Chingching Chang. 1995. "Effects of Gender Schematic Processing on the Reception of Political Commercials for Men and Women Candidates." *Communication Research* 22: 430–58.

Huddy, Leonie. 1997. "Feminists and Feminism in the News." In *Women, Media, and Politics,* ed. Pippa Norris. New York: Oxford University Press.

Hyman, Herbert H. 1959. *Political Socialization.* Glencoe, Ill.: Free Press.

Iyengar, Shanto, Nicholas A. Valentino, Stephen Ansolabehere, and Adam F. Simon. 1997. "Running as a Woman: Gender Stereotyping in Women's Campaigns." In *Women, Media, and Politics,* ed. Pippa Norris. New York: Oxford University Press.

Jennings, M. Kent, and Richard G. Niemi. 1974. *The Political Character of Adolescence.* Princeton: Princeton University Press.

Johnson, Sammy, and William G. Christ. 1988. "Women Through 'Time': Who Gets Covered?" *Journalism Quarterly* 65: 889–97.

Kahn, Kim Fridkin. 1996. *The Political Consequences of Being a Woman: How Stereotypes Influence the Conduct and Consequences of Campaigns.* New York: Columbia University Press.

Kernell, Samuel. 1993. *Going Public: New Strategies of Presidential Leadership.* Washington, DC: Congressional Quarterly Press.

Kinder, Donald R., and Thomas R. Palfrey. 1993. "On Behalf of an Experimental Political Science." In *Experimental Foundations of Political Science,* ed. Donald R. Kinder and Thomas R. Palfrey. Ann Arbor: University of Michigan Press.

Mills, Kay. 1997. "What Difference Do Women Journalists Make?" In *Women, Media, and Politics,* ed. Pippa Norris. New York: Oxford University Press.

Okin, Susan Moller. 1990. "Thinking Like a Woman." In *Theoretical Perspectives on Sexual Difference,* ed. Sue Thomas and Clyde Wilcox. New Haven: Yale University Press.

Owen, Diana, and Jack Dennis. 1992. "Sex Differences in Politicization: The Influence of Mass Media." *Women and Politics* 12: 19–41.

Paletz, David L. 1999. *The Media in American Politics: Contents and Consequences.* New York: Longman.

Poole, Barbara. 1993. "Should Women Identify Themselves as Feminists When

Running for Political Office." Paper presented at the annual meeting of the American Political Science Association, Washington, DC.

Rakow, Lana F., and Kimberlie Kranich. 1991. "Women as Sign in Television News." *Journal of Communication* 4: 8–23.

Smith, Kevin B. 1997. "When All's Fair: Signs of Parity in Media Coverage of Female Candidates." *Political Communication* 14: 71–82.

Terkildsen, Nayda, and Frauke Schnell. 1997. "How Media Frames Move Public Opinion: An Analysis of the Women's Movement." *Political Research Quarterly* 50: 879–92.

Vande Berg, Leah R., and Diane Streckuss. 1992. "Prime-Time Television's Portrayal of Women and the World of Work: A Demographic Profile." *Journal of Broadcasting and Electronic Media* 36: 195–208.

Weaver, David, and G. Cleveland Wilhoit. 1996. *The American Journalist in the 1990's: U.S. News People at the End of an Era.* Mahwah, NJ: Lawrence Erlbaum.

Williams, Leonard. 1998. "Gender, Political Advertising, and the 'Air Wars.'" In *Women and Elective Office: Past, Present, and Future,* ed. Sue Thomas and Clyde Wilcox. Oxford: Oxford University Press.

8 ❖ A Portrait of Continuing Marginality: The Study of Women of Color in American Politics[1]

Cathy J. Cohen

❖ INTRODUCTION: THE INVISIBILITY OF WOMEN OF COLOR[2]

It seems only appropriate that we begin this discussion of the study of women of color in American politics with a painfully obvious, yet no less troubling admission. Namely, in 2000 we still know very little about the political activity, ideologies, and attitudes of African American, Latina, Asian and Pacific Islander, and Native American women, especially in comparison to the knowledge we have gained about other groups such as white men. Clearly, we know a bit more than we did when I first penned this piece in the mid-1990s, having experienced such symbolic events as the media's frenzy over the vote of soccer moms, largely constructed as white, middle-class, suburban women. However, despite such periodic interest in women's political activity, we are still in desperate need of more research that can provide increasing detail to the skeletal picture we have of the political behavior of women of color. And while there exist numerous reasons for this pattern of neglect, in this chapter I will briefly comment on what I consider to be four significant causes.

First and foremost, any examination into the invisibility of women of color in the field of American politics must begin with some understanding of what has traditionally been defined as political by the mainstream of the discipline, namely voting and other formal institutional activity. In contrast to accepting this bounded and limited notion of what is political, feminist scholars have long pointed out how an adherence to an artificial dichotomy between public and private domains works to hide the various ways in which women participate politically (Hopkins 1993; Pateman 1989). These researchers argue that the dominant focus on electoral forms of participation in the study of American politics has diverted attention away from the extra-systemic and more social forms of political participation in which many women, in particular women of color, concentrate their activity. Thus, lost in American politics' very narrow definition of what constitutes noteworthy political participation is the non-traditional political activity of women of color. This type of political behavior is evident, for example, in the organizing of women of color through their local churches and neighborhood schools (Higginbotham 1993). Such activities, which many researchers have designated the private actions of individual women, have proven over the years to facilitate a collective political consciousness on the part of women of color that leads to increased electoral behavior and mobilization in communities of color (Jackson 1987). Thus, without some broader understanding and definition of what counts as political, the political work and attitudes of all women will continue to be only partially acknowledged and understood in political science.[3]

A second circumstance leading to the absence of information on the political activity of women of color in studies of American politics undoubtedly centers around the increasing reliance on survey data as the evidence of choice in political science. Because of the preoccupation of researchers with mounting national public opinion surveys and the willingness of large foundations to support these efforts, national databases are now where we turn (at least those of us who want to be published in the major journals) for information on the political behavior of those in the populace. As we know, women of color, especially when pulled out of a national study and then disaggregated by racial group, rarely comprise a sub-sample large enough to examine rigorously. And even when attention is paid to over-sampling, a trend that has come into favor among researchers, this process can produce a skewed view of the community of color under consideration, disproportionately including those who live in neighborhoods predominated by the racial group being over-sampled. So, while over-sampling may produce, for example, more African Americans in a sample, there is no guarantee that the over-sampling will provide an accurate picture of all the members of the group, allowing for sophisticated statistical analysis of their political activity. Finally, even in those rare instances when data on women of color have been gathered at sufficient levels, often the survey questions were designed with a focus on the majority of respondents, specifically white respondents, and thus the questions are unable to tease out the variation and unique political behavior and circumstances of Latina, Asian and Pacific Islander, Native American, and African American women.

A third reason for the invisibility of women of color in studies of American politics has been the limited way in which political science has sought to diversify and expand its curriculum and legitimize fields of research. Specifically, as political scientists have increasingly begun at least to recognize the fields of Latino politics, Black politics, Asian politics, Native American politics, and women and politics as areas worthy of scholarly pursuit and interest, the framework through which we engage in this work has not changed accordingly. For example, inclusion of a Black politics course in a political science department does not guarantee any systemic examination of the politics of Black women. Instead, courses on Black politics, like courses on other marginal communities, have generally meant the study of Black leaders or more specifically Black men, with limited attention given to the distinct political histories and activities of Black women. Even in the most progressive courses, the professor will often designate only one or two weeks out of an entire semester to talk about issues of gender, of course conflating the study of women with the study of gender. Similarly, courses and research on women and politics generally assume whiteness as the norm and reference women of color in an additive manner. As a result, in both cases Asian, Latina, Native American, and Black women are subsumed under more easily identifiable and supposedly inclusive categories, such as race or gender. These categories, while suggestive of inclusion, are capable in the wrong hands of enacting their own form of exclusion or secondary marginalization (Cohen 1999).

Finally, I would be remiss if I did not mention, as a fourth reason for the invisibility of women of color in the study of American politics, the general demographics of those who teach and research in the fields of American politics and women in politics. Clearly the abundance of white men who overpopulate the ranks of those we call political scientists affects the choices of who gets studied, independent of their personal, ideological and/or political leanings. It is only "natural" that researchers focus their attention, consciously and subconsciously, on those thought to look, act, and share similar experiences with the person sitting behind the computer. It seems that scholars (at least in American politics) gravitate toward those understood as the norm, those who have been studied in the past (thus there is a literature to build on), and those whose observation is likely to win you the esteem of your colleagues, the attention of publishers, and eventually, tenure from your institution. Needless to say, a similar, though I hope less deterministic, version of this phenomenon goes on among those who study women and politics. Thus, considering such patterns of replication between researcher and subject, it is not surprising that research on women of color is inadequately pursued and represented in the field of American politics.

Of course, I could spend the rest of this paper delineating additional reasons for the absence of work on women of color in the study of American politics, and clearly that discussion has to happen if we are to move forward. However, part of the purpose of this chapter is to identify what we do know and, from the information provided in that literature, make some assessment of what we need to know in the future.

❖ CATHY J. COHEN

❖ PAST AND PRESENT RESEARCH: THE LITERATURE?

Despite the overall lack of information or scholarly inquiry into the political behavior of women of color found in the main journals of political science, information on this subject has grown and continues to grow over the years.[4] Specifically, while political scientists have definitely benefitted from this expanding literature detailing the past and present political activity of women of color, in no way can we take full or partial credit for this development. Supplementing the sparse amount of work on women of color in political science are the writings of those researchers and writers, many historians and journalists, who have documented the ways Native American, Latina, Asian, and Black women have organized historically around issues of inequality, marginalization, and their individual and community survival. Thus, the process of building a field centered on the study of the politics of women of color means rejecting the narrow boundaries and definitions of politics offered by political science. Instead, we must see this as an interdisciplinary project, bolstered in large part by the work of scholars in various disciplines outside of political science.

In terms of what we do know, and where there are established literatures on women of color and politics, there seem to be three general categories of knowledge that I will employ for this paper. The first is extra-systemic participation (social movements, labor and grassroots organizing). The second is traditional political behavior (electoral activity and public opinion). Finally, the third category I will use centers on elite leadership activities (elected and appointed public officials). Before I begin a very brief review of those literatures, highlighting just some of the themes and writings to be found in an extensive search of these areas, let me point out that the documented or written knowledge on the political involvement of women of color is not evenly distributed across racial groups. There has been significantly more written on the experiences of Black women within and outside of traditional modes of political expression. Unfortunately, the political actions and ideas of other women of color have only recently made their way onto the research agendas of those who study women and politics, those who study the politics of specific racial and ethnic groups, and those who claim to study American politics generally. In part, this disturbing phenomenon is due to the limited way in which political scientists continue to conceptualize issues of race, namely in terms of a simple dichotomy between whites and Blacks. However, as was stated earlier, issues of methodology, racial and gender makeup of those in the discipline (faculty and graduate students), and the funding decisions of foundations also contribute to the reification of such a static and increasingly nonfunctional racial and gender schema.[5]

❖ Extra-systemic Participation

Of those areas in which we do have information about the politics of women of color, their activity in extra-systemic social movements and political organizations seems to be the most extensive. This is a trend evident across racial groups. Not surprisingly, it is in this area of analysis, where case studies detailing the political organizing efforts of individual and groups of women of color predominate, that historians continue to be among the most consistent contributors (Brown 1994; DuBois and Ruiz 1990; White 1999). Increasingly, however, scholars in other fields such as sociology, anthropology, and political science have provided important contributions, marshaling evidence of the long history of political activism among women of color and challenging prevailing explanations of the invisibility of women of color as resulting from their general apathy for things political. Specifically, mainstream explanations of politics, which attempt to justify the lack of published work on the political behavior of women of color by suggesting, for example, that these women are adverse to political activity or that they hold gendered roles in their communities that demand less political consciousness and activity, are directly and effectively challenged by this evolving field of study.

Examples of this type of work are numerous, and thus, I will only mention a few. Angela Davis, in her 1971 article "Reflections on the Black Woman's Role in the Community of Slaves," details the lived experiences and acts of resistance of enslaved Black women. Paula Giddings, in her 1984 book *When and Where I Enter*, tells the stories of politically active Black women, many of whom served as members and leaders of movements working for the liberation of their communities. Elsa Barkley Brown (1994), in her exceptional article "Negotiating and Transforming the Public Sphere: African Political Life in the Transition from Slavery to Freedom," focuses on the electoral arena and documents the communal political participation of Black women during reconstruction when denied an individual vote. Alice Chai (1982), in her article "Korean Women in Hawaii, 1903–1945," traces the history of Korean women immigrating to Hawaii and their participation in the Korean independence movement. Patricia Zavella (1988), in her article "The Politics of Race and Gender: Organizing Cannery Workers in Northern California," details the efforts of Chicana cannery workers and their struggle to unionize. Vicki Ruiz (1987), in her book *Cannery Women/Cannery Lives: Mexican Women, Unionization, and the California Food Processing Industry, 1930–1950*, examines the many dimensions of Mexican women, including their political work as labor union activists. Finally, Alison Bernstein (1984), in her article "A Mixed Record," explores the political participation of Native American women in tribal and state politics through their enfranchisement during the 1930s.

❖ Cᴀᴛʜʏ J. Cᴏʜᴇɴ

While there is much to be learned from these historical analyses of the participation and organizing of women of color prior to the formal end of segregation, there is also a well-defined literature focusing on their participation in the social movements and identity politics of the 1960s through 1990s. As we might expect, much of the work highlighting the recent social and political activism of women of color poses questions that explore the relationship of Black, Native American, Asian and Pacific Islander, and Latina women to the officially defined women's movement. Many of these recent works also explore the struggle of women of color to define an equal and visible position within their own indigenous racial, ethnic, and sexual liberation movements. Diane-Michele Prindeville's and John G. Bretting's 1998 article "Indigenous Women Activists and Political Participation"; Belinda Robnett's 1997 book *How Long? How Long?: African American Women in the Struggle*; Sandhya Shukla's 1997 article "Feminisms of the Diaspora both Local and Global: The Politics of South Asian Women against Domestic Violence"; Mary Pardo's book *Mexican American Women Activists: Identity and Resistance in Two Los Angeles Neighborhoods* (1998); and Esther Ngan-Ling Chow's 1989 article, "The Feminist Movement: Where Are All the Asian American Women?" are just a few examples of the more recent additions to this literature. Through the work of these writers, and many more, researchers have begun to learn the diverse ways in which women of color continuously labor to pursue their politics in ways that are meaningful to their multiple identities and communities. These works, at their best, build on the theoretical ground work laid by scholars such as hooks (1984), King (1988), Crenshaw (1991) and Collins (1990, 1998), which highlight the intersectional nature of the lives and politics of women of color, and present a complex understanding of the daily struggles and political work of women in these communities.[6]

❖ Traditional Political Behavior

In conjunction with our growing understanding of women's extra-systemic political activity, there has also occurred an expansion in what we know regarding how women of color participate in traditional avenues of politics. Undoubtedly, the acquisition and use of the vote represents the area in which we have gained the greatest knowledge of how women of color participate in electoral and government systems. However, we must remember that while white women gained the vote in 1920 with the passage of the nineteenth amendment, many women of color have struggled over the years for real enfranchisement (Gordon et al. 1997). Whether because of oppressive voter registration and immigration laws, racial discrimination through Jim Crow in the south, or the denial of the vote through strict language requirements, women of color have only recently acquired consistent access to the ballot. Correspondingly, only in the last twenty to thirty years has there emerged any serious work on the electoral participation of women of color, with most such studies highlighting the participation of Black women.

One of the earliest and most significant efforts to document the political participation of Black women was found in the pages of Githens' and Prestage's 1977 edited volume, *A Portrait of Marginality*. It was in this book that we learned that, despite low measures on all those characteristics thought to be important in facilitating voting (e.g., income, education), electoral activity among Black women was increasing at a rate greater than for any other group in the population (Lansing 1977). Furthermore, we were also made aware in this volume that not only were Black women voting in increasing numbers, they were participating at a rate at least equal to that of Black men. It was much of this early work, in particular that which focused on Black women, that informs our current work and comprehension of voting differences between women and men of color and between women of color and white women.

Consistent with earlier work, our continued exploration into the voting patterns of women of color has revealed some interesting developments. For example, through the research of Jewel Prestage (1991) we now know that African American women seem to participate not at the same level, but at a higher rate, at least in the realm of voting, than do African American men. Prestage notes that "as of 1988, African American women were reported to be 4 percentage points more likely to cast ballots than were African American men of comparable socioeconomic status." Furthermore, data gathered by the U.S. Bureau of the Census indicates that the gap in both voting and registration between African American women and men has expanded slightly, standing currently at about 6 percentage points. In the 1996 election, 60% of African American men were registered to vote compared to 66% of African American women. Similarly, 47% of African American men reported voting in the 1996 presidential election, while a majority of African American women, 54%, reported voting in the same election (Casper and Bass 1998). This gap in voting and registration between Black men and women is slightly larger than the approximate 2.5 percentage point difference in voting and registration evident between white women and men.[7]

While the gap between white men and women is smaller than that between African American men and women, the gap between Latinas and Latino men is consistent with that observed among Blacks. For example, in the 1996 presidential election 33% of Latino males said they were registered, while 24% reported voting. Among Latinas, 39% indicated they were registered to vote, while 29% reported voting in the election (Casper and Bass 1998). Again, these data are consistent with early work that examined the voting patterns of Latinas and Latinos. Brischetto and de la Garza (1983), in their book *The Mexican American Electorate: Political Participation and Ideology*, write that a Hispanic woman who was single was more likely to register to vote than a comparable single

Hispanic male. Carol Hardy-Fanta, in her book *Latina Politics, Latino Politics*, supports this finding, noting, "In the 1988 presidential election, Latina women were registered and voted at rates slightly higher than those of Latino men: 37.4 percent of women compared to 33.5 percent of men were registered; 30.1 percent of women voted compared to 27.4 percent of men" (1993, 202).

The general trend of women of color registering and voting at rates higher than men in their racial group is challenged somewhat when we examine data detailing Asian and Pacific Islander communities. Evidence provided by the United States Bureau of the Census (1993) indicates that Asian and Pacific Islander men voted and registered at rates nearly equal to their female counterparts. For example, 32% of Asian and Pacific Islander men registered to vote in the 1992 election, similar to the 30.6% of Asian and Pacific Islander women who were registered. Further, 28% of Asian and Pacific Islander men voted in 1992, while nearly as many, 26.7%, of Asian and Pacific Islander women voted. Interestingly, the 1996 election data suggest, ever so subtly, that Asian and Pacific Islander women may be on their way to out-participating the men in their group, like other women of color. In 1996, 32% of Asian and Pacific Islander men were registered to vote, while 33% of Asian and Pacific Islander women were registered. Of those reporting actually voting on election day, 26% of both Asian and Pacific Islander men and women indicated they went to the polls (Casper and Bass 1998).

Unfortunately, while we have increasing knowledge of the voting patterns and decisions of women of color, we have only limited understanding of their political activity through other forms of participation such as petition writing, campaign contributions, or political party activity. From what we do know, however, it seems that, like in the realm of voting, women of color are generally as active politically as the men in their racial and ethnic groups. For example, Jane Junn (1997) in her article "Assimilating or Coloring Participation? Gender, Race and Democratic Political Participation," looks briefly at the different forms of political participation engaged in by women and men generally and more specifically white women and different groups of women of color. Junn bases her conclusions on data from the 1990 Citizen Participation Study that included an over-sampling of communities of color. Junn's findings suggest that once disparities in resources are controlled for, very few significant differences remain in the political activity of men and women.

In contrast to the general similarity between men's and women's participation, Junn does find that white women participate at higher rates in most political activities than do women of color, with the realm of political protest or civil disobedience being the exception. Finally, when Junn disaggregates the category of women of color, she finds that African American women are more likely than Asian or Latina women to approach the levels of participation demonstrated by white women. While much of the variation in participation rates evident between different groups of women can be accounted for by variables such as citizenship, education, and income, Junn asks for caution in simply pushing for more participation by women of color. She argues "advocating more participation by women is justifiable only under circumstances where the structure and institutions of the process of decision making incorporate difference, and when the conceptualization of the citizen is contested and fluid. When the structures are biased, and when concepts of political beings are fixed, advocating more participation does not empower or emancipate those who have been previously dominated" (1997, 395).

In addition to the type of large-scale statistical analysis undertaken by Junn, case studies, ethnographic work, and small-scale surveys have also been helpful in detailing the patterns of political participation pursued by women of color. Specifically, while statistical analysis of participation by women of color provides some clarity about general trends, case study analyses, ethnographic research, and smaller survey studies provide us with the additional details needed to fill in the picture of political participation by women of color. For example, Carol Hardy-Fanta's work (1993) on Latina and Latino political participation in Boston is helpful in this regard. Through the use of in-depth interviews and sustained participation in community activity, Hardy-Fanta is able to explore the many factors contributing to and limiting participation among Latinas living in Boston. Beyond reporting the percentage of those participating, Hardy-Fanta describes the culturally specific processes of social ization that influence the political activity of these Latinas, an achievement that could never be reached by simply relying on statistical analysis.

Similar to our increased knowledge of the electoral actions of women of color, we have also experienced expanding insights into the political attitudes of women of color. With the increasing availability of public opinion data and national and local surveys, some researchers have used these resources to examine the distinct attitudes of different women of color as well as their beliefs in comparison to those of white women (Robinson 1987; Marshall 1990; Wilcox 1990a; Mansbridge and Tate 1992; Lynxwiler and Gay 1996; Montoya 1996; Gay and Tate 1998). As we might expect, much of the writing in this area has been limited to those subject areas and questions found on most national political surveys. Questions of efficacy, policy preferences, party allegiance, and one's feelings toward concepts like feminism have been and continue to be explored, emphasizing in particular how the attitudes of women of color differ either from men in their racial group or from white women.

For example, Yvette Alex-Assensoh and Karin Stanford (1997), using data from a small survey of residents in severely impoverished neighborhoods in Columbus, Ohio, present a very interesting examination of the political lives of poor African American women. In their essay entitled "Gender, Participation and the Black Urban Underclass," the authors examine differences in the political attitudes and behavior of African American men and women who live in areas of concentrated poverty. Similar to the findings of Prestage and others, the authors discover that while few differences exist in the expressed political attitudes of Black women and men, significant differences are identifiable in their levels of political participation. Specifically, the authors found that "black men and women harbor similar impressions of and attitudes about the political system. . . . [However,] the similarities in political attitudes and outlook do not translate into similar levels of political participation. Overwhelmingly, Black women participate in more types of activities and participate more frequently than their Black male counterparts" (408). Only in the area of civil disobedience did the Black men in this study exhibit higher rates of approval for this form of participation than did Black women.

Other researchers like Gay and Tate (1998) and Montoya (1996) have looked specifically at the role of gender consciousness in shaping public opinion. In both instances, while the authors find some difference in the expressed attitudes of men and women of the same racial and ethnic group, the power of racial and ethnic consciousness cannot be denied. Specifically, while a gender gap is evident in certain topic areas within race and ethnic groups, a significant race and ethnicity gap also exists, in particular, between white women and women of color. Gay and Tate explain the complexity that underlies their findings:

> Even if race remains the dominant political screen for black women, our results still soundly repudiate the popular view that gender is irrelevant for black women. The core theoretic essence of our findings is that the patterns that characterize the political attitudes and behavior of black women, and of groups that belong to more than one social category, are extremely complex. On nongendered policy matters and issues, racial solidarity promotes a liberal perspective. Yet, with complicated issues and events that pit race against gender and gender against race, gender remains politically relevant for black women, in this case working against collective pressures to support the interests of blacks over those of women. (1998, 182)

Finally, one last group of studies that deserve mention are those projects that explore differences, primarily in policy preferences, between white women and women of color, most often Black women. These works have produced important, and often unexpected, results. Examples include research documenting African American women's greater support than that found among white women for both the ERA and legalized abortion, when religiosity is controlled for (Wilcox 1990*a*, 1990*b*). And while all of these studies have been helpful in expanding our comprehension of women of color and their political behavior, it has been the work of authors such as Gay and Tate (1998) that move us toward a more complex understanding of the factors driving public opinion among women of color. I highlight their work because far too often left unexamined in these traditional public opinion analyses are the multiple reasons women of color differ in their attitudes and behavior from men in their racial group and from white women.

The unique processes of attitudinal development among women of color have largely gone unexplored, ignoring how their specific existence, in part as the targets of racist and/or sexist and/or classist and/or heterosexist oppression, has altered not their vote in the next election, but more likely how they think about, relate to, identify with, and resist the political system. We have failed to push for and utilize research designs that allow us to fully explore the specificity of women's experiences, especially as those experiences vary for different groups of women of color. Our neglect in this area seems especially devastating since questions of consciousness, political ideology, and general worldview are critically important in understanding not only if individuals will participate in the American political process, but also how their inclusion might transform the system.

❖ Elite Leadership Activities

The last area I want to discuss briefly is that of the election and appointment of women of color to public office. This is a subject in which our knowledge of the activities and progress of women of color has been clearly documented. For example, data collected by the Center for American Women and Politics (CAWP 2001) informs us that of the 73 women who served in the 107th U.S. Congress, 20, or 27.4%, were women of color.[8] Further, of the 89 women who served in statewide elective office in 2001, 5, or 5.6%, were women of color.[9] Finally of the 1,665 women who served in state legislatures across the country, 269, or 16.2%, were women of color.[10] And while the general trend for women of color in public office, even at the local/municipal level, has been one of expansion and increasing numbers, recent judicial attacks on majority–minority districts as well as on affirmative action put all of these advances at risk.

There are, of course, a number of other important dimensions to the analysis of women of color public officials beyond the particulars of how many women hold office. For example, the works of Darcy, Hadley, and Kirksey (1997); Darcy, Welch, and Clark (1994); Welch and Herrick (1992); Rule (1992); Moncrief, Thompson, and Schuhmann (1991); Carroll and Strimling (1983); and Baxter and Lansing (1980) have all helped to construct a framework for understanding the numerous issues surrounding voting schemes and campaign laws that influence who gets elected. For instance, through the work of Darcy, Hadley, and Kirksey (1997) we know that election systems affect the potential election of women of color, with Black women benefitting from multi-member districts. Scholars in this area of research have also discovered that the trend of white women being underrepresented in elected or appointed public office is similarly found in the experiences of women of color.

❖ Cathy J. Cohen

Thus, while in 1991 African American men held 91% of their expected lower house seats, as calculated through their percentage of the population, African American women held only 36% of their expected seats (Darcey, Hadley and Kirksey 1997).

In addition to research on election systems, the work of Paule Cruz Takash (1997), in her article "Breaking Barriers to Representation: Chicana/Latina Elected Officials in California," includes important information on the political trajectories of women of color elected officials, as exemplified in the histories of Latina elected officials in California. She asks, "Can we speak of a distinct Latina politics that differs from that of their non-Latina female and Latino counterparts?" (1997, 414). Cruz Takash mounted an extensive survey of all Latina public officials in California, examining their routes to elected office, their perception of politics, and the nature of their representational styles. She found that many of the elected officials she interviewed made their way into these offices by first engaging in local community political work. Further, Cruz Takash also suggests that while many of these women exhibit what some might label a feminist consciousness, these Latina officials seem to prioritize those issues perceived as affecting the entire Latino community, issues such as employment and education. This work on Latina elected officials should be read as part of a larger literature, focusing on the routes women of color take to elected and appointed office. Research on Black women, for instance, has emphasized the role of the Black church, the Civil Rights movement, and the Black Power movement in shaping the consciousness and political agenda of Black women officeholders (Robnett 1997; Crawford, Rouse, and Woods 1993; Jordan and Hearon 1979; Chisolm 1970).

Analysis of women of color as elected leaders is also one of the few areas in American politics where we can identify the active pursuit of information on women of color other than Black women, although this research is still heavily skewed in that direction.[11] For example, Darcy, Welch, and Clark (1994) find that Hispanic women, while still under-represented in local positions, have become increasingly visible as local officeholders. They note that while Hispanics hold few mayoral positions across the country, Hispanic women account for 13% of those positions. Further, the authors report that Hispanic women have increased their proportional city council representation from 0.11 in 1978 to 0.23 in 1988. Unfortunately, the authors were unable to pursue research on the patterns of local officeholding among Asian and Pacific Islander and Native American women, writing that "there is almost no information about Asian and Native American women's representation" (1994, 33).

A slight departure from that pessimistic, yet true, statement is Melanie McCoy's 1992 article, "Gender or Ethnicity: What Makes a Difference? A Study of Women Tribal Leaders." In her article, McCoy examines the relationship or applicability of research on white women elected to public office to the experiences of Native American women involved in tribal politics. McCoy questions whether earlier work that found that white women elected officials pursued a legislative agenda emphasizing "'traditional women's issues,' that is policies concerning children, nurturance, child welfare, reproduction and education," was appropriate for predicting the type of political agenda women tribal leaders would adopt. McCoy's analysis suggests that, like the Latina elected officials in Cruz Takash's study, women tribal leaders did not differ significantly from male tribal leaders in the issues they considered most important. She states, "tribal leaders, regardless of gender, seem to give priority to issues which concern the survival of their people. Women tribal leaders rank the same issue first as do men leaders, tribal economic development" (1992, 64).

In contrast to McCoy's finding of a negligible gender influence on the political agenda of female tribal officials, Prindeville and Gomez discover that "both gender and ethnic identity are significant influences for Indian women holding public offices in New Mexico" (1999, 17). The authors conclude that the observed difference in results between the two studies is related to the different samples of women leaders examined. Specifically, Prindeville and Gomez write:

> To a large degree, we are challenging the conclusions of Melanie McCoy's study of female tribal leaders. While our research questions are quite similar our findings are substantially different. The primary reason for this lies in the tribal membership of the leaders interviewed. Unfortunately, McCoy did not identify the tribal affiliation of her 19 subjects. However, based on her findings, we speculate that the majority of women in her sample serve in what we call "inclusive" tribes . . . In contrast, our sample consists of 13 women from "inclusive" (7), "transitional" (3), or "traditional" (3) tribes . . . "Traditional" tribes prohibit women's participation in tribal politics . . . We speculate that when Indian women are members of such "transitional" or "traditional" tribes, gender becomes a salient issue influencing their policy agendas and ultimately motivating their participation in politics outside of the tribe. (1999, 20–21)

Finally, I would direct the reader's attention to additional information on women of color and representation found not in the pages of social science journals, but in other publications. For example, new demographic information on Asian and Pacific Islander women in public office can be found in the 2000 *National Asian Pacific American Political Almanac* (UCLA Asian American Studies Center). Discussion of the experiences of Asian Pacific American women as public officials, while limited, can also be found in articles such as Judy Chu's 1989 article, "Asian Pacific American Women in Mainstream Politics." Further, there have been a number of biographical books written on the lives of women of color who served in leadership positions. For example, the autobiography of Wilma Mankiller (1993), elected chief of the Cherokee Nation, the largest tribe in the United States, provides us with a detailed discussion of an alternative form of elected leadership by a woman of color. There are also sections and chapters in larger books that deal with the activities of women of color in public office. Marla N. Powers (1986), in her book *Oglala Women: Myth, Ritual and Reality*, takes up the question of women's leadership in tribal politics. Similarly, Maurilio Virgil (1987) writes of the 1986 United States Senate bid of Linda Chavez.

In conclusion, I want to once again remind the reader that this broad discussion of trends in the literature on women of color in American politics should not be considered exhaustive of what we know, but instead illustrative of the kind of knowledge and information that is being generated. It now becomes our task to figure out what future research and analysis should focus on and give priority to when detailing, theorizing, and broadly examining the political experiences of women of color.

❖ WHAT WE NEED TO FIND OUT: THE FUTURE AGENDA

As we proceed through the new millennium there are at least five general points that I believe we should consider as we build a research agenda on women of color in American politics. The first point may be the most basic, and that is the need to disaggregate the category of women of color. It should be clear by now that the distinct social, political, economic, and cultural experiences individuals live through and with intensely influence their political outlook and activity. Thus, any attempt to understand or explain the political activity and outlook of women of color must pay direct attention to and account for those unique experiences that define their opportunity structure. This is not to say that there are no systemic trends influencing the life chances of women of color, and we should surely be in the business of drawing universal conclusions when they are appropriate. However, the varied lived experiences of women of color, as well as the unequal and skewed distribution of the limited knowledge we do have, necessitates that we further break down our categories of analysis. I am, of course, calling for the type of disaggregation that would include a separation of the category women of color into distinct racial groups. I would, however, go further than that to include an analysis of the specific political attitudes and behavior of women with distinct histories and national identities within these separate racial categories. For example, within the racial and ethnic category of Latina, we need to look separately at the different political patterns of Puerto Rican women as distinct from Chicana women as unique from Cuban women.

A second general principle that should guide our future research agenda is the need to broaden our definition of what is political. I make mention of this issue because, increasingly, as women of color experience greater success in the realm of electoral politics and officeholding, energy and material resources will undoubtedly be directed toward the study of their inclusion. Partly, this trend will develop in response to the fact that as more women populate public office, research on their activities becomes easier. Further, the mass media in its search for the quick and easy story will focus on this phenomenon, creating commercialized slogans like "the year of the woman." There is also the fact that more conservative elites will use the increasing numbers of women of color in public office as justification for their calls for the abolition of policies thought to "advantage" women and people of color. And with public recognition and discourse being increasingly focused on the political careers of women of color, we may also find more willingness on the part of foundations to fund research in this area. However, while attention to those gaining official positions is undoubtedly warranted, I worry that the local and community-based political activity, daily struggles, and attempts at empowerment undertaken by the masses of women of color will be largely neglected. Thus, a redefinition of not only what is political, but also what is politically important, seems in order. This means that while traditional acts of political participation and the election of women of color to public positions will no doubt continue to draw our attention, we must prioritize research which examines the efforts of women working locally to intervene politically in those institutions and systems perceived as structuring their lives.

A third issue which should inform our future research is the controversial question of the purpose and reason for our scholarship. Specifically, I believe that our work on the political behavior of women of color can and should be more than just an academic exercise. The oppression and marginalization experienced by women of color suggests that their empowerment at both the national and local level is required if many in their communities are to survive. Therefore, a redistribution not only of goods and services, but also of fundamental power in our society is desperately needed to improve the lived reality of most people of color. To the degree that research on women of color in American politics not only can facilitate their participation as full actors in this system, but also can aid these same women in transforming the oppressive structures, institutions, and practices they confront, then we must shape our research agendas with this purpose, among others, in mind. To that end, part of our research must focus not only on measuring levels of inclusion or alienation, but also on creating policy and grassroots interventions which can improve the everyday lives of women of color. As politically conscious researchers, we are faced with the task of producing rigorous social science research, while also facilitating the popular dissemination of these findings in ways that can be used in politically grounded environments.

A fourth and closely connected issue to the previous discussion, is the question of how we should engage in this work. Repeatedly, when I sit on panels discussing research on women of color, issues of control and direction of this scholarship emerge. Specifically, it is my belief that we must design our research so that the process and end result is one that leads toward the empowerment of those individuals and communities we study. I am not suggesting that we refrain from publishing those findings that seem critical of or disturbing to the individuals being studied. Instead, I am arguing for a process where not only the researcher, but also the subjects get to comment on and interpret the findings. Thus, when possible, our research should give voice to the experiences, systems of domination, and strategies of resistance Latina, Native American, African American, and Asian and Pacific Islander women embody. When possible, the words and actions of these women should be included and highlighted in our work.

Again, I am not suggesting that the use of data sets for the study of women of color is inappropriate. Instead, I want to push for the complete and complex presentation of the barriers and opportunities different women of color encounter. To that end, additive approaches to the study of identities must be abandoned and replaced with intersectional framings developed and utilized by feminist scholars, many of color. This, of course, dictates a process of reeducation where we reconceptualize the topic area as well as the manner in which we do our work. This reevaluation will hopefully challenge simple and superficial dichotomies between "objective social science" and, for instance, participatory observation, which asks the researcher to locate herself in and contribute to those communities with whom she is interacting and from whom she is learning. It is my belief, I must admit, that the complex process of bringing to the forefront the experiences of women of color as well as reorienting the discipline will be led by women of color scholars—those individuals who already find themselves and their communities alienated, invisible, and marginalized in the field of political science.

Finally, I believe that our future research must look a little like our past and continue to develop basic knowledge on the political activity and political thought of women of color. Undoubtedly, this may seem mundane to those unfamiliar with this field. The reality, however, is that we are still in a state of catch-up, designing research agendas to probe questions already asked of other groups. So, for example, we must identify ways to facilitate the ongoing work of those who engage in case studies and historical analyses of Asian and Pacific Islander, Latina, Native American, and African American women. This type of historic and case study analysis has great value if only for the legacy of struggle it documents. We must, however, also pay attention to the real world applicability of this work. Scholars involved in such projects might be advised to spend more time detailing the specific means through which women of color have previously found their way into political organizing and mobilization, as well as addressing the question of how such activities are relevant to current organizing efforts. Are there identifiable routes through which women of color have continuously become politicized and active in political organizations? How in the past have women of color acquired the resources necessary for their political work? There are a plethora of basic questions about organizing where knowledge of the ways women of color have historically set out to better their condition might be helpful.

At the same time that we want to maintain our interest in the historical political activity of women of color, we need desperately to expand what we know about the worldviews, policy preferences, and general political activity of women of color today. In most cases these data can be generated most easily through national or local surveys that seek to measure the opinions and actions of respondents across numerous domains. This work, however, calls for a reassessment of what we ask in our surveys. Surveys as they currently exist, in particular national surveys, have been defined largely by white male researchers whose subjects of interest (other whites) are presumed to concentrate their political activity in formally recognized acts. By diversifying the research team (especially those in control) and the target population under examination, I believe we can begin to significantly alter what we ask on surveys. Specifically, sections in national surveys that attempt to measure the patterns of political participation of respondents might be redesigned to include significantly more questions measuring local or community-based acts of participation, where women of color direct most of their political energy. Clearly, the literature has already established that it is most often through local activity, personal interactions, and social networks that women of color and people generally become politicized. So questions that explore the connection between participation and leadership in local churches, parent-teacher associations, or other civic activity and social capital sources may prove to be more important in understanding the political behavior of women of color than questions focused on formal political activity. Further, survey questions designed to measure the policy preferences of respondents should be restructured to include more topics that disproportionately impact on women, in particular women of color. Policy questions on welfare reform, sexual harassment, the prosecution of pregnant women for drug use, reproductive choices, the prevalence of racism *and* sexism in work and social institutions, as well as other questions which center on living conditions in poor, isolated communities where many women of color live, must be a part of our new research agenda.

Finally, with regard to survey data, I would make a strong plea that we spend more time looking at the ways in which people organize and process information. What are the general ideologies and frameworks that people, in particular women of color, use to make sense of the world? How do women of color cognitively organize their multiple and intersecting identities? Only through understanding how women of color come to negotiate their unique position as targets of, at the very least, racist and sexist oppression, can we begin to develop effective interventions. Of course, survey data can provide us with some of this material at a very general level. However, we will need to

❖ CATHY J. COHEN

build on this work through the use of in-depth interviews and ethnographic research.

Interestingly, as I noted earlier, we do have some knowledge about women of color and white women as elected public officials and appointees. So with this information in hand, it may now be time to demonstrate the applicability of general theories of women in elected office to the experiences of Latina, Native American, Asian and Pacific Islander, and African American women elected officials. For example, to what extent do women of color in elected offices pursue a legislative agenda significantly different from their male colleagues of the same racial group or from white women? Do these women have a different "homestyle" with their constituencies? Do they pursue or are they given different committee assignments? What about their re-election chances? Does incumbency have the same impact and power for women of color? Based on the knowledge that women of color might be advantaged by multi-member districts in state elections, how might the underrepresentation of women of color be impacted by the continuing fight to undermine majority–minority single-member districts? With regard to institutional participation, do traditional party mechanisms work to enhance the election chances of women of color?

Methodological approaches to pursuing this research are limited. Because of the small number of women of color at the national level, statistical analysis of this specific group should be pursued with caution. However, a broader survey of women of color at local, state, and national levels would seem in order, although complex. As I mentioned above, the composition of such a survey would need to reflect the specific issues and conditions faced by women of color officeholders at multiple levels. The use of case studies is another approach that has been used with some success. This type of in-depth interviewing allows the researcher to focus on the details of one woman's experience, often spending time with the officeholder in numerous settings. The data generated through in-depth interviewing, ethnographic work, or case studies can then be compared, identifying general theories of recruitment and advancement for women of color officeholders.

❖ CONCLUSION

In conclusion, I want first to remind the reader that while papers which attempt to review and highlight the specific experiences and political actions of women are color are not only necessary, but essential in building the field of women and politics, this subject area cannot remain relegated to "special" women of color papers, panels, or journal editions. Such a process only reinforces the marginalization of this sector within the larger field of women and politics. I am not suggesting, however, that a panel at a conference designed to deal with the politics of women of color exclusively is uncalled for or inherently problematic. Instead, I believe that designating one panel to deal with the specific issues encountered by women of color, without requiring every other panel at a conference to include *significant* attention to the plight of African American, Asian and Pacific Islander, Native American, and Latina women, is irresponsible. We must expect all those who study women and politics to consistently address the issues confronted by women of color, challenging the unspoken normative standard of whiteness in this field and making central the interaction of gender, race, and ethnicity in our research.

Second, as increasing numbers of those in our discipline feel alienated from the methodologies and publications that purportedly define the field of political science, it is time for those of us committed to the study of women and politics and gender issues to push for an expansion in what is considered political and who are deemed worthy political actors. Specifically, I would encourage all those in American politics to think more critically about the role and importance of gender and race in their own work. For example, if you somehow believe that studying Congress does not automatically include important questions concerning gender and race, especially as maleness and whiteness is constructed and privileged in that institution, then your understanding of the research is clearly limited. However, beyond mobilizing researchers, publishers and foundations must also be held accountable for the lack of representation and attention given to research on women of color. No longer can we allow foundations, principal investigators, and research institutes to design national surveys, hold large conferences, and make policy recommendations that only, at best, tangentially and periodically address the needs and experiences of women of color.

Finally, let me return to the point from which I began. While we have increased our knowledge about women of color in American politics, there is still much to learn. And as one might expect, it has been difficult to lay out a detailed research agenda for the future because so many of the basic building blocks are still absent. The particular role and history of women of color in American politics have yet to be even minimally explored, especially as we disaggregate the racial groups under examination. However, the lack of research on women of color must be addressed if we hope to make research on women a vehicle for change, as opposed to yet another exercise in academic passivity. We must remember that research on women of color in American politics can serve as an important bridge between academia and activism. It seems almost impossible to study women whose life chances are so intimately tied to systems of oppression and exploitation without also committing ourselves to making our research work toward their empowerment. Research on women of color and political participation provides us with a rare opportunity, not often found in political science, when the work we pursue could actually better the lives of those we study. I can only hope that some of us are willing to seize this opportunity.

❖ Notes

1 The title for this chapter comes from the ground-breaking book edited by Marianne Githens and Jewel L. Prestage, *A Portrait of Marginality: The Political Behavior of the American Woman.*

2 The author thanks Joshua Gamson, Alan Gerber, Lynne Huffer, Kathleen Jones, Tamara Jones, Alexis Lori McGill, and Deborah Minkoff for their helpful comments and assistance. All shortcomings are the full responsibility of the author.

3 Interestingly, while feminist scholars have long pointed out the political nature of, in particular, voluntary activity, it has only been recently at the urging of Robert Putnam, through his work on civil society, that members of the discipline have taken seriously this argument, demonstrated in the outpouring of recent research in this area.

4 By mainstream journals in the field of American politics, I mean journals such as the *American Political Science Review*, the *American Journal of Political Science*, and the *Journal of Politics.*

5 While the limited construction of issues of race in American politics and the over-all lack of documented knowledge limit my discussion of the participation and politics of women of color other than Black women, I also want to take responsibility for my own lack of knowledge/expertise in the lives and resistance of women of color outside of my chosen academic field of Black politics and outside my lived experience as a Black woman. This inability to transcend our limited groupings not only points to the in-adequacy of our educational systems and personal educational decisions, but also highlights the need to disaggregate the category of women of color and recognize the distinct and important issues to be identified and explored within the experiences of each group of women.

6 In addition to the authors mentioned in the text, other scholars more familiar to political scientists such as Mae C. King (1973), Shelby Lewis (1982), Alma M. Garcia (1980), and A. Mirande and E. Enriquez (1981), among others, have also examined the political and theoretical implications of multiple identities as embodied in women of color.

7 The U.S. Bureau of the Census, Current Population Reports P20-504, estimated that 66% of white men and 69% of white women were registered to vote in 1996. In the same year approximately 55% of white men and 55% of white women voted in the presidential election (Casper and Bass 1998).

8 There were 13 African American women, six Latinas, and one Asian American woman elected to the 107th U.S. Congress. Two additional female delegates served in that Congress. One was African American and the other was Caribbean American (Center for American Women and Politics 2001).

9 The racial breakdown of women of color serving as statewide elected officials in 2001 was as follows: one African American woman, two Latinas, one Native American

woman, and one Asian American woman (Center for American Women and Politics 2001).

10 One hundred eighty-two African American women, 56 Latinas, 20 Asian and Pacific Islander women, and 10 Native American women served as state legislators in 2001 (Center for American Women and Politics 2001).

11 Again, I want to remind the reader that in no way am I suggesting that there is too much work pursued on African American women. Instead, there has been far too little work pursued on *any* specific grouping of women of color. The fact remains, however, that most often when research has been initiated on women of color, it has centered disproportionately on the experiences of African American women.

❖ REFERENCES

Alex-Assensoh, Yvette, and Karin Stanford. 1997. "Gender, Participation and the Black Urban Underclass." In *Women Transforming Politics: An Alternative Reader*, ed. Cathy J. Cohen, Kathleen B. Jones, and Joan C. Tronto. New York: New York University Press.

Baxter, Sandra, and Marjorie Lansing. 1980. *Women and Politics: The Invisible Majority.* Ann Arbor: University of Michigan Press.

Bernstein, Alison. 1984. "A Mixed Record: The Political Enfranchisement of American Indian Women During the Indian New Deal." *Journal of the West* 23(3): 13–20.

Brischetto, Robert, and Rodolfo O. de la Garza. 1983. "The Mexican American Electorate: Political Participation and Ideology." Occasional Paper No. 3, *The Mexican American Electorate Series.* San Antonio: Southwest Voter Registration and Education Project.

Brown, Elsa Barkley. 1994. "Negotiating and Transforming the Public Sphere: African American Political Life in the Transition from Slavery to Freedom." *Public Culture* 7(1): 107–46.

Carroll, Susan J., and Wendy S. Strimling. 1983. *Women's Routes to Elective Office.* New Brunswick, NJ: Center for the American Woman and Politics.

Casper, Lynne M., and Loretta E. Bass. 1998. "Voting and Registration in the Election of November 1996," P20-504. *Current Population Reports.* United States Bureau of the Census. Washington, DC: U.S. Government Printing Office.

Center for American Women and Politics. 2001. "Women of Color in Elective Office 2001." Fact Sheet. New Brunswick, NJ: Center for American Women and Politics.

Chai, Alice. 1982. "Korean Women in Hawaii, 1903–1945." In *Asian and Pacific American Experiences: Women's Perspectives*, ed. Nobuya Tshchida. Minneapolis: Asian/Pacific American Learning Resource Center, University of Minnesota.

Chisolm, Shirley. 1970. *Unbought and Unbossed.* New York: Avon.

Chow, Esther Ngan-Ling. 1989. "The Feminist Movement: Where Are All the Asian American Women." In *Making Waves: An Anthology of Writings By and About Asian American Women*, ed. Asian Women United of California. Boston: Beacon Press.

Chu, Judy. 1989. "Asian Pacific American Women in Mainstream Politics. In *Making Waves: An Anthology of Writings By and About Asian American Women*, ed. Asian Women United of California. Boston: Beacon Press.

Cohen, Cathy J. 1999. *The Boundaries of Blackness: AIDS and the Breakdown of Black Politics.* Chicago: University of Chicago Press.

——Kathleen B. Jones, and Joan C. Tronto, eds. 1997. *Women Transforming Politics: An Alternative Reader.* New York: New York University Press.

Collins, Patricia Hill. 1990. *Black Feminist Thought: Knowledge, Consciousness, and the Politics of Empowerment.* Boston: Unwin Hyman.

——1998. *Fighting Words: Black Women and the Search for Justice.* Minneapolis: University of Minnesota Press.

Crawford, Vicki L., Jacqueline Anne Rouse, and Barbara Woods, eds. 1993. *Women in the Civil Rights Movement: Trailblazers and Torchbearers, 1941–1965.* Bloomington: Indiana University Press.

Crenshaw, Kimberle. 1991. "Mapping the Margins: Intersectionality, Identity Politics, and Violence Against Women of Color." *Stanford Law Review* 43(6): 1241–99.

Cruz Takash, Paule. 1997. "Breaking Barriers to Representation: Chicana/Latina Elected Officials in California." In *Women Transforming Politics: An Alternative Reader,* ed. Cathy J. Cohen, Kathleen B. Jones, and Joan C. Tronto. New York: New York University Press.

Darcy, R., Susan Welch, and Janet Clark. 1994. *Women, Elections and Representation.* Lincoln: University of Nebraska.

——Charles D. Hadley, and Jason F. Kirksey. 1997. "Election Systems and the Representation of Black Women in American Legislatures." In *Women Transforming Politics: An Alternative Reader,* ed. Cathy J. Cohen, Kathleen B. Jones, and Joan C. Tronto. New York: New York University Press.

Davis, Angela. 1971. "Reflections on the Black Woman's Role in the Community of Slaves." *Black Scholar* 3(December): 2–15.

DuBois, Ellen Carol, and Vicki L. Ruiz, eds. 1990. *Unequal Sisters: A Multicultural Reader in U.S. Women's History.* New York: Routledge.

Garcia, Mario T. 1980. "The Chicano in American History: The Mexican Women of El Paso, 1880–1920: A Case Study." *Pacific Historical Review* 49(May): 315–37.

Gay, Claudine, and Katherine Tate. 1998. "Doubly Bound: The Impact of Gender and Race on the Politics of Black Women." *Political Psychology* 19(1): 169–84.

Giddings, Paula. 1984. *When and Where I Enter: The Impact of Black Women on Race and Sex in America.* New York: William Morrow.

Githens, Marianne, and Jewel L. Prestige, eds. 1977. *A Portrait of Marginality: The Political Behavior of the American Woman.* New York: McKay.

Gordon, Ann D., with Bettye Collier-Thomas, John H. Bracey, Arlene Voski Avakian and Joyce Avrech Berkman, eds. 1997. *African American Women and the Vote 1837–1965.* Amherst, Mass.: University of Massachusetts Press.

Hardy-Fanta, Carol. 1993. *Latina Politics, Latino Politics: Gender, Culture, and Political Participation in Boston.* Philadelphia: Temple University Press.

Higginbotham, Evelyn Brooks. 1993. *Righteous Discontent, The Women's Movement in the Black Baptist Church, 1880–1920.* Cambridge, Mass.: Harvard University Press.

hooks, bell. 1984. *Feminist Theory: From Margin to Center.* Boston: South End Press.

Hopkins, Anne H. 1993. "Observations on Gender in Political Science and the Academy." *Journal of Politics* 55(3): 561–68.

Jackson, Byron. 1987. "The Effects of Racial Group Consciousness on Political Mobilization in American Cities." *Western Political Quarterly* 40(December): 631–46.

Jordan, Barbara, and Shelby Hearon. 1979. *Barbara Jordan: A Self-Portrait.* New York: Doubleday.

Junn, Jane. 1997. "Assimilating or Coloring Participation? Gender, Race, and Democratic Political Participation." In *Women Transforming Politics: An Alternative Reader*, ed. Cathy J. Cohen, Kathleen B. Jones, and Joan C. Tronto. New York: New York University Press.

King, Deborah. 1988. "Multiple Jeopardy, Multiple Consciousness: The Context of a Black Feminist Ideology." *Signs: Journal of Women in Culture and Society* 14(1): 42–72.

King, Mae C. 1973. "The Politics of Sexual Stereotypes." *Black Scholar* 14(March–April): 12–23.

Lansing, Marjorie. 1977. "The Voting Patterns of American Black Women." In *A Portrait of Marginality: The Political Behavior of the American Woman*, ed. M. Githens and J. L. Prestage. New York: McKay.

Lewis, Shelby. 1982. "A Liberation Ideology: The Intersection of Race, Sex and Class." In *Women Rights, Feminism and Politics in the United States*, ed. M. L. Shanley. Washington, DC: American Political Science Association.

Lynwiler, John, and David Gay. 1996. "The Abortion Attitudes of Black Women: 1971–1991." *Journal of Black Studies* 27(2): 260–77.

Mankiller, Wilma, and Michael Wallis. 1993. *Mankiller: A Chief and Her People.* New York: St. Martin's Press.

Mansbridge, Jane, and Katherine Tate. 1992. "Race Trumps Gender: Black Opinion on the Thomas Nomination." *PS: Political Science and Politics* 25: 494–511.

Marshall, Susan E. 1990. "Equity Issues and Black–White Differences in Women's ERA Support." *Social Science Quarterly* 71(2): 299–314.

McCoy, Melanie. 1992. "Gender or Ethnicity: What Makes a Difference? A Study of Women Tribal Leaders." *Women & Politics* 12(3): 57–68.

Mirande, Alfredo, with Evangelina Enriquez. 1981. *La Chicana: The Mexican–American Woman.* Chicago: University of Chicago Press.

Moncrief, Gary F., Joel A. Thompson, and Robert Schuhmann. 1991. "Gender, Race and the State Legislature: A Research Note on the Double Disadvantage Hypothesis." *Social Science Journal* 28(October): 481–87.

Montoya, Lisa J. 1996. "Latino Gender Differences in Public Opinion: Results from the Latino National Political Survey." *Hispanic Journal of Behavioral Sciences* 18(May): 255 76.

Pardo, Mary S. 1998. *Mexican American Women Activists: Identity and Resistance in Two Los Angeles Neighborhoods.* Philadelphia: Temple University Press.

Pateman, Carole. 1989. *The Disorder of Women: Democracy, Feminism, and Political Theory.* Stanford: Stanford University Press.

Powers, Marla N. 1986. *Oglala Women: Myth, Ritual and Reality.* Chicago: University of Chicago Press.

Prestage, Jewel L. 1991. "In Quest of the African American Political Woman." *The Annals of the American Academy of Political Science* 515(May): 88–103.

Prindeville, Diane-Michele, and John G. Bretting. 1998. "Indigenous Women Activists and Political Participation: The Case of Environmental Justice." *Women & Politics* 19(1): 39–58.

——and Teresa Braley Gomez. 1999. "American Indian Women Leaders, Public Policy, and the Importance of Gender and Ethnic Identity." *Women & Politics* 20(2): 17–32.

Robinson, Deborah M. 1987. "The Effect of Multiple Group Identity Among Black Women on Race Consciousness". Ph.D. diss. University of Michigan.

Robnett, Belinda. 1997. *How Long? How Long?: African American Women in the Struggle*. New York: Oxford University Press.

Ruiz, Vicki L. 1987. *Cannery Women/Cannery Lives: Mexican Women, Unionization, and the California Food Processing Industry, 1930–1950*. Albuquerque: University of New Mexico Press, 1987.

Rule, Wilma. 1992. "Multimember Legislative Districts: Minority and Anglo Women's and Men's Recruitment Opportunity." In *United States Electoral Systems: Their Impact on Women and Minorities*, ed. Wilma Rule and Joseph F. Zimmerman. New York: Greenwood.

Shukla, Shandhya. 1997. "Feminisms of the Disaspora Both Local and Global: The Politics of South Asian Women against Domestic Violence." In *Women Transforming Politics: An Alternative Reader*, ed. Cathy J. Cohen, Kathleen B. Jones, and Joan C. Tronto. New York: New York University Press.

U.S. Bureau of the Census. 1993. "Voting and Registration in the Election of November 1992," P20-466. *Current Population Reports*. Washington DC: U.S. Government Printing Office.

Virgil, Maurilio E. 1987. *Hispanics in American Politics: The Search for Political Power*. New York: University Press of America.

Welch, Susan, and Rebekah Herrick. 1992. "The Impact of At-Large Elections on the Representation of Minority Women." In *United States Electoral Systems: Their Impact on Women and Minorities*, ed. Wilma Rule and Joseph F. Zimmerman. New York: Greenwood Press.

White, Deborah G. 1999. *Too Heavy a Load: Black Women in Defense of Themselves, 1894–1994*. New York: W. W. Norton.

Wilcox, Clyde. 1990*a*. "Black Women and Feminism." *Women & Politics* 10(3): 55–84.

——1990*b*. "Race Differences in Abortion Attitudes: Some Additional Evidence." *Public Opinion Quarterly* 54: 248–55.

Zavella, Patricia. 1988. "The Politics of Race and Gender: Organizing Cannery Workers in Northern California." In *Women and the Politics of Empowerment*, ed. Sandra Morgen and Ann Bookman. Philadelphia: Temple University Press.

9 ❖ Broadening the Study of Women's Participation

Martha A. Ackelsberg

Why should we be concerned with broadening the study of women's participation in U.S. politics?[1] One might well argue that such efforts are unnecessary: rates of participation by women in conventional politics are rising and fast approaching those of men; women are making gains in the electoral–political arena, especially at the local level, but increasingly at the state and (though more slowly) federal levels. And, further, what have traditionally been defined as "women's issues"—ranging from access to abortion and birth control to maternity/parental leave to child care to healthcare to welfare to education—are making it onto the mainstream national political agenda. Isn't it sufficient to assume that these trends will continue and to go about measuring and/or studying women's participation in traditional channels—i.e., those addressed by other chapters in this volume, including recruitment of candidates, fundraising, the role of the media, the relationship to parties, issues of leadership, race and class differences, organizational strategies, and the like?

Yet, without diminishing the significance of these gains (and the importance of research that will allow us to explore their limits and what can be done to overcome them), it remains the case that a focus on the electoral arena, and on traditional forms of participation, offers us only a partial view of politics and participation in this country, and, in particular, the participation of women. For large numbers of women have been, and remain, active *outside* traditional political arenas—or in other than traditional ways. Such activities have a significant impact on the formal electoral/political arena and would be worth studying if only for those effects. But, as I have argued elsewhere (1988), these activities also constitute important forms of politics in themselves and deserve study, as such. Most basically, non-electoral forms of what is sometimes termed "collective behavior" (e.g., demonstrations, protests, the creation of alternative institutions) can exert pressure on mainstream organizations and may make them more amenable to change from traditionally structured groups.[2] At times the alternative organizations and/or modes of behavior they create can serve as models for, or challenges to, existing institutions and practices.[3] And, more broadly, these activities express ways of engagement with, or involvement in, the "public business" that effectively broaden our understandings of that "business," i.e., of politics, itself.

In short, and most immediately, broadening our study of women's participation is critical to an accurate understanding of the full range and extent of women's activism in what is generally termed public life. It challenges us to break through dichotomized ways of thinking about political participation versus social mobilization or collective behavior, for example, to recognize that "politics," properly understood, necessarily includes both and that, in fact, the distinction is more misleading than helpful. More significantly, and in the longer range, attention to a broader concept of *women's* participation has much to contribute to a rethinking of the meanings and practice of citizenship and participation for *everyone* as we prepare to meet the challenges of the twenty-first century.

❖ DEMOCRACY AND WOMEN'S PARTICIPATION: THE CHALLENGE OF THEORY AND HISTORY

❖ Public, Private, and the Definition of the Political

Much early feminist work, in both history and the social sciences, focused on the supposed separation between public and private domains, pointing out that the division obscured the exercise of power within the private realm, masked the maleness of the public realm, and ignored the relationship between the relegation of women to the private domain and their subordination in the public (see Rosaldo 1974; Bourque and Grossholtz 1974; Eisenstein 1978; Elshtain 1974). More recent work (e.g., Pateman 1988, 1989; Ackelsberg and Shanley 1996; Rosaldo 1980; Okin 1989; and Boling 1996) challenged that dichotomization further, pointing out the gendered nature of both public and private domains, and the interdependence of each on the other. And some critics have added to this discussion of the public/private dichotomy a related critique of the construction of the categories of "dependence" and "independence" as similarly gendered and raced (Ackelsberg 1994; Gordon and Fraser 1994; Nelson 1984; Mink 1990, 1995, 1998, 2000).

These dichotomies affect definitions of politics and participation in critical ways. Carole Pateman, for example, has argued (1979, 1980) that the concept of a social contract, which anchors U.S. political self-understanding, is grounded in a dichotomous (and gendered) understanding of public and private. The myth of a *social* contract, which purports to unite free and equal individuals, obscures the *sexual* contract on which it depends and which assures that both citizenship and the paid work that has come to be identified with "independence" are defined in totally male terms—and, further, depend on the support of women in the "private" realm. Our common understandings of both citizen and worker assume that each will have someone at home to take care of his needs and make it possible for him to work or to engage in public/political life.[4] Politics is "public business" that takes place in the "public" (i.e., male) domain. In short, our most basic understandings of citizenship and public participation, and the institutions through which they are realized and expressed, are gendered at their core. Women *cannot but remain* second-class citizens (a kind of support-staff of public life) as long as these institutions continue to define and structure our politics. On these grounds alone, then, we could make a claim for the necessity of "broadening the study of women's participation"!

Further, Pateman argues, the metaphors of consent and contract that ground our political institutions are flawed in other ways as well. At best, we as citizens have the option of voting or not voting, but we have little role in defining or structuring what will be voted on, or whether we consent to a regime as such. While she draws on metaphors of male–female relationships, Pateman's critique of contract—and of contractual understandings of political life—goes considerably beyond questions of gender:

> Consent must always be given *to* something; in the relationship between the sexes, it is always women who are held to consent to men . . . An egalitarian sexual relationship cannot rest on this basis; it cannot be grounded in "consent". . . . Perhaps the most telling aspect of the problem of women and consent is that we lack a language through which to help constitute a form of personal life in which two equals freely agree to create a lasting association together. ([1980] 1989, 84; also 1988, 183–88)

If that is true for marriage, however, the force of her argument is that it is similarly true for social and political relationships: no more do we have a language through which to help constitute a form of *social* life in which *any* equals (*however differently constituted*) freely agree to create lasting relationships. The limits of consent and equality in marriage, then, point also to the limits of consent and equality in liberal democratic politics. We need new models and new metaphors to constitute a more broadly inclusive and democratic politics. Attention to women's participation in a wide range of activities may give us some clues as to how to move beyond the limits of existing models and practices of democracy (on this point see also Ackelsberg 1988).

❖ Activism without Access: Women and the Welfare State

Related to this questioning of the construction of politics and democracy in the liberal state (and the U.S. in particular) is a series of questions about "the state" and its relation to women. In its broadest formulation, the question takes the form: "Is the state an arena for the domination of women or for their empowerment?" The literature on this topic is vast, and much of it focuses on the construction and operation of welfare state policies and programs.[5] Early work by Frances Fox Piven (1984; Piven and Cloward 1982) and Zillah Eisenstein (1984), for example, argued that welfare programs arose from women's struggles and have provided important contexts for women's empowerment. These perspectives were challenged by Jean Elshtain (1983, 1984), Isaac Balbus (1982), Kathy Ferguson (1984), Irene Diamond (1994), and others, who focused on the welfare system as a site for the bureaucratic and disciplinary regulation of sexuality and family life.

Recent work by a wide range of authors has continued to explore this complex and multi-faceted relationship, noting the role of welfare policies and institutions in controlling women at the same time that it emphasizes women's roles in the *construction* of those same welfare state policies. The issues here are many and can only be touched on briefly in a paper of this length. These recent studies begin from a recognition that neither power nor participation can most effectively be studied in dichotomous ways: modern social and political life is complex and ambiguous. Practices are neither *simply* emancipatory nor simply oppressive.[6] Nevertheless, and at the same time, these scholars point to women's roles in opening up new avenues for women's participation—and, importantly, for dramatically changing societal understandings of the domain of politics itself—even at a time when women, themselves, were denied formal access to mainstream politics. As William Chafe put it, "women's history [of the Progressive Era] has caused scholars to reconsider the definition of politics itself, broadening that area of inquiry to include informal networks of influence that helped shape public policy and highlighting the intersection of the personal and the political" (1993, 102).

Thus, Seth Koven and Sonya Michel (1990), Barbara Nelson (1990*a*, 1990*b*), Gwendolyn Mink (1990, 1995, 1998), Theda Skocpol (1992), Kathryn Kish Sklar (1993), Wendy Sarvasy (1992, 1997), and Linda Gordon (1994*a*, 1994*b*), among others, have all explored the roles of women in creating what came to be major welfare state programs, especially AFDC, Social Security, unemployment benefits, and Workman's Compensation. None of these studies sees women's accomplishments as unproblematic: the institutions they created were fundamentally structured by race and class even as they attempted to address the problems of relatively powerless women and children. Nevertheless, each study also provides important evidence of the ways women's activities outside the formal political realm (since women did not have official access to that realm) were critical to the development of these institutions.

In fact, attention to women's activism does much more than provide information about the construction of the U.S. welfare state: it offers clues to a fuller understanding of the changing nature and practices of politics and citizenship. Thus, Suzanne Lebsock, focusing on the broad range of women's voluntary associations in the nineteenth century, argues that "long before they [women] were voters, they were political actors" (1990, 35). Through their activism, the WCTU, club women (white and black), settlement house workers, labor union activists, "direct action radicals" such as Emma Goldman, Margaret Sanger, and Elizabeth Gurley Flynn, and suffragists "helped change the political landscape in the forty years surrounding the turn of the century" (1990, 36). Paula Baker (1990) has suggested that the ideology (and practice) of separate spheres— that defined "politics" as male and "domesticity" as female while exclud- ing women from formal electoral/political participation—effectively created a separate arena of women's politics characterized by voluntarism and an atten- tion to social needs. As white women were eventually included in the formal political arena, they brought with them this penchant for voluntary association (rather than party-type organization) and an attention to "social issues", both of which profoundly influenced the practice of politics in the United States (see also Hewitt 1984, 1993). Black women—effectively excluded from formal political participation in many areas until the mid-1960s—nevertheless continued to perform important "public" work in their communities, to raise issues, and to create institutions to meet communal needs (Gilkes 1980, 1988; White 1993; Hine 1993).[7] Women's activism broadened the shape and domain of politics, and eventually redefined what counted as "political" for everyone. Sarvasy (1992, 1997; see also Lebsock 1990; Baker 1990; Hewitt 1993) draws on this history (with all its race and class biases!) to argue that women's activism in the early part of this century offers us a manifestation of "social citizenship" that can provide important models for contemporary revisionings.[8] In short, we cannot properly understand "politics," let alone political change, unless we broaden our understanding of the varieties of (women's) participation to include activities which, at any given moment, might well be considered "beyond the pale."

❖ "Insiders" and "Outsiders"

As I suggested earlier, attention to those activities considered "outrageous" and "inappropriate" has been another important focus of feminist research and revisionism in the study of American politics. On the one hand, as any number of studies have suggested, branding certain types of activities "disorderly" or "unseemly" has been a way both of excluding women (and others) from formal political life and of denying the *political* significance of activities they have undertaken (Banfield 1974; Hall 1986; Hall et al. 1987; Ackelsberg 1991; Tobias 1997; Kaplan 1997; Naples 1998a, 1998b; Rosen 2000). Thus, it is important to examine the boundaries of what is considered appropriate political behavior, for they both define its limits and offer an opportunity to explore differences in those limits by race, class, or gender.

In addition, other feminists have directed our attention to the relationship between "radicals" and "traditionalists," or between those who work "inside" and those who work "outside" formal political institutions. While, as Mary Katzenstein (1990, 1998) reminds us, women are never wholly inside, nor wholly outside institutions, nevertheless, there are differences in strategies and tactics between those who operate in "protest" modes and those who try to work within institutions (what she has termed "unobtrusive mobilization"). Her work (1998), and that of Joyce Gelb (1989), Gelb and Marian Palley (1987), Viven Hart (1994), Janet Flammang (1997), Cathy Cohen (1999), and Sheila Tobias (1997) remind us of the complicated relationships among women "inside" and those "outside," and their interdependence. Once again, they insist, we cannot fully comprehend the success and failure, or even the strategies and tactics, of those inside institutions if we fail to take account of their relationships with (or, at the very least, awareness of) those acting more autonomously, or in more contestatory modes outside them. Or, to put it more generally, we cannot assume that there is a dichotomous distinction between "insider" politics and that of "outsiders"; as in so many other areas, feminist explorations point to the ways that dichotomous assumptions can blind us to the much more complex character of political life.

❖ Questions/Topics for Further Research

This brief theoretical and historically oriented overview has demonstrated the importance of broadening the study of women's participation. Feminist historians and sociologists have pioneered the exploration of "women's culture and politics," and have, as I have suggested, increasingly attempted to draw out the implications of women's activities in this broader context for politics and social change in the more narrowly constructed arena. But feminist political scientists have been somewhat slower to take up this challenge, especially with respect to studies of contemporary U.S. activism. Much feminist political science research still focuses primarily on questions of who gets involved in elections, parties, running for office, lobbying politicians, or working in the bureaucracy. While there are studies of contemporary grassroots movements, few have seriously addressed their implications for politics and citizenship more generally.[9]

One of the main reasons for this narrowness of focus has to do with methodological biases within the discipline of political science itself, and especially within the field of U.S. politics. Since the 1950s, the study of U.S. politics has been dominated by the "behavioral" approach—a focus on quantitative studies, based on survey research, of supposedly "objective" phenomena, such as voting patterns, rates of turnout, party identification, and comparative measures of "interest" in politics. Since these methodologies defined (and continue to define) the discipline for years—affecting, for example, patterns of research funding and evaluation of research for purposes of tenure and promotion—a great deal of feminist research on women and politics has conformed to this norm. Of course, feminist behavioral research in political science differs from traditional mainstream work in its insistence on the significance of examining *women's* particular patterns of participation and the ways they are similar to, or different from, those of men (e.g., Amundsen 1977; Beckwith 1986; Baxter and Lansing 1983; Phillips 1991). Nevertheless, as Janet Flammang has noted, studies undertaken with quantitative methodologies necessarily focus on actions and behaviors and have tended to be much less concerned with the *meanings* people (and especially women) attach to those behaviors (Flammang 1997, especially chs. 3–4; see also Hawkesworth 1989; Hekman 1987).

In order to address the sorts of questions that historians and theorists have raised for us—questions that, I am arguing, are necessary for a fuller under-standing of women's participation in politics—scholars will need to challenge the dominance of these narrowly quantitative methodologies and to supple-ment them with more qualitative methods, including participant observation, interviews, and case studies. Ferree and Miller would take the methodological challenges even further: "analysis of participation in terms of cognitive struc-ture and organizational strategies of recruitment, rather than in terms of the specific motives *or* incentives individuals have for joining movements, reintro-duces the old problem of participation in a new and potentially productive manner" (1985, 55). Of course, given the hegemony of behavioral methods within the discipline as a whole, these new approaches will probably not meet with easy acceptance. Nevertheless, as recent works amply demonstrate, they have much to offer, not only to the study of women and politics specifically, but also to the broader study of political science (see, for example, Cohen, Jones, and Tronto 1997; Cohen 1999; Sparks 1997; Brettschneider 1996; Buker 1987; Ferguson 1988).

I will suggest four general areas in which new research might be undertaken and then look more specifically at the issues to be addressed under each rubric: (1) What are the patterns of women's mobilization into politics: who gets involved and why? (2) What are the patterns of consciousness-change: what happens to those who participate in "non-traditional" political activism? what is the relationship between grassroots activism and "politicization" more gener-ally? (3) How do we evaluate the effectiveness of various strategies and/or approaches to activism, e.g., "outsiders" vs. "insiders," efforts to create alterna-tive institutions, protest vs. policy-making? and (4) What are the places where we are "stuck" either theoretically or politically, and can the study of non-traditional forms of participation contribute to addressing these dilemmas?

❖ Martha A. Ackelsberg

❖ *Mobilization: Who Gets Involved in Activism and Why?*

Over the past decade or so, historians and feminist theorists have offered a variety of models to explain patterns of participation (or nonparticipation) by women. Temma Kaplan claimed that many women are mobilized/activated by what she termed "female consciousness" (the understanding of what it is to be a woman that is specific to a particular culture and historical moment), a perspective that, although derived from prevailing sexual divisions of labor, may nevertheless generate compelling concepts of rights and obligations that can provide a context for quite radical collective action. And, she suggested, under certain circumstances, relatively conservative "female consciousness" can be transformed into a more contestatory "feminist consciousness" (Kaplan 1980, see also 1997). Others have argued that it is women's concern for the safety and continuity of their families and communities that seems to engage them in political activity. Sara Ruddick (1989) and Jean Elshtain (1982, 1983) have suggested that it is not so much a female consciousness as "maternal thinking" that characterizes the worldview of many women activists and provides a framework for understanding their mobilization and goals.

Mary Dietz, by contrast, has suggested (1985, 1987) that both female consciousness and maternal thinking are too limited in focus and that women are activated by (and ought to be mobilized around) notions of citizenship and inclusivity. Darlene Clark Hine (1993), Cheryl Gilkes (1988), Nancy Naples (1998*a*), Deborah Gray White (1993), and others have argued that, in the case of many black women activists, a key mobilizing factor is some notion of "race uplift." And, as we have seen, Wendy Sarvasy has suggested (1997) that what motivated many women activists in the early years of this century was a notion of "social citizenship," which might be seen as another version of what Jane Addams referred to as "municipal housekeeping."

Studies of women activists could explore whether any of these perspectives are helpful in understanding either patterns of mobilization or the construction of agendas for activism. Further, are there differences in patterns of engagement, or in grounds of mobilization, by race? class? age? region? Do participants' understandings of the grounds of their participation change over time? as a consequence of activism? in what ways? Do some of these perspectives/ideologies appeal to particular groups more than to others? If so, which ones, and why?

There is room here for both historical and contemporary studies. Existing historical studies of communities and organizations can be reexamined for what light they shed on patterns of mobilization and for what they say about the relationship between the larger cultural/political context and women's participation. Do openings in more formal electoral or bureaucratic arenas seem to mean more or less nontraditional participation by women? Are there

variations by class, race, or ethnicity? What is the relationship between changing definitions of politics and women's participation in both formal and informal arenas? New studies of women's organizations might focus on some of
these questions with an eye to their implications for participants' understandings of politics, participation, and citizenship. Do those who engage in so-called
non-traditional forms of participation see it as second-best to electoral participation? Or do they see themselves as engaging in "politics by other means"? Do
they understand themselves to be engaging in a critique of "normal politics" or
to be struggling to change definitions of "the political"?

Beyond these questions is that of the contexts in which women *come* to
politics: do their paths follow those predicted/described by pluralist models
(i.e., of coming to an awareness of an interest, finding others who share it, and
joining with them to insert their interest into the general political fray)? Or,
does (women's) activism reflect a different understanding of the relationship
between individuals, communities, and politics?[10] In some of my earlier work, I
suggested that much women's activism belies both the distinction between
public and private and the extreme individualism which ground dominant
theories of political behavior. And I argued that attention to women's activism
could lead us to question the relevance of those individualist models to men as
well as to women, leading perhaps to broader understandings of citizenship.
Research on women who are engaged in such activities could help to shatter
false dichotomies and determine whether the apparent challenges to these ways
of thinking and to individualist understandings of mobilization into politics
hold more broadly, and what their applications might be for how we understand both the domain of politics and the possibilities of citizenship.

❖ Patterns of Consciousness Change

What happens to participants once they engage in political activism, however
defined? Temma Kaplan wrote (1980, 564) of the possibility of a shift from
"female consciousness" to "feminist consciousness" as activism contributes to a
consciousness of broader political issues. Other studies of activists have suggested that a sense of empowerment comes from engaging with others in collective action. As one of Cynthia Cockburn's informants expressed it (1977, 67),
"when you start getting involved, you find you're not a cabbage any more.
You've got a mind and can do things . . ." How common are such transforma-
tions? of a sense of self? in relation to other family members? to the larger
community? to other organizations? to the political system more generally?
What are the contexts in which such changes occur? What factors in the
social/political context affect the likelihood of that transformation, and how do
they vary by class, ethnicity, race, age, and sexual orientation? Do the patterns or
processes differ between formal and informal types of participation?

❖ MARTHA A. ACKELSBERG

And what about that broader consciousness, or sense of empowerment, the recognition that one is "not a cabbage anymore"? Does it transfer from one issue to another? Can we talk of people or groups empowered by their experiences in ways that change their orientation to politics and participation more generally? Or, to put it another way, is activism "addictive"? Many studies of politics and participation have suggested that *unsuccessful* activism has serious negative consequences—i.e., that those with experiences of protest without success are more likely than ever to be resigned to their fate (e.g., Lipsky 1968; Parenti 1970; Piven and Cloward 1977). Can these factors be overcome? Is *any* success better than none? Does the significance of the issues addressed matter (see, for example, Castells 1983, chs. 6, 13, 15, 25–26; Alinsky 1969; Katznelson 1981; Medoff and Sklar 1994)? What is the relationship (if any) between "cooptation" and consciousness-change? Does a changed consciousness lead to less likelihood of cooptation (as some studies might suggest)? What do we mean by "cooptation" in this sense? Do we understand it to mean (as many critics do) entry into the more formal or traditional political arena? If so, do we need to rethink its connotations?

More generally, it would also be important to know about crossover or carry-over between grassroots/oppositional activism and more mainstream participation. Participation in civil rights movement organizations is one sort of case: there are well-known examples of male activists moving from civil rights movement organizations into electoral politics (e.g., Julian Bond, Jesse Jackson) and also of white women, for example, moving from activism in the civil rights movement into more explicitly feminist activities. The consequences of women's participation in the National Welfare Rights Organization, however, are much less well known. Although that organization had been established mainly by black male activists, the majority of its activists were women recipients of AFDC. Many of them, apparently, were politicized by their experiences and experienced themselves as more effective politically as a result of their participation. It would be important to explore further both what happened to their consciousness about the nature and meaning of politics and what effect their participation had on their later activism in other contexts.[11] How many women become active in their neighborhood or community in collective actions of one sort or another (e.g., school-related issues, environmental concerns, abortion rights, and healthcare) and move from that into more conventional politics? What factors make such crossovers likely? or unlikely? Are there different patterns for people who get involved in different issues? Do patterns differ by age, race, class, sexual orientation? Are there differences between women and men? In short, do participants see these various forms of participation along a continuum (challenging, in yet another context, dichotomous ways of thinking about participation), or do they perceive a stepwise difference between grassroots and mainstream politics?

Finally, and related to this, what is the relationship between grassroots activism (or collective action) and politicization more generally? How, if at all, does participation in activities outside of the mainstream political arena affect women's overall interest in politics? Does it affect patterns of voting? of lobbying? of following local or national issues? Again, is there a continuum of politics that effectively includes informal, as well as formal, participation? Are there differences in awareness, in behavior, in attitudes between those who are engaged in mainstream institutions and practices and those who engage in more non-traditional forms? What institutional/structural factors affect mobilization into different types of activism or the change in consciousness that does (or does not) take place as a result of it? Is the distinction that political scientists (and many politicians) tend to make between activism in organizations *versus* electoral participation a valid or helpful one?

❖ *Alternative Strategies: Strengths and Limits*

One set of questions concerning strategies has to do with the relationship between the "insiders"—those working as elected policy-makers and bureaucrats (policy implementers)—and "outsiders"—protesters, demonstrators, those who attempt to establish alternative institutions, and the like. Rather than pose the question of the relative value of insider vs. outsider perspectives—thereby reinforcing a dichotomous understanding of these phenomena—I think the more fruitful research would look at the relationship between the two modes or contexts of activism. Gelb (1989), Gelb and Palley (1987), Katzenstein (1998), and Hart (1994), for example, all point to the mutual interdependence of activists outside institutions and insiders. The activists need people in positions of authority and/or responsiblity within institutions who can put into effect the policies they desire; the insiders need external pressure groups both to serve as support networks for them and to keep pressure on the institutions. More research needs to be done as to what these relationships are, how the different groups perceive their roles, and what they count as successes. Also, how do those relationships vary with the different dimensions of policy-making—e.g., getting issues onto the agenda, legislating or otherwise formulating policy, and implementing policy? What are the relationships among women (and women's groups) at each stage? How do they vary? Do they change with different policy domains?

What about different *forms* of activism? At the turn of the century, women were active both in lobbying those with political power to address social issues such as women's labor, child labor, and the needs of poor mothers at the same time that they (or others) were developing programs and institutions to meet some of the needs not being addressed by social policy. In our own day, there are those who create shelters for battered women, set up abortion/birth control clinics, develop assistance for those "squatting" in abandoned housing, or build housing for homeless women and their families; those who protest and lobby and devote their energies to getting these issues onto the public/political agenda; others who lobby policy-makers to ensure that those issues on the agenda will actually be translated into meaningful programs; and still others who are in positions to develop and implement these policy changes. What do relationships look like in each context? Are different types of activism more or less effective in different contexts? How does each group of actors view the others? their relationships? the political process as a whole?

How do these different types of participation affect contemporary understandings of the boundaries of politics? What kinds of activities tend to be labelled "disorderly" or "inappropriate"? Does the application of those labels vary with the class, race, age, or sexual orientation of the participants? Does participation initally labelled disorderly become accepted as orderly or appropriate? If so, how? What is the process? What is the relationship between disorderly participants and political insiders? When, and how, have nontraditional forms of participation broadened the boundaries of politics—either by widening the definition of what constitutes legitimate political action/participation or by forcing the inclusion of new issues onto the political agenda?

❖ Activism and Contemporary Theoretical Dilemmas

Finally, can broadening the study of women's participation contribute anything to the resolution of (or at least to addressing) some of the critical issues confronting contemporary feminist activists, politicians, and theorists? Here, I would mention two arenas in particular although there are surely many more.

Tensions surrounding "identity politics" and coalition-building. Both at the level of theorizing, and at the level of political practice, many groups—feminist and otherwise—have been caught up in attempting to address questions of equality and difference among women. These questions, of course, followed from those with which feminists initially engaged: questions of equality/difference between women and men. Early efforts focused on what differences "made a difference." That is to say, feminists recognized that men and women were socialized differently in most societies and that they differed along biological/genetic lines. Much early feminist work addressed questions such as how relevant biological differences were to gender-based patterns of dominance and subordination. On what grounds could one argue for equality between men and women while acknowledging the ways the differences between them might well require different treatment (e.g., Rosaldo and Lamphere 1974; Butler and Scott 1992; Rhode 1990; Kessler-Harris 1985, 1994)? More recently, analogous questions have arisen with respect to differences (of class, sexuality, race/ethnicity, age) *among* women. Growing numbers of feminists—especially those who are not white, middle-class, able-bodied, Christians—argue that too much feminist theorizing and activism presupposes some notion of a "universal woman," analogous to that of "universal man," independent of any cultural/ethnic/class context—a notion that, in fact, denies the complex ways in which gender, race, class, sexuality, and ethnicity are socially structured and mutually interdependent. At the same time, much postmodernist, post-structuralist feminist theorizing challenges the usefulness of fixed identity categories of any sort. The question these critiques pose for feminist theorizing—and for studies of women's participation—is a critical one: How can we move toward some sort of broad-based solidarity among women without, on the one hand, denying the differences of class, race, ethnicity, sexuality, and so forth that exist among us or, on the other hand, reifying them and turning them into immutable and unbridgeable differences?[12]

We can find important clues to an answer by looking at the real political activities in which people (especially women) have engaged. With a few exceptions, we have not looked as carefully as we might at those moments where people from a variety of "identity categories" have engaged in real-life political struggle and resistance. We ought to be looking at grassroots participation around issues such as housing cost and availability, school desegregation, and toxic wastes as resources for theory. Much, I think, can be learned from those who are acting and attempting to effect change—people who work with others who share various identity characteristics and at the same time form coalitions on the basis of those characteristics with others "unlike" themselves—even while experiencing the contingent and contested nature of their identities.[13]

Attention to such activities can also help us think about the relationship between identity(ies), activism, and coalition-building. What is the relationship between political participation (whether in the broad or narrow sense) and identity? Does grassroots participation engage and/or affect participants with respect to issues of identity differently than does electoral participation?[14] Is there a relationship between participation in politics, however defined, and willingness to engage in coalition-building? If so, in what direction? Is there a difference in the effects of traditional vs. non-traditional participation on these sorts of changes?

Creating alternatives to contemporary policy. Politically, we are at a major turning point in national policy debates about health care, welfare reform, and violence; racism, education, and the persistence of poverty in the midst of affluence, while not formally part of the discussions, have also been on the public consciousness. We have also seen that there are real limits to the boundaries of those debates and to the creativity and imagination apparently available to policy-makers (and even policy analysts and critics). And yet, there are groups and organizations of women who have been addressing these issues "on the ground" for years—contemporary equivalents of the club women of the late-nineteenth and early-twentieth centuries, of the settlement house workers, of those who were attempting to establish what Wendy Sarvasy (1992, 1997) refers to as "social citizenship." As historians look back on that period, they now recognize (e.g., Chafe 1993; Lebsock 1990; Baker 1990; Sklar 1993) that activities that were *not* seen as "political" then were, in fact, essential components of the larger political landscape and had important implications for what eventually met more narrow definitions of politics.

While the larger context of political participation has certainly changed since then, there are, nevertheless, contemporary equivalents of those actors: those who are building housing for homeless women and their children, those who are members of organizations like Arise (a low-income and poor people's rights organization in Springfield, Massachusetts, that focuses on community organizing around welfare rights, health care reform, criminal justice, grassroots strategies to end violence against women, housing and homelessness issues, and the like). Cynthia Enloe has commented ironically, in another context (1993, 39), that "the more a government is preoccupied with what it calls national security, the less likely its women are to have the physical safety necessary for sharing their theorizing about the nation and their security within it." But this is true not only in the case of national security issues; the same could be said of us: have we looked to the women who are organizing around these issues for any directions in policy-making? I suspect that the answer is, "Not nearly as much as we might." After all, they are neither politicians nor policy-makers, and most of their activity is taking place outside what we tend to recognize as the political arena. But that does not mean that there is not much we might learn from it; studies of women's activism in these areas might well help expand our limited imaginations with respect to policy, just as women's activism at the turn of the twentieth century dramatically affected understandings of what issues were appropriate to politics and what could be done to address them.

In a variety of ways, then, a broadened study of women's participation becomes an essential component of any research agenda on women in American politics in the twenty-first century. Broadening the range of our attention will certainly make possible a more textured understanding of what happens (and why) within the traditional domain of politics. But there is more. Historically, women's participation has created new spaces for politics and dramatically expanded our understandings of what politics is about. There is no reason to expect any less from contemporary activism (by both women and men). In the end, I would argue, such attention has the potential not only to assist in addressing some critical problems, but also to expand and deepen our perspectives on the nature and possibilities of politics and citizenship in the twenty-first century.

❖ NOTES

1 I am grateful to Janet Flammang, Carol Hardy-Fanta, and other participants in the conference on "Research on Women and American Politics: Agenda-Setting for the Twenty-First Century" for engaging conversations and helpful comments on earlier drafts of this paper.

2 See, e.g., Gelb and Palley 1987 and Katzenstein 1998.

3 I have in mind here such activities as Margaret Sanger's birth control clinics in the early years of this century in the U.S.; the children's aid programs and mothers' support groups that volunteer clubwomen established in both the U.S. and Western Europe at roughly the same time and that served as "models" for later government programs; the battered women's shelter movement; and many others. I discuss this phenomenon in more detail below.

4 Pateman 1988. On the complicated (and changing) relationship between economic self-support and citizenship in the United States, see also Shklar 1991. For a more extended discussion of these issues, see Ackelsberg 1998.

5 Irene Diamond and I (1987, 512–14) summarized some of the contours of this debate; see also Ackelsberg 1992, 2001; Mink 1995, 1998; and Gordon 1994*a*, 1994*b*.

6 See, e.g., Cohen 1985, especially 712–16; this perspective is, of course, as critical to the work of Michel Foucault and his followers as it is to Habermas on whose analysis Cohen draws.

7 Note also the work of Mary Church Terrell ([1904] 1990) and Ida B. Wells Barnett ([1893] 1990, [1901] 1977, and 1970) on anti-lynching struggles.

8 There has also been an enormous amount of feminist writing in recent years on reconceptualizing citizenship, writings that address many questions related to the definition and "contents" of politics. See, among others, Lister 1997; Sparks 1997; Bickford 1997; Rosen 2000; Mouffe 1996; Mansbridge 1996; Phillips 1991; Fraser 1989, 1997; Benhabib 1996; Calhoun 1997. See also Ackelsberg 2001 and sources reviewed there.

9 Some exceptions to this generalization include Hardy-Fanta 1993; Sparks 1997; Cohen 1999; Flammang 1997; and Cohen, Jones, and Tronto 1997.

10 Writings on the civil rights movement and its rootedness in existing community networks represent one counter to this perspective. Do the same findings hold, for example, for the women who became active in the National Welfare Rights Organization? Other movements and organizations located primarily within the African American community? What about other ethnic/minority-based organizations? Some clues may be found in recent studies reported in Blee 1998; Jetter, Orleck, and Taylor 1997; Naples 1998*b*.

11 Nancy Naples' recent book (1998*a*) provides some fascinating material for such a study. On the women of the welfare rights movement themselves, see West 1981; Hertz 1977; Pope 1990.

❖ MARTHA A. ACKELSBERG

12 The citations here could easily fill a book. The classics include Lorde 1984; Lewis 1977; Simons 1979; Dill 1983; Lugones and Spelman 1983; Beck 1989; Klepfisz 1990; Kaye/Kantrowitz 1992. For a recent attempt to incorporate these perspectives into a politics of "specificity," see Phelan 1994. I explored these issues at greater length in Ackelsberg 1996.

13 See, e.g., Brettschneider 1996, Introduction.

14 There is an extensive and growing literature on patterns and/or determinants of women's participation in politics. See Payne 1990; Romer 1990; Katzenstein and Mueller 1987; and more recently, Flammang 1997; Cohen, Jones, and Tronto 1997.

❖ REFERENCES

Ackelsberg, Martha. 1988. "Communities, Resistance, and Women's Activism: Some Implications for a Democratic Polity." In *Women and the Politics of Empowerment*, ed. Ann Bookman and Sandra Morgen. Philadelphia: Temple University Press.

——1991. *Free Women of Spain: Anarchism and the Struggle for the Emancipation of Women*. Bloomington: Indiana University Press.

——1992. "Review Essay: Feminist Analyses of Public Policy." *Comparative Politics* 24: 477–93.

——1994. "Dependency or Mutuality: A Feminist Perspective on Dilemmas of Welfare Reform." *Rethinking Marxism* 7: 73–86.

——1996. "Identity Politics, Political Identities: Thoughts Toward a Multicultural Politics." *Frontiers: A Journal of Women's Studies* 16: 87–100.

——1998. "Embracing Ambiguities: Exclusivity, Inclusivity, Activism and Citizenship." Paper presented at the 1998 Annual Meeting of the American Political Science Association, Boston.

——2001. "(Re)Conceiving Politics? Women's Activism and Democracy in a Time of Retrenchment." *Feminist Studies* 27(2): 391–418.

——and Irene Diamond. 1987. "Gender and Political Life: New Directions in Political Science." In *Analyzing Gender: A Handbook of Social Science Research*, ed. Beth B. Hess and Myra Marx Ferree. Newbury Park: Sage.

——and Mary Lyndon Shanley. 1996. "Privacy, Publicity and Power: A Feminist Rethinking of the Public-Private Distinction." In *Revisioning the Political: Feminist Reconstructions of Traditional Concepts in Western Political Theory*, ed. Nancy Hirschman and Christine DiStefano. Boulder, Colo.: Westview Press.

Alinsky, Saul. 1969. *Rules for Radicals*. New York: Random House.

Amundsen, Kristen. 1977. *A New Look at the Silenced Majority*. Englewood Cliffs, NJ: Prentice-Hall.

Baker, Paula. 1990. "The Domestication of Politics: Women and American Political Society, 1780–1920." In *Women, the State, and Welfare*, ed. Linda Gordon. Madison: University of Wisconsin Press.

Balbus, Isaac. 1982. *Marxism and Domination*. Princeton: Princeton University Press.

Banfield, Edward C. 1974. "Rioting Mainly for Fun and Profit." In *The Unheavenly City Revisited*, ed. Edward C. Banfield. Boston: Little, Brown.

Baxter, Sandra, and Marjorie Lansing. 1983. *Women and American Politics: The Visible Majority.* Ann Arbor: University of Michigan Press.

Beck, Evelyn Torton, ed. 1989. *Nice Jewish Girls: A Lesbian Anthology.* Revised and updated ed. Boston: Beacon Press.

Beckwith, Karen. 1986. *American Women and Political Participation.* New York: Greenwood Press.

Benhabib, Seyla, ed. 1996. *Democracy and Difference: Contesting the Boundaries of the Political.* Princeton: Princeton University Press.

Bickford, Susan. 1997. "Anti-Anti-Identity Politics: Feminism, Democracy and the Complexities of Citizenship." *Hypatia* 12(4): 111–31.

Blee, Kathleen, ed. 1998. *No Middle Ground: Women and Radical Protest.* New York: New York University Press.

Boling, Patricia. 1996. *Privacy and the Politics of Intimate Life.* Ithaca, NY: Cornell University Press.

Bourque, Susan C., and Jean Grossholtz. 1974. "Politics an Unnatural Practice: Political Science Looks at Women's Participation." *Politics and Society* 4: 225–66.

Boyte, Harry. 1995. "Beyond Deliberation: Citizenship as Public Work." *The Good Society* 5(2): 15–19.

Brettschneider, Marla, ed., 1996. *The Narrow Bridge: Jewish Perspectives on Multiculturalism.* New Brunswick: Rutgers University Press.

Buker, Eloise. 1987. "Storytelling Power: Personal Narratives and Political Analysis." *Women & Politics* 7: 29–46.

Butler, Judith, and Joan Scott. 1992. *Feminists Theorize the Political.* New York: Routledge.

Calhoun, Craig, ed. 1997. *Habermas and the Public Sphere.* Cambridge, Mass.: MIT Press.

Castells, Manuel. 1983. *The City and the Grassroots.* Berkeley: University of California Press.

Chafe, William. 1993. "Women's History and Political History." In *Visible Women: New Essays on American Activism,* ed. Nancy A. Hewitt and Suzanne Lebsock. Urbana, Ill., and Chicago: University of Illinois Press.

Cockburn, Cynthia. 1977. "When Women Get Involved in Community Action." In *Women in the Community,* ed. Marjorie Mayo. London: Routledge and Kegan Paul.

Cohen, Cathy J. 1999. *The Boundaries of Blackness: AIDS and the Breakdown of Black Politics.* Chicago: University of Chicago Press.

——Kathleen B. Jones, and Joan Tronto, eds. 1997. *Women Transforming Politics: An Alternative Reader.* New York: New York University Press.

Cohen, Jean. 1985. "Strategy or Identity: New Theoretical Paradigms and Contemporary Social Movements." *Social Research* 52: 663–716.

Diamond, Irene. 1994. *Fertile Ground.* Boston: Beacon Press.

Dietz, Mary. 1985. "Citizenship with a Feminist Face." *Political Theory* 13: 19–37.

——1987. "Context Is All: Feminism and Theories of Citizenship." *Daedalus:* 1–24.

Dill, Bonnie Thornton. 1983. "Race, Class and Gender: Prospects for an All-Inclusive Sisterhood." *Feminist Studies* 9: 131–50.

Eisenstein, Zillah, ed. 1978. *Capitalist Patriarchy and the Case forSocialist Feminism.* New York: Monthly Review Press.

—— 1984. *Feminism and Sexual Equality: Crisis in Liberal America.* New York: Monthly Review Press.

Elshtain, Jean. 1974. "Moral Woman and Immoral Man: A Consideration of the Public-Private Split and Its Ramifications." *Politics and Society* 4: 453–73.

—— 1982. Feminism, Family and Community." *Dissent* 29: 442–49.

—— 1983. "Antigone's Daughters." In *Families, Politics and Public Policies,* ed. Irene Diamond. New York: Longman.

—— 1984. "Reclaiming the Socialist-Feminist Citizen." *Socialist Review* 74: 21–27.

Enloe, Cynthia. 1993. *The Morning After: Sexual Politics at the End of the Cold War.* Berkeley: University of California Press.

Ferguson, Kathy E. 1984. *The Feminist Case Against Bureaucracy.* Philadelphia: Temple University Press.

—— 1988. "Subject Centeredness in Feminist Discourse." In *The Political Interests of Gender,* ed. Kathleen B. Jones and Anna G. Jonasdottir. London: Sage Publications.

Ferree, Myra Marx, and Frederick D. Miller. 1985. "Mobilization and Meaning: Toward an Integration of Social-Psychological and Resource Mobilization Perspectives on Social Movements." *Sociological Inquiry* 55(1): 38–61.

Fraser, Nancy. 1989. *Unruly Practices: Power, Discourse and Gender in Contemporary Social Theory.* Minneapolis: University of Minnesota Press.

—— 1997. "Rethinking the Public Sphere: A Contribution to the Critique of Actually Existing Democracy." In *Habermas and the Public Sphere,* ed. Craig Calhoun. Cambridge, Mass.: MIT Press.

Flammang, Janet. 1997. *Women's Political Voice: How Women Are Transforming the Practice and Study of Politics.* Philadelphia: Temple University Press.

Gelb, Joyce. 1989. *Feminism and Politics: A Comparative Perspective.* Berkeley, Calif.: University of California Press.

—— and Marian Lief Palley. 1987. *Women and Public Policies.* Princeton: Princeton University Press.

Gilkes, Cheryl. 1980. "'Holding Back the Ocean with a Broom.'" In *The Black Woman,* ed. LaFrances Rodgers-Rose. Beverly Hills, Calif.: Sage.

—— 1988. "Building in Many Places." In *Women and the Politics of Empowerment,* ed. Ann Bookman and Sandra Morgen. Philadelphia: Temple University Press.

Gordon, Linda. 1994a. "Black and White Visions of Welfare: Women's Welfare Activism, 1890–1945." In *Unequal Sisters: A Multi-Cultural Reader in U.S. Women's History,* 2nd ed., ed. Vicki L. Ruiz and Ellen Carol Dubois. New York: Routledge.

—— 1994b. *Pitied But Not Entitled.* New York: Basic Books.

—— and Nancy Fraser. 1994. "A Genealogy of Dependency: Tracing a Keyword of the U.S. Welfare State." *Signs* 19: 309–36.

Hall, Jacquelyn Dowd. 1986. "Disorderly Women." *Journal of American History:* 354–82.

—— Nancy Hewitt, Ardis Cameron, and Martha Ackelsberg. 1987. "Disorderly Women: Gender, Politics and Theory." Roundtable discussion. Berkshire Conference of Women Historians, Wellesley College, June.

Hardy-Fanta, Carol. 1993. *Latina Politics, Latino Politics: Gender, Culture and Political Participation in Boston.* Philadelphia: Temple University Press.

Hart, Vivien. 1994. *Bound by Our Constitution: Women, Workers, and the Minimum Wage*. Princeton: Princeton University Press.

Hawkesworth, Mary E. 1989. "Knowers, Knowing, Known: Feminist Theory and Claims to Truth." *Signs* 14: 533–57.

Hekman, Susan. 1987. "The Feminization of Epistemology: Gender and the Social Sciences." *Women & Politics* 7: 65–83.

Hertz, Susan. 1977. "The Politics of the Welfare Mothers Movement: A Case Study." *Signs* 2: 600–11.

Hewitt, Nancy. 1984. *Women's Activism and Social Change*. Ithaca, NY: Cornell University Press.

——1993. "In Pursuit of Power: The Political Economy of Women's Activism in Twentieth Century Tampa." In *Visible Women: New Essays on American Activism*, ed. Nancy Hewitt and Suzanne Lebsock. Urbana, Ill., and Chicago: University of Illinois Press.

Hine, Darlene Clark. 1993. "The Housewives' League of Detroit: Black Women and Economic Nationalism." In *Visible Women: New Essays on American Activism*, ed. Nancy Hewitt and Suzanne Lebsock. Urbana, Ill., and Chicago: University of Illinois Press.

Jetter, Alexis, Annelise Orleck, and Diana Taylor, eds. 1997. *The Politics of Motherhood: Activist Voices from Left to Right*. Hanover, NH: University Press of New England.

Kaplan, Temma. 1980. "Female Consciousness and Collective Action: The Case of Barcelona." *Signs* 5: 545–66.

——1997. *Crazy for Democracy: Women in Grassroots Movements*. New York: Routledge.

Katzenstein, Mary Fainsod. 1990. "Feminism within American Institutions." *Signs* 16: 27–54.

——1998. *Faithful and Fearless: Moving Feminist Protest Inside the Church and Military*. Princeton: Princeton University Press.

——and Carol McClurg Mueller, eds. 1987. *The Women's Movements in the United States and Western Europe*. Philadelphia: Temple University Press.

Katznelson, Ira. 1981. *City Trenches*. New York: Pantheon.

Kaye/Kantrowitz, Melanie. 1992. *The Issue Is Power: Essays on Women, Jews, Violence and Resistance*. San Francisco: Aunt Lute.

Kessler-Harris, Alice. 1985. "The Debate over Equality for Women in the Workplace: Recognizing Differences." In *Women and Work: An Annual Review*, ed. Laurie Larwood, et al. Vol. 1: 141–61. Beverly Hills, Calif.: Sage.

——1994. "Equal Employment Opportunity versus Sears, Roebuck and Company: A Personal Account." In *Unequal Sisters: A Multicultural Reader in U.S. Women's History*, 2nd ed., ed. Vicky L. Ruiz and Ellen Carol Dubois. New York: Routledge.

Klepfisz, Irena. 1990. *Dreams of an Insomniac: Jewish Feminist Essays, Speeches, and Diatribes*. Portland, Or.: Eighth Mountain Press.

Koven, Seth, and Sonya Michel. 1990. "Womanly Duties: Maternalist Politics and the Origins of Welfare States in France, Germany, Great Britain, and the United States, 1880–1920." *American Historical Review* 95: 1076–108.

Lebsock, Suzanne. 1990. Women and American Politics: 1880–1920." In *Women, Politics and Change*, ed. Louise Tilly and Patricia Y. Gurin. New York: Russell Sage.

❖ Martha A. Ackelsberg

Lewis, Diane K. 1977. "A Response to Inequality: Black Women, Racism, and Sexism." *Signs* 3: 339–61.

Lipsky, Michael. 1968. "Protest as a Political Resource." *American Political Science Review* 62: 1144–58.

Lister, Ruth. 1997. "Dialectics of Citizenship." *Hypatia* 12(4): 6–26.

Lorde, Audre. 1984. *Sister Outsider*. Trumansburg, NY: Crossing Press.

Lugones, Maria C., and Elizabeth V. Spelman. 1983. "Have We Got A Theory for You! Feminist Theory, Cultural Imperialism, and the Demand for 'The Woman's Voice'." *Women's Studies International Forum* 6: 573–81.

Mansbridge, Jane. 1996. "Reconstructing Democracy." In *Revisioning the Political: Feminist Reconstructions of Traditional Concepts in Western Political Theory*, ed. Nancy Hirschman and Christine DiStefano. Boulder, Colo.: Westview Press.

Medoff Peter, and Holly Sklar. 1994. *Streets of Hope*. Boston: South End Press.

Mink, Gwendolyn. 1990. "The Lady and the Tramp: Gender, Race, and the Origins of the American Welfare State." In *Women, the State, and Welfare*, ed. Linda Gordon. Madison: University of Wisconsin Press.

——1995. *The Wages of Motherhood*. Ithaca, NY: Cornell University Press.

——1998. *Welfare's End*. Ithaca, NY: Cornell University Press.

——2000. *Whose Welfare?*. Ithaca, NY: Cornell University Press.

Mouffe, Chantal. 1996. "Democracy, Power, and the 'Political'." In *Democracy and Difference: Contesting the Boundaries of the Political*, ed. Seyla Benhabib. Princeton: Princeton University Press.

Naples, Nancy A. 1998a. *Grassroots Warriors: Activist Mothering, Community Work, and the War on Poverty*. New York: Routledge.

——ed. 1998b. *Community Activism and Feminist Politics: Organizing Across Race, Class, and Gender*. New York: Routledge.

Nelson, Barbara. 1984. "Women's Poverty and Women's Citizenship." *Signs* 10: 209–31.

——1990a. "The Origins of the Two-Channel Welfare State." In *Women, the State and Welfare*, ed. Linda Gordon. Madison: University of Wisconsin Press.

——1990b. "The Gender, Race, and Class Origins of Early Welfare Policy and the Welfare State." In *Women, Politics and Change*, ed. Louise Tilly and Patricia Gurin. New York: Russell Sage.

Okin, Susan Moller. 1989. *Justice, Gender, and the Family*. New York: Basic Books.

Parenti, Michael. 1970. "Power and Pluralism: The View from the Bottom." *Journal of Politics* 32: 501–30.

Pateman, Carole. 1979. *The Problem of Political Obligation*. New York: John Wiley.

——1988. *The Sexual Contract*. Stanford, Calif.: Stanford University Press.

——[1980] 1989. "Women and Consent." *Political Theory* 8: 149–68. Repr. in *The Disorder of Women: Democracy, Feminism and Political Theory*. Stanford, Calif.: Stanford University Press.

——1989. *The Disorder of Women: Democracy, Feminism, and Political Theory*. Stanford, Calif.: Stanford University Press.

Payne Charles. 1990. " 'Men Led, But Women Organized': Movement Participation of Women in the Mississippi Delta." In *Women and Social Protest*, ed. Guida West and Rhoda Lois Blumberg. New York: Oxford University Press.

Phelan, Shane. 1994. *Getting Specific: Postmodern Lesbian Politics.* Minneapolis: University of Minnesota Press.

Phillips, Anne. 1991. *Engendering Democracy.* University Park: Pennsylvania State University Press.

Piven, Frances Fox. 1984. "Women and the State: Ideology, Power, and the Welfare State." *Socialist Review* 74: 11–19.

—— and Richard A. Cloward. 1977. *Poor People's Movements.* New York: Pantheon.

—— 1982. *The New Class War.* New York: Pantheon.

Pope, Jackie. 1990. "Women in the Welfare Rights Struggle: The Brooklyn Welfare Action Council." In *Women and Social Protest*, ed. Guida West and Rhoda Lois Blumberg. New York: Oxford University Press.

Rhode, Deborah, ed. 1990. *Theoretical Perspectives on Sexual Difference.* New Haven: Yale University Press.

Romer, Nancy. 1990. "Is Political Activism Still a 'Masculine' Endeavor?" *Psychology of Women Quarterly* 14: 229–43.

Rosaldo, Michelle Zimbalist. 1974. "Woman, Culture and Society: A Theoretical Overview." In *Woman, Culture and Society*, ed. Michelle Zimbalist Rosaldo and Louise Lamphere. Stanford, Calif.: Stanford University Press.

—— 1980. "The Use and Abuse of Anthropology." *Signs* 5: 389–417.

—— and Louise Lamphere, eds. 1974. *Women, Culture and Society.* Stanford, Calif.: Stanford University Press.

Rosen, Ruth. 2000. *The World Split Open: How the Modern Women's Movement Changed America.* New York: Penguin Putnam.

Ruddick, Sara. 1989. *Maternal Thinking: Toward a Politics of Peace.* Boston: Beacon Press.

Sarvasy, Wendy. 1992. "Beyond the Difference versus Equality Policy Debate: Postsuffrage Feminism, Citizenship, and the Quest for a Feminist Welfare State." *Signs* 17: 329–62.

—— 1997. "Social Citizenship from a Feminist Perspective." *Hypatia* 12: 54–73.

Shklar, Judith. 1991. *American Citizenship: The Quest for Inclusion, The Tanner Lectures on Human Values.* Cambridge, Mass.: Harvard University Press.

Simons, Margaret A. 1979. "Racism and Feminism: A Schism in the Sisterhood." *Feminist Studies* 5: 389–410.

Sklar, Kathryn Kish. 1993. "The Historical Foundations of Women's Power in the Creation of the American Welfare State." In *Mothers of a New World*, ed. Seth Koven and Sonya Michel. New York: Routledge.

—— Anja Shuler, and Susan Strasser, eds. 1998. *Social Justice Feminists in the United States and Germany: A Dialogue in Documents.* Ithaca, NY: Cornell University Press.

Skocpol, Theda. 1992. *Protecting Soldiers and Mothers: The Political Origins of Social Policy in the United States.* Cambridge, Mass.: Harvard University Press.

Sparks, Holloway. 1997. "Dissident Citizenship: Democratic Theory, Political Courage, and Activist Women." *Hypatia* 12, 4: 74–110.

Terrell, Mary Church. [1904] 1990. "Lynching from a Negro's Point of View." Repr. in *Quest for Equality: The Life and Writings of Mary Eliza Church Terrell, 1863–1954*, ed.

❖ Martha A. Ackelsberg

Beverly Washington Jones. Vol. 13 of *Black Women in United States History*. Brooklyn, NY: Carlson Publishing, Inc.

Tobias, Sheila. 1997. *Faces of Feminism: An Activist's Reflections on the Women's Movement*. Boulder, Colo.: Westview Press.

Wells, Ida B. 1970. *Crusade for Justice: The Autobiography of Ida B. Wells*, ed. Alfreda M. Duster. Chicago: University of Chicago Press.

Wells-Barnett, Ida B. [1893] 1990. "Lynch Law in All Its Phases." Repr. in *Ida B. Wells-Barnett: An Exploratory Study of an American Black Woman, 1893–1930*, ed. Mildred I. Thompson. Vol. 15 of *Black Women in United States History*. Brooklyn, NY: Carlson Publishing, Inc.

—— [1901] 1977. "Lynching and the Excuse for It." Reprint. In "Lynching and Rape: An Exchange of Views," by Jane Addams and Ida B. Wells, ed. with introd. by Bettina Aptheker. Occasional Paper No. 25. New York: American Institute for Marxist Studies.

West, Guida. 1981. *The National Welfare Rights Movement: The Social Protest of Poor Women*. New York: Praeger.

White, Deborah Gray. 1993. "The Cost of Club Work, The Price of Black Feminism." In *Visible Women: New Essays on American Activism*, ed. Nancy Hewitt and Suzanne Lebsock. Urbana, Ill.: University of Illinois Press.

❖ Index